# IRON MAN 2020

# IRON MAN 2020

**WRITERS:** Fred Schiller, Ken McDonald, Tom DeFalco, Simon Furman, Walt Simonson & Daniel Merlin Goodbrey with Barry Windsor-Smith & Bob Wiacek

**PENCILERS/BREAKDOWNS:** Mark Beachum, Herb Trimpe, Barry Windsor-Smith, Bryan Hitch, Bob Wiacek, William Rosado & Lou Kang with Manny Galan

**INKERS/FINISHERS:** Bob Wiacek, Barry Windsor-Smith, Bryan Hitch & Craig Yeung with Jim Amash

**COLORISTS:** Bob Sharen, Barry Windsor-Smith, Euan Peters, Christie Scheele & Chris Sotomayor with Joe Andreani

**LETTERERS:** Jim Novak, Michael Higgins, Diana Albers, Janice Chiang, Annie Halfacree, John Costanza & Dave Sharpe

**ASSISTANT EDITORS:** Mike Marts, Michael Horwitz & Jody LeHeup with Paula Foye

**EDITORS:** Jim Owsley, Larry Hama, Steve White, Nel Yomtov, John Barber & Nicole Boose with Rob Tokar

**DIGITAL PRODUCTION:** Joe Sabino
**DIGITAL PRODUCTION MANAGER:** Tim Smith 3
**DIGITAL COORDINATOR:** Harry Go
**DIRECTOR OF DIGITAL CONTENT:** John Cerilli

**FRONT COVER ARTIST:** Bob Wiacek
**BACK COVER ARTIST:** Barry Windsor-Smith
**COVER COLORIST:** Veronica Gandini

**COLLECTION EDITOR & DESIGN:** Nelson Ribeiro
**ASSISTANT EDITOR:** Alex Starbuck
**EDITORS, SPECIAL PROJECTS:** Mark D. Beazley & Jennifer Grünwald
**SENIOR EDITOR, SPECIAL PROJECTS:** Jeff Youngquist
**RESEARCH:** Daron Jensen, Stuart Vandal & Jeph York
**LAYOUT:** Jeph York
**PRODUCTION:** ColorTek
**SVP OF PRINT & DIGITAL PUBLISHING SALES:** David Gabriel

**EDITOR IN CHIEF:** Axel Alonso
**CHIEF CREATIVE OFFICER:** Joe Quesada
**PUBLISHER:** Dan Buckley
**EXECUTIVE PRODUCER:** Alan Fine

**IRON MAN 2020.** Contains material originally published in magazine form as AMAZING SPIDER-MAN ANNUAL #20, MACHINE MAN #1-4, DEATH'S HEAD #10, IRON MAN 2020 #1, ASTONISHING TALES: IRON MAN 2020 #1-6 and WHAT IF? #53. First printing 2013. ISBN# 978-0-7851-6735-8. Published by MARVEL WORLDWIDE, INC., a subsidiary of MARVEL ENTERTAINMENT, LLC. OFFICE OF PUBLICATION: 135 West 50th Street, New York, NY 10020.  **Printed in the U.S.A.** ALAN FINE, EVP - Office of the President, Marvel Worldwide, Inc. and EVP & CMO Marvel Characters B.V.; DAN BUCKLEY, Publisher & President - Print, Animation & Digital Divisions; JOE QUESADA, Chief Creative Officer; TOM BREVOORT, SVP of Publishing; DAVID BOGART, SVP of Operations & Procurement, Publishing; RUWAN JAYATILLEKE, SVP & Associate Publisher, Publishing; C.B. CEBULSKI, SVP of Creator & Content Development; DAVID GABRIEL, SVP of Print & Digital Publishing Sales; JIM O'KEEFE, VP of Operations & Logistics; DAN CARR, Executive Director of Publishing Technology; SUSAN CRESPI, Editorial Operations Manager; ALEX MORALES, Publishing Operations Manager; STAN LEE, Chairman Emeritus. For information regarding advertising in Marvel Comics or on Marvel.com, please contact Niza Disla, Director of Marvel Partnerships, at ndisla@marvel.com. For Marvel subscription inquiries, please call 800-217-9158. **Manufactured between 2/27/2013 and 3/22/2013 by R.R. DONNELLEY, INC., SALEM, VA, USA.**

10 9 8 7 6 5 4 3 2 1

MARVEL
25TH
ANNIVERSARY
© 1986 MARVEL COMICS GROUP
$1.25 US
$1.50 CAN
20•1986
02921
APPROVED BY THE COMICS CODE AUTHORITY
GIANT-SIZED ANNUAL
the AMAZING SPIDER-MAN ANNUAL
HE'S BACK!
THE IRON MAN OF 2020!
AND SPIDEY'S IN FOR THE FIGHT OF HIS LIFE!

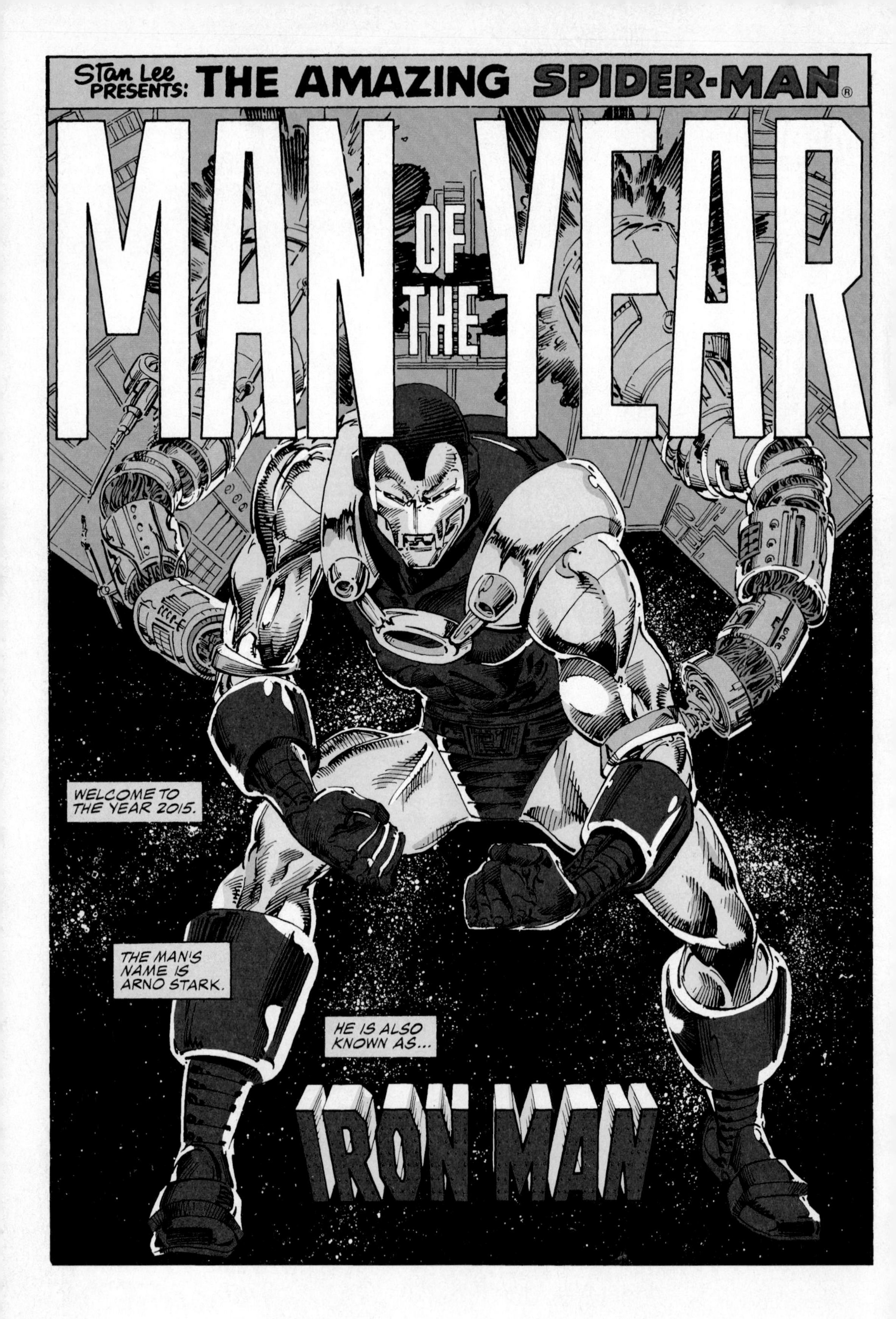
Stan Lee PRESENTS: THE AMAZING SPIDER-MAN®
MAN OF THE YEAR
WELCOME TO THE YEAR 2015.
THE MAN'S NAME IS ARNO STARK.
HE IS ALSO KNOWN AS...
IRON MAN

HIS ARMOR IS THE MOST ADVANCED TECHNOLOGICAL MARVEL OF THIS AGE.

WHEN HE WEARS IT...

...IT MAKES HIM THE SINGLE MOST DANGEROUS MAN ON THE PLANET.
HOW'S THIS, GUYS?
GREAT, MR. STARK.
HOLD IT RIGHT THERE, MR. STARK.

THESE SHOTS WILL LOOK GREAT IN TOMORROW'S EDITION.
ARNO STARK... INVENTOR OF THE FIRST WORKABLE TIME DISPLACEMENT DEVICE, AND FRONT RUNNER FOR TIME MAGAZINE'S "MAN OF THE YEAR" AWARD!
ALL THAT, AND I CAN SING, TOO!
PRESS
PHOTO STAFF
UPI
HOW DO YOU FEEL ABOUT THE MAN OF THE YEAR NOMINATION, MR. STARK?

HOW DO YOU THINK I FEEL?
EVER SINCE I PURCHASED STARK ENTERPRISES FROM THE LATE TONY STARK'S ESTATE, I'VE KEPT MY HEAD BURIED IN THE LAB...

...REFINING STARK'S RATHER CRUDE DESIGNS ...DEVELOPING NEW TECHNOLOGIES.
FAR AS I'M CONCERNED, IT'S HIGH TIME SOMEONE NOTICED!
MR. STARK --CALL ON COMLINK THREE.

ARNO?! WHAT ARE YOU DOING THERE?!
WONDERFUL.

HI, CYNTHIA.
DON'T "HI, CYNTHIA" ME, MISTER. YOU'VE GOT AN APPOINTMENT, REMEMBER?
HI, DADDY.
I'VE GOT LOTS OF APPOINTMENTS, HONEY.
HI, SON.

IF YOU THINK I'M GOING TO STAND FOR ONE MORE CANCELED WEEKEND...
SWEETHEART, I'M DOING THE BEST I CAN...
...YOU'VE GOT A BIG SURPRISE COMING FOR YOU, PAL, 'CAUSE I DO NOT INTEND...
ARNO!! ARNO, WHERE ARE YOU?!
HAWK'S CALLING, DARLING.
TO HADES WITH HAWK! I'M TALKING TO YOU, NOW...

ARNO! YOU PROMISED!
THIS WEEKEND FOR YOUR WIFE AND KID. REMEMBER US, ARNO?
IF NOT FOR US, YOU'D HAVE NO PICTURES ON YOUR DESK!
BLAST YOU, ARNO!! WHERE ARE YOU HIDING?!?
IGNORE HIM, ARNO. TELL HAWK TO--


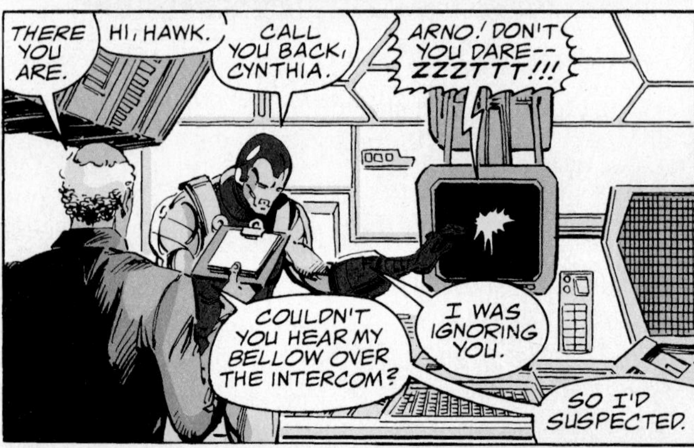

THERE YOU ARE.
HI, HAWK.
CALL YOU BACK, CYNTHIA.
ARNO! DON'T YOU DARE-- ZZZTTT!!!
COULDN'T YOU HEAR MY BELLOW OVER THE INTERCOM?
I WAS IGNORING YOU.
SO I'D SUSPECTED.

"THEY'RE WAITING FOR YOU IN LAB "B." I SUGGEST YOU HURRY."
TIME MACHINE'S STILL GOT A FEW BUGS IN IT...
GOT TO WORK THEM OUT BEFORE MAN OF THE YEAR JUDGING BEGINS...
GOTTA BE FRIENDLY TO THEM... THE MILITARY GOONS WAITING FOR ME...
...I HATE BUILDING MUNITIONS... BUT THE MONEY'S GOT TO COME FROM SOMEPLACE...
...WONDER WHAT'S FOR LUNCH...?
WHAT WAS IT CYNTHIA WANTED?
ARNO!!!
OH WELL, I'LL SEND HER ROSES.
SHUT UP, HAWK. I'M ON MY WAY.

I LOVE THIS.
INVESTING MY FATHER'S FORTUNE IN STARK'S DESIGNS WAS THE BEST MOVE I'VE EVER MADE.
IT'S GIVEN MY LIFE MEANING... MADE ME WHOLE.
NOW, WITH MY TIME MACHINE, I CAN FINALLY STEP OUT OF STARK'S SHADOW...
...AND ESTABLISH A REPUTATION OF MY OWN.
ARNO! BEFORE YOU ARRIVE AT LAB "B", LET ME RUN DOWN YOUR ITINERARY FOR THIS WEEKEND...
DON'T BOTHER.
GOT TO DISCONNECT THAT DIRECT CHANNEL HAWK ALWAYS CHIRPS ON...
YOUR FLYOVER WITH THE MILITARY BRASS--
--CORPORATE SUMMIT WITH NAKAIMONO LTD.--
--THE GERMANS WILL BE WATCHING THAT ONE--
CLICK!
CLICK!
--MORE START-UP TESTING ON THE TIME MACHINE--
--AND THEN, AFTER LUNCH--
YEAH, YEAH.
HAWK, DON'T YOU EVER GET TIRED OF NAGGING ME?
NEVER, MY BOY.
I LIVE FOR THE EXPERIENCE.
STRAIGHTEN UP, ARNO. THE MILITARY IS, AFTER ALL, YOUR BREAD AND BUTTER.
KEEPING THEM HAPPY MAKES IT POSSIBLE FOR YOU TO TINKER WITH TIME MACHINES--
--AND WIN MAN OF THE YEAR AWARDS.
FOR PITY'S SAKE, AT LEAST RETRACT THE ROLLER SKATES.

DECORUM IS ESSENTIAL TO GOOD BUSINESS PRACTICES.

Main gates secured, all decks.
Priority clearance one activated.
Hello, Mr. Stark. Welcome to Lab "B."
Would you like some tea?
Or, perhaps a nice cup of coffee?
YOU DON'T KNOW HOW TO MAKE A NICE CUP OF COFFEE, SX-9.
Then, perhaps you should reprogram me, Mr. Stark.
GENTLEMEN. SORRY TO KEEP YOU WAITING.
0900 HOURS MEANS 0900 HOURS, STARK. KEEP ME WAITIN' AGAIN--
--AN' YOU'LL BE BACK SELLIN' USED HOVERCRAFT...
General, I can recalibrate my time data charts so that Mr. Stark will in fact have arrived a few minutes early . . .
...AN' I HATE YOUR SMART-DUCK COMPUTER.

LET'S GET DOWN TO IT. WEAPON MK-3--THE PLANET BUSTER BOMB.
A GREAT ADVANCEMENT TO MANKIND--THOUGH NOBODY KNOWS ABOUT IT. ALL NUCLEAR WEAPONS WERE OUTLAWED IN THE SALT VI AGREEMENTS.
OUR ABILITY TO LIVE FREE AND ENJOY OUR HUMAN RIGHTS HANGS ON OUR ABILITY TO DESTROY THE ENEMY.
QUICKLY AND CLEANLY.

IT'S FRIGHTENING HOW COMFORTABLE THESE GUYS LOOK STANDING IN FRONT OF THAT BOMB.
THE RADION COUNT OVER THAT PROTOTYPE WE EXPLODED LAST NIGHT SHOULD BE DOWN TO ACCEPTABLE LEVELS.
THE ION SCREEN YOU PLACED OVER THE AREA KEPT THE RUSKIES FROM EVER KNOWING ABOUT IT.

YEAH, YOU'RE REAL SLICK, MISTER.
JUST DON'T FORGET WHO'S CALLING THE SHOTS AROUND HERE.

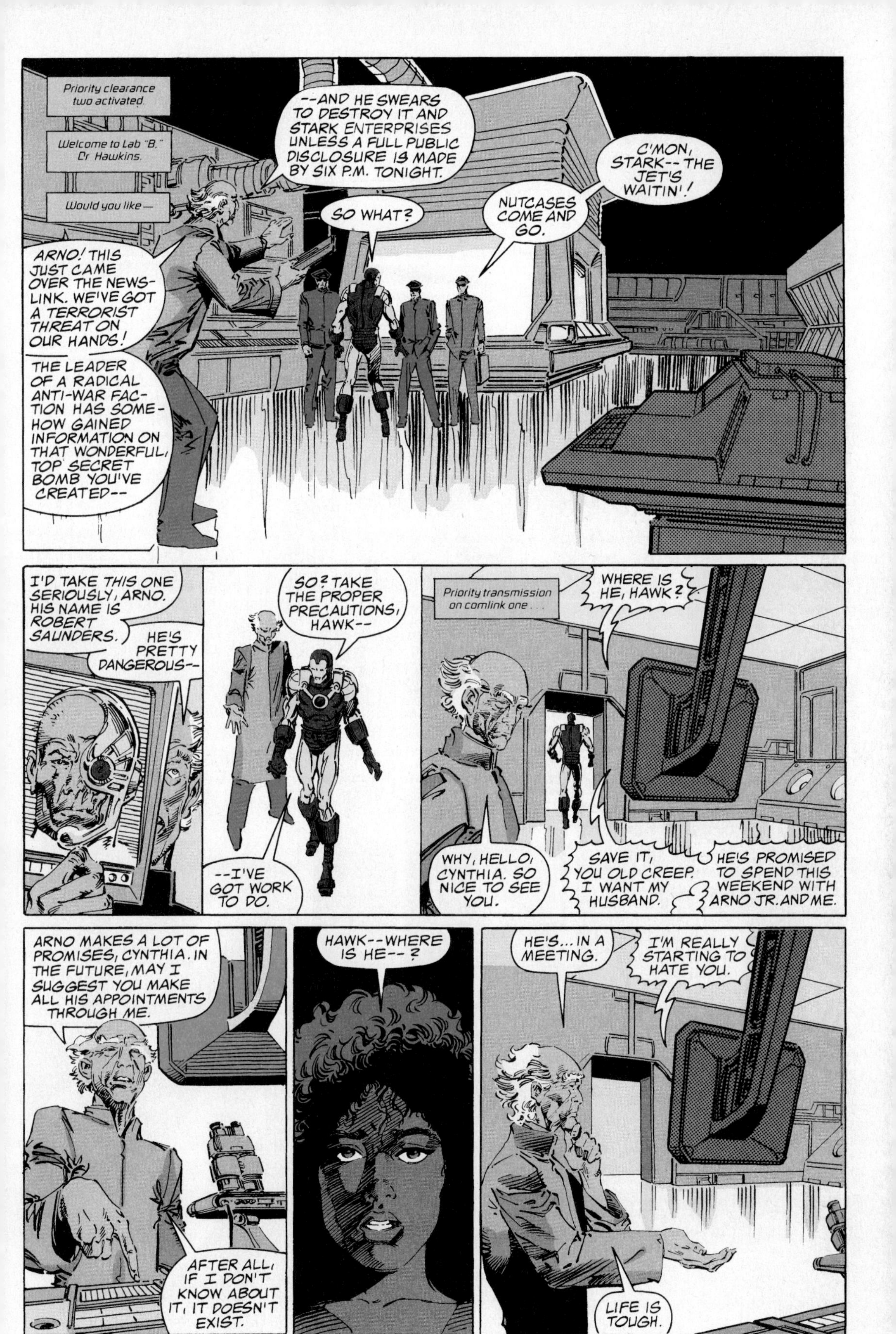
Priority clearance two activated.
Welcome to Lab "B," Dr. Hawkins.
Would you like —
ARNO! THIS JUST CAME OVER THE NEWS-LINK. WE'VE GOT A TERRORIST THREAT ON OUR HANDS!
THE LEADER OF A RADICAL ANTI-WAR FACTION HAS SOMEHOW GAINED INFORMATION ON THAT WONDERFUL, TOP SECRET BOMB YOU'VE CREATED--
--AND HE SWEARS TO DESTROY IT AND STARK ENTERPRISES UNLESS A FULL PUBLIC DISCLOSURE IS MADE BY SIX P.M. TONIGHT.
SO WHAT?
NUTCASES COME AND GO.
C'MON, STARK-- THE JET'S WAITIN'!
I'D TAKE THIS ONE SERIOUSLY, ARNO. HIS NAME IS ROBERT SAUNDERS.
HE'S PRETTY DANGEROUS--
SO? TAKE THE PROPER PRECAUTIONS, HAWK--
--I'VE GOT WORK TO DO.
Priority transmission on comlink one . . .
WHERE IS HE, HAWK?
WHY, HELLO, CYNTHIA. SO NICE TO SEE YOU.
SAVE IT, YOU OLD CREEP. I WANT MY HUSBAND.
HE'S PROMISED TO SPEND THIS WEEKEND WITH ARNO JR. AND ME.
ARNO MAKES A LOT OF PROMISES, CYNTHIA. IN THE FUTURE, MAY I SUGGEST YOU MAKE ALL HIS APPOINTMENTS THROUGH ME.
AFTER ALL, IF I DON'T KNOW ABOUT IT, IT DOESN'T EXIST.
HAWK--WHERE IS HE--?
HE'S... IN A MEETING.
I'M REALLY STARTING TO HATE YOU.
LIFE IS TOUGH.

HAWK!!
HE CUT THE COMLINK--
HOW DARE HE?!
ARNO'S IN ON THIS, TOO! THOSE TWO OUGHT TO GET MARRIED!
TWO OF A KIND.
THEY'RE OVER IN THE LAB HAVING A GOOD TIME...

...I'M STUCK HERE AT HOME, SURROUNDED BY HUNGRY REPORTERS!
REPORTERS WHO ALL WANT A GLIMPSE OF THE MAN OF THE YEAR!!

WE'D LIKE A GLIMPSE OF HIM, TOO, WOULDN'T WE?
ALWAYS PUTS ME ON HOLD.
YES, MOM.
NEVER COMES HOME WHEN HE SAYS HE'S COMING HOME...
NEVER SPENDS ANY TIME WITH HIS FAMILY...
WELL, HE'S NOT GETTING AWAY WITH IT THIS TIME...

YOUR CAR IS READY, MA'AM.
COME HERE.
LET'S GET YOU BUTTONED UP.
WE'RE GOING DOWN TO YOUR FATHER'S LAB.
HE'S NOT GETTING AWAY WITH STANDING US UP AGAIN.
HOLD STILL.

I'M GOING TO SHOW HIM.
YES, MOM.

WHO DOES HE THINK HE IS...?

MUCH LATER...
Time lapse: detonation plus eleven point three hours.
Radiation levels 19.772 hg. units.
GOTTA GET THOSE STATS UP, BOY.
85% vegetation destroyed by flash-burn. 14% vegetation destroyed by radiation.
15% WORTH'A RUSKIE CAN FIRE A REAL NASTY COUNTER-STRIKE.
72% animal life destroyed by flash-burn. 13% animal life destroyed by radiation.
Kill-through ratios are as follows:
THIS STINKS.
Projected cities kill-through at 92% on impact at ground-zero.
87% kill-through on impact within ten-mile radius of ground zero . . .
. . . error factor of 12% plus or minus . . .
IT REALLY STINKS.
HOW MUCH HAVE I SOLD OUT?
HOW MUCH OF MYSELF HAVE I TRADED IN JUST TO GRAB A FEW HEAD-LINES?
TELL YOU WHAT, BOY--
--YOU WORK THE BUGS OUTTA THIS THING--GET THOSE KILL STATS UP--
--AND MAYBE WE'LL KEEP FUNDIN' YOUR TIME MACHINE.
AND MAY-BE YOU'LL ACTUALLY MAKE MAN OF THE YEAR.
MAYBE.

SOON, BACK AT STARK INTERNATIONAL...
ARMED
ZZAAXX!!

HIS NAME IS ROBERT SAUNDERS.

HE WARNED THEM NOT TO BUILD THE BOMB. HE PLEADED WITH THEM.
NOW, HE MUST ACT.
HEY!!

HAVE YOU SEEN MY DADDY?
STARK'S SON, ARNO JR.
WHAT'S HE DOING HERE?

I DON'T KNOW WHO YOUR FATHER IS, SON.
WHY, HE'S ARNO STARK! HE'S THE BOSS HERE!
ARNO! STOP PESTERING THAT TECHNICIAN!

COME ON, LET'S CHECK OUT LAB "B".
GOOD THING YOUR FATHER GAVE ME A SECURITY THREE CLEARANCE...
GOOD-BYE, MISTER!
THE BOY... SO YOUNG.

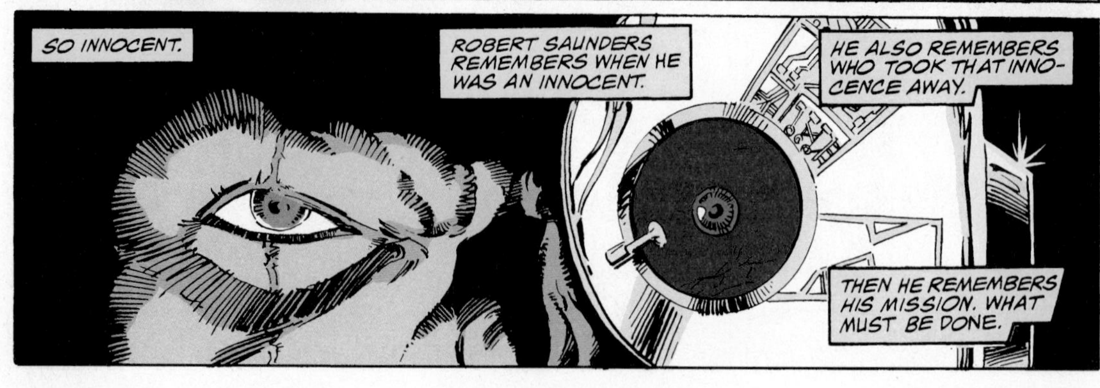
SO INNOCENT.
ROBERT SAUNDERS REMEMBERS WHEN HE WAS AN INNOCENT.
HE ALSO REMEMBERS WHO TOOK THAT INNOCENCE AWAY.
THEN HE REMEMBERS HIS MISSION. WHAT MUST BE DONE.

LESS THAN AN HOUR LATER...
RED ALERT
HAVE WE GOT IT ISOLATED?
YES, SIR, DR. HAWKINS-- LAB "B"!
THE ONE WITH THE BOMB IN IT...?!
THAT'S THE ONE.
OH, GOOD.
Security shutdown sequence sector 6 . . .
Security shutdown sequence sector 7 . . .
Security shutdown sequence sector 8 . . .
Security shutdown sequence section 11 . . .
Security shutdown sequence sector 12 . . .
ComLink with Air Transport Seven scrambled and locked, Dr. Hawkins . . .
WHAT'S UP, HAWK?
REMEMBER THAT TERRORIST I WARNED YOU ABOUT EARLIER, ARNO?
LOOK, I'M A LITTLE BUSY HERE, HAWK.
WE'VE GOT A FULL SCALE LOCKOUT RUNNING, ARNO. NO GAMES.

SOMEHOW THAT SAUNDERS NUT HAS LOCKED US OUT OF LAB "B"... HE'S ARMED THE PLANET BUSTER BOMB...
Security shutdown sequence sector 21 . . .
Security shutdown sequence sector 22 . . .
HAWK... PLEASE...JUST HANDLE IT, OKAY?
HE'S GOT YOUR WIFE, ARNO.

STARK!!!
HAVE YOU GONE NUTSO?!?
HAWK-- SECURE ALL STATIONS. LOCK ALL CHANGES OUT.
NOBODY LEAVES 'TILL I GET THERE.
YOU'RE MAKIN' A CAREER DECISION, MISTER--
AND, JAM THE COMLINK THE GOOD GENERAL'S USING!
GET BACK HERE, MISTER!! NOW!!
STARK INTERNATIONAL.
ALL AUTOMATIC SECURITY SYSTEMS HAVE KICKED IN. THE DOME IS CLOSING.
IN SECONDS, THE PLANT WILL BE TOTALLY SECURE. NO ONE WILL GET IN OR OUT.
SAUNDERS DOESN'T HAVE MUCH TIME.
All changes locked out.
Security chiefs check in on scramble code seven.
All changes locked out.
Security chiefs check in on scramble code eight.

THERE!!
THAT GUY'S GOT NO CLEARANCE TAGS--HE'S STEALING THAT SCOOTER--!!

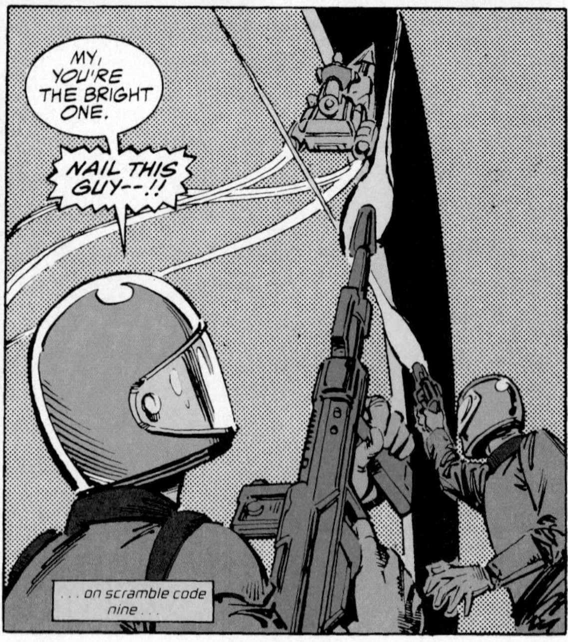
MY, YOU'RE THE BRIGHT ONE.
NAIL THIS GUY--!!
. . . on scramble code nine . . .

STARK'S WIFE AND CHILD ARRIVING WHEN THEY DID WAS AN INCREDIBLE STROKE OF LUCK.
SAUNDERS HAS NO INTENTION OF ACTUALLY DETONATING THE BOMB... HE JUST WANTS THE WAR-MONGERS TO SWEAT A LITTLE.
HE'LL CANCEL THE ARMING SEQUENCE FROM HIS SAFEHOUSE IN THE HILLS. AT THE LAST POSSIBLE MOMENT.
BUT FIRST, THE SWEAT.
STARK!!!
WHAMMM!
STATUS, HAWK?
CAN'T GET INTO THE LAB, ARNO. WE'RE DOING WHAT WE CAN.
CYNTHIA IS REALLY ANNOYED.
ARE WE SECURE?
ALL BUT THAT ONE.
I'M ON HIM.

SAUNDERS FIRES A HIGH INTENSITY PLASMA BOLT AT IRON MAN.
HE MIGHT JUST AS WELL HAVE SPIT AT HIM FOR ALL THE EFFECT IT HAS.
ARNO, I THINK THAT'S OUR BOY. BE CAREFUL WITH HIM.
I'LL SNAG HIM WITH MY RETRACTOR BEAM.
SAUNDERS GUNS HIS ENGINES, MAKING A LAST ATTEMPT TO GET THROUGH THE SWIFTLY NARROWING GAP IN THE DOME'S CLOSING WALLS.
IRON MAN'S BEAM COMES TOO LATE.
THIS JUST ISN'T HIS DAY.
KAABLOOM!
LOST HIM, HAWK.
I NOTICED.
BAD NEWS, ARNO--
--ROBERT SAUNDERS WAS OUR ONLY HOPE. NOW HE'S SPREAD ALL OVER THE EAST DOME.
MR. STARK-- COULD WE HAVE A STATEMENT... ?
HOW DO YOU FEEL--
YOUR WIFE AND KID...
GET OUT OF HERE...
... BEFORE I THROW YOU OUT!
SHEESH... SOME "MAN OF THE YEAR!"
WOTTA GROUCH...

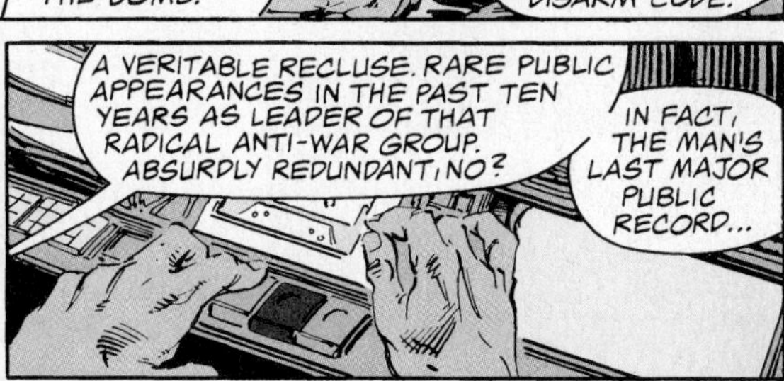

THE SPIDER-MAN MENACE

12 YEAR-OLD HONOR STUDENT INJURED IN SUPER-HERO SLUG-FEST

NEW YORK CITY.
TODAY.
SPIDER-MAN!!!
KILL HIM!!!
YEAH, YEAH...
...MAKE ME SCARED.

YOU'LL LAUGH OUT OF THE OTHER SIDE OF YOUR HEAD, CLOWN-- WHEN YOU TANGLE WITH...
...THE BLIZZARD!!!
NO, NO, NO!!
YOU'VE GOT IT ALL WRONG, BUNKIE!
YOU SUPER BADDIES HAVE TO SHOUT YOUR NAME WITH MORE RESONANCE! YOUR DELIVERY LACKS CONVICTION!
HERE, WATCH...

YOU'LL LAUGH OUT OF THE OTHER SIDE OF YOUR HEAD, CLOWN, WHEN YOU DARE EMBRACE AND/OR CHALLENGE THE POWER OF...
...SNOW CONE MAN!!!
SEE HOW IMPRESSED HE IS?
WORKS EVERY TIME!

I HOPE MY AUTOMATIC CAMERA'S GETTING ALL THIS. I'D HATE TO THINK MY SONG AND DANCE BIT WAS ALL FOR NOTHING.
AFTER ALL, SOMEONE WITH THE PROPORTIONAL STRENGTH AND AGILITY OF A SPIDER COULD MOP UP THESE CLOWNS IN HIS SLEEP!

HECK, MY AUNT MAY COULD MOP UP THESE CLOWNS IN HER SLEEP!
SINCE WHEN DOES THIS "BLIZZARD" GUY START ROBBING BANKS, ANYWAY? I THOUGHT HE WAS INTO HEAVIER STUFF.
OH WELL. BETTER WRAP THIS UP.

PARDON ME.
THWIP!!
DON'T GO AWAY.

IS HE... IS HE STILL BEHIND US...? MAN, WHAT A NUT...
GUY CRACKS JOKES WHILE HE BASHES OUR HEADS IN! DUDE AIN'T HUMAN!

SPLATT!

BETTER TELL YOUR GUYS TO WATCH WHERE THEY'RE RUNNING NEXT TIME, BLIZ!
YOU NEVER KNOW WHERE A WALL OF WEBBING'S GONNA POP UP.
YOU SMART-MOUTHED JERK!!

NOBODY MAKES FUN OF ME, PAL.

MY BATTLE SUIT GIVES ME THE POWER TO CONDENSE MOISTURE ALL AROUND ME AT WILL.
NOW THAT'S A HANDY ONE TO WHIP OUT AT PARTIES!
SZZAAP!

LOOK, PAL, CAN'T WE CUT A DEAL OR SOME-THING?
SAY, YOU DON'T ROB BANKS, I DON'T CALL YOU NAMES!

WELL, I TRIED.
THWIP!! THWIP!!

MISSED ME, DOPE!

YOU, FOR SURE!

BUT I DID MANAGE TO SNAG THAT HUNK OF ICE OVER YOUR HEAD!

SHEESH.
WHAT A WAY TO MAKE A LIVING!
CLICK!

THERE'S GOTTA BE AN EASIER GIG IN TOWN THAN GOING THREE OUT OF FIVE FALLS WITH MR. FROSTY BACK THERE.
THOUGH, HOPEFULLY MY AUTOMATIC CAMERA PICKED UP ENOUGH GOODS TO PAY MY RENT.

WHAT'S IT SAY?
NOTE? WHAT NOTE?!
SEZ: "COMPLIMENTS OF YOUR FRIENDLY, NEIGHBORHOOD SPIDER-MAN!"

I'D SAY GOOD THING I HAPPENED BY THE BLIZZARD ROBBING THAT BANK--
--BUT I HESITATE CALLING FROSTBITE IN AUGUST A "GOOD THING."
HOPE MY CITY EDITOR, MS. KATHYRN CUSHING, GOES FOR THESE PIX. SHE'S REALLY BEEN DOWN ON ME LATELY.
BUT EVEN SHE'S GOT TO ADMIT SPIDEY GOING TOE-TO-TOE WITH ONE OF THE DEADLIEST... WELL...
...HMMM. MAKE THAT ONE OF THE MOST OBSCURE, LITTLE-KNOWN, TWO-BIT BADDIES.
I'M DOOMED.

WELL, NOTHING VENTURED, NOTHING GAINED. MY LANDLADY, THE EVER-CHARMING MRS. MUGGINS, IS ON THE PROWL AGAIN.
THE RENT IS LATE AGAIN.
AND SO, I'M TRYING TO SELL SPIDEY ACTION PHOTOS AGAIN. EVEN THOUGH I KNOW NO ONE WANTS 'EM.
AIN'T IT GREAT HOW LIFE COMES FULL CIRCLE LIKE THIS?
WELL, HERE GOES NOTHING. TIME TO STRIP OFF THE UNION SUIT AND LET PETER PARKER BREATHE AGAIN.
DAILY
HOPE CUSHING'S IN A GOOD MOOD...

KATE'S NOT IN, PETER. DENTIST APPOINTMENT.
GUESS YOU'LL HAVE TO WAIT FOR ROBBIE
AND HE'S REAL BUSY.
AND THE BANKS CLOSE AT THREE...
I SHOULD'VE KEPT ONE OF THOSE MONEY BAGS I RECOVERED FROM THE HEIST.
HONESTY AND POVERTY MUST GO HAND IN HAND SOMEHOW...

HUH?
IS THAT KID... IMITATING ME...?

WHO'S THE ELF?
HE'S BOBBY SAUNDERS, ONE OF THE BUGLE STOCK-HOLDER'S KIDS. MR. JAMESON IS HAVING A SHOW AND TELL IN THE CONFERENCE ROOM.
BOBBY, THIS IS PETER PARKER ONE OF OUR FREELANCE PHOTOGRAPHERS.
PLEASED TO MEET YOU, MR. PARKER. I'M VERY FAMILIAR WITH YOUR WORK.
YOU SEEM TO GET ALL THOSE HARD-TO-GET SHOTS. I MEAN, THE IMMEDIACY OF THE NEWS ITEM AND THE INVENTIVE CAMERA ANGLES YOU USE...
...MORE THAN MAKE UP FOR YOUR WORK'S GRAINY FINISH AND POOR COMPOSITION.

ER... THANKS.
ANY TIME.
I'M RUNNING, PETER. YOU WANTED TO SEE ME?

YEAH, ROBBIE ...I'VE GOT THESE PIX--
CUSHING HANDLES PHOTOS.
SHE'S AT THE DENTIST.
SHE'LL BE BACK.

I NEED THE MONEY...
CUSHING HANDLES MONEY.
SEE YOU, ROBBIE.

'BYE, PETE. OH, YEAH--
--I HOPE THOSE AREN'T MORE SPIDER-MAN SHOTS.

I AM DOOMED.

I'VE ALREADY GOT PEOPLE OVER THERE, BUT I DON'T TRUST THAT FOREIGN BUREAU CHIEF. HE'LL SNAG ALL THE GOOD PIX AND SEND ME THE REFUSE.
DON'T GIVE ME ANY OF YOUR "I'M TIRED OF BEING SHOT AT" GUFF, PARKER. I REALIZE THE ASSIGNMENTS I USUALLY GIVE YOU FOR "NOW" TEND TO PLACE YOU IN DANGEROUS SITUATIONS.
BUT THIS ONE IS A CAKEWALK. THE MOST THAT CAN HAPPEN IS A TERRORIST ATTACK OR TWO.
I NEED A TOPFLIGHT WORLD CLASS PHOTOG ON THE SCENE RIGHT AWAY. AND SINCE I COULDN'T GRAB ANY OF THEM, I'M OFFERING THE JOB TO YOU.
AND DON'T HAGGLE ON RATE. YOU'LL GET TOP BUCKS. WELL, WHAT'S YOUR ANSWER?!

WE'RE IN THE MO--NEY...
WE'RE IN THE MO-- NEY...
I'M SO HAPPY I COULD CRY...
I DON'T KNOW THE LYRICS...
THAT'S IT. NOT ANOTHER DRINK AS LONG AS I LIVE.
EVERYTHING'S COM-MING UP RO-SES...
WH-WHAT?!
PETER--
--HOW DARE YOU COME SWINGING IN MY WINDOW--
--DRESSED LIKE THAT?!!
RELAX, MARY JANE, I WAS REAL CAREFUL. NOBODY SPOTTED ME.
I'M SAVED! MY LIFE IS SAVED BY A CIGAR-SUCKING WEASEL WITH A CREW CUT!
WHAT ARE YOU TALKING ABOUT?
GE-NEE-VAH! GE-NEE-VAH! MY KIN-DA TOWN...!
I LEAVE TOMORROW.
NO, YOU DON'T.
YOU'VE FORGOTTEN WHAT TOMORROW IS, HAVEN'T YOU?
--:
NO. THAT'S NEXT WEEK.
TOMORROW.

TOMORROW.
MY AUNT MAY'S BIRTHDAY.
THE DAY I ALWAYS SPEND WITH HER.

THE WOMAN RAISED ME LIKE I WAS HER OWN SON. SHE'S SACRIFICED SO MUCH FOR ME...
...NOW I'M RUNNING OUT ON HER. OH, SURE, ALL I HAVE TO SAY IS, "I HAD TO WORK..."
SHE'D UNDERSTAND.
IT STILL STINKS, THOUGH. BUT, IF I DON'T TAKE THIS JOB, I'LL GET EVICTED.

I'LL DO THE HONORABLE THING. CALL HER FROM THE AIRPORT.

WHOOPS! THERE'S MRS. MUGGINS... LOADED FOR BEAR.

IF SHE SEES ME, I'M DEAD. I'VE GOT TO DUCK HER 'TILL I GET PAID FOR THIS JOB.

SHORTLY...
IT'S TIMES LIKE THESE WHEN HAVING A DUAL IDENTITY COMES IN HANDY!
ALL I'VE GOTTA DO IS CLIMB UP OUT OF MY SKY-LIGHT AND...

WAIT... WHY'S MY SPIDER-SENSE TINGLING...?
OH, GREAT. MY NEIGHBORS, CANDI AND RANDI, ARE UP HERE SUN-BATHING AGAIN.

NOW WHAT?
AH-HA!
GOT IT!

THIS IS A DUMB IDEA! THIS IS A VERY DUMB IDEA.
I FIND IT HARD TO BELIEVE ANYONE WHO KNOWS ME AND RAN INTO ME WEARING THIS OUTFIT...
...WOULD HAVE ANY TROUBLE FIGURING OUT WHO'S UNDER THE MASK.
STILL, THERE ARE SEVERAL APARTMENTS UP HERE. SHE WOULDN'T KNOW EXACTLY WHICH ONE I CAME OUT OF...

...WOULD SHE?
THIS IS A DUMB IDEA.
HEY! YOU'RE SPIDER-MAN!

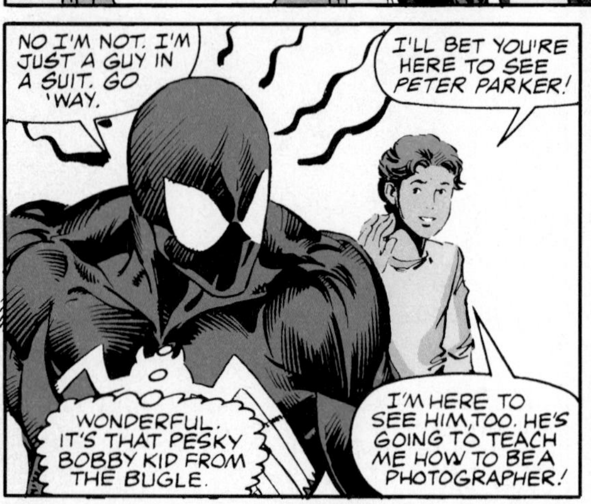
NO I'M NOT. I'M JUST A GUY IN A SUIT. GO 'WAY.
I'LL BET YOU'RE HERE TO SEE PETER PARKER!
WONDERFUL. IT'S THAT PESKY BOBBY KID FROM THE BUGLE.
I'M HERE TO SEE HIM, TOO. HE'S GOING TO TEACH ME HOW TO BE A PHOTOGRAPHER!

MUGGINS HEARD MY NAME MENTIONED... NOW SHE'S SUSPICIOUS.
HOW'D YOU GET HIS ADDRESS?
YOU KIDDING? MY DAD'S A STOCK-HOLDER!

I TELL YOU, GUYS...
...THE CRIMINAL JUSTICE SYSTEM AIN'T SQUAT. I GET NAILED FOR ATTEMPTED ROBBERY YESTERDAY...

...I'M BACK ON THE STREET TODAY. AND, I'M LOOKIN' FOR REVENGE.

FINDING SPIDER-MAN WON'T BE EASY... BUT WORD ON THE STREET HAS IT HE BUZZES PAST THE DAILY BUGLE EVERY SO...
...I DON'T BELIEVE IT! THERE HE IS!

LOOK, BOBBY, SINCE YOU WON'T TELL ME WHERE YOU GO TO SCHOOL, AND YOU WON'T TELL ME WHERE YOU LIVE...
...I FIGURE THE BUGLE WILL HAVE TO DO. I'M SURE THEY'LL LET YOU CALL YOUR FOLKS OR WHATEVER.
BUT...
GOT A PLANE TO CATCH, PAL.

TOO LATE TO NAIL HIM...
...BUT WE SURE AS HECK CAN SNATCH HIS LITTLE FRIEND!

SWING THE VAN AROUND!
HUH...?

GOT HIM!
MMMMPPHHZZRRTT!!

OWWW!!
SLAP!!
THE BRAT BIT ME!!

THUMMP!
THERE! SPIDER-MAN LANDED ON THE ROOF!!
THAT'S IT, BIG MAN.
COME AND GET IT.

TimePhase transfer engage plus 10.726 minutes.
All s.istems normal.
Engaging combat-ready Defense Condition Four.
Repulsor energy cannons cycling up.
10.326 seconds to DefCon Four engagement.
RRIIIPPP!!!
IRON MAN?!?
WHAT'S HE DOING HERE...?!

HEY! COME BACK WITH THAT KID!!
6.725 seconds to DefCon Four engagement.
HE'S IGNORING ME... JUST FLYING OFF!
TREATING ME LIKE I DIDN'T EVEN EXIST!!

JUST LIKE ALWAYS.
I'VE CLASHED WITH THAT ARMORED IDIOT MORE TIMES THAN I'D LIKE TO REMEMBER. HE'S ALWAYS TRASHED ME AND FLOWN OFF...
JUST LIKE HE'S DOING NOW.
WELL, I'VE GOT A SURPRISE FOR HIM.

THE COPS CONFISCATED MY ORIGINAL BLIZZARD OUTFIT.
BUT, THEY MISSED THIS ONE, MY NEW EXPERIMENTAL MODEL. IT'S EVEN MORE POWERFUL THAN THE ORIGINAL.
THE ARMORED AVENGER'S IN FOR A REAL CHILLY RECEPTION!
HEY-- IRON MAN--
--NEVER TURN YOUR BACK--
--ON A BLIZZARD!!
Rapid shell temperature degeneration.
System inoperative.
System inoperative.
Malfunction.
Housekeeping units responding.
Refractory systems compensating.
Engaging emergency Combat Defense Condition 0.
KERRR-RRAAASSHH!!

CAUGHT ME OFF GUARD.
TIME DISPLACEMENT EFFECT... REALLY TAKES THE WIND OUT OF YOU...
SYSTEMS GARBLED... SLUGGISH...
...BUT THEY'LL WORK WELL ENOUGH.

ALL RIGHT, AVENGER--
...THIS IS THE END OF THE LINE!!

I'VE GOT NO TIME FOR THIS... CLOWN!
SSSZZZZZ
AAAAHH!
SORRY THAT HAD TO HAPPEN, BUT THIS IS AN EMERGENCY SITUATION.
HE JUST GOT IN THE WAY.

THWIPP!
NOT MUCH TIME LEFT.

WHAT--?!

HIYA, SHELL-HEAD.
HOW'S TRICKS?

STAY OUT OF THIS, SPIDER-MAN.
THIS IS AN EMERGENCY SITUATION.

Engage repulsor IM6P77.
KRAAKK!!
INTERFERE, AND BE DESTROYED!
WHAT'S WITH HIM?

GOOD THING I DECIDED TO DOUBLE BACK AND MAKE SURE BOBBY GOT UPSTAIRS!
I DON'T KNOW WHAT'S GOING ON HERE, BUT IRON MAN'S SURE ACTING WEIRD!
GOTTA SNAG THAT CHUNK OF BUILDING BEFORE IT HITS THE KID!!

THEN I'LL FIGURE OUT WHAT IRON MAN'S PROBLEM IS.

THEN I'LL GET BOBBY UPSTAIRS!

THEN, JUST MAYBE, I'LL CATCH MY PLANE!
CRUNNCH!

THE... RETINA SCANNER...
...YOU'VE DESTROYED IT!!

DIDN'T COUNT ON THIS. GETTING SAUNDERS' RETINA PATTERNS IS SUCH A SIMPLE TASK!
I ONLY BROUGHT ONE INSTRUMENT WITH ME. I COULD JERRY-RIG ANOTHER, BUT I DON'T HAVE THE TIME.
EVEN THOUGH I'M TRAVELING THROUGH TIME, REAL TIME CONTINUES BACK HOME. I CAN'T CHEAT THE CLOCK!
I'VE GOT ABOUT TWENTY MINUTES BEFORE THE PLANET BUSTER BOMB EXPLODES. I'VE NO CHOICE--

--I'VE GOT TO TAKE THE BOY WITH ME!!
SOUNDS LIKE OUR EXIT CUE, BOBBY.
SOMETHING TELLS ME I REALLY TICKED GOLDEN BOY OFF WHEN I DROPPED HIS THINGAMAWOOGIT.

SPIDER-MAN!!
FFRRAAZZTT!!
HAND OVER THE BOY IMMEDIATELY!
Engage repulsors IM6P77-78.

KAA-BLOOM
SOMETHING'S SERIOUSLY WRONG, HERE.
HEY BOBBY-- YOU ROB A BANK OR SOMETHING?

N...NOT LATELY...
Engage repulsor IM6P78.
IRON MAN'S LOSING IT. THIS MAKES NO SENSE.

BUT, THEN AGAIN, HE IS AN AVENGER! FOR ALL I KNOW THIS KID COULD BE A DANGEROUS MONSTER FROM THE PLANET XENON!
SMART MONEY'S ON THE IRON GUY. HE CAN WIPE UP THE STREET WITH FRIENDLY, NEIGHBORHOOD WEB-SLINGERS ALL DAY LONG!
BUT WHY WON'T HE TALK TO ME?
WHAT'S THIS ALL ABOUT?!

I'M HANDLING THIS ALL WRONG. SPIDER-MAN IS OBVIOUSLY SOME SORT OF LAW-ENFORCEMENT AGENT.
I WISH I COULD SIT DOWN WITH HIM AND EXPLAIN THINGS... LIKE HOW THAT BOY HE'S TRYING TO PROTECT...
...WILL GROW UP UP TO BE ONE OF THE DEADLIEST TERRORISTS OF MY AGE?!
Engage repulsors IM6P77-78.
THERE'S NO TIME. GOT TO GRAB SAUNDERS AND GET BACK!!

S-SPIDER-MAN... SLOW DOWN... I... I... CAN'T CATCH... MY BREATH...
KID, THAT GUY IN THE TIN SUIT'S TRYING TO DO YOU SOME PERMANENT DAMAGE!
KEEP GOING.
WITH YOU ALL THE WAY.

I DON'T WANT TO HURT YOU, SPIDER-MAN.
I'M TOUCHED.
Engage disruptor field AX707.
WHAT ABOUT THE KID?

I DON'T CARE ABOUT SAUNDERS! AS LONG AS THERE'S TANGIBLE REMAINS...
ZZAAPP!!
TANGIBLE REMAINS?! GROSS!
HE... HE KNOWS MY NAME!!
LUCKY GUESS.
WHAT AM I GONNA DO?! CAN'T JUST KEEP RUNNING LIKE THIS!!

I'M REALLY BLOWING THIS.
Engage disruptor beam AX706.
I'M HAMSTRUNG BY MY OWN TECHNOLOGY! ALL OF THE ARMOR'S OFFENSIVE WEAPONRY IS DESIGNED FOR TOTAL DESTRUCTION!
CAN'T CONFRONT SPIDER-MAN DIRECTLY WITHOUT RISKING INCINERATING BOTH HIM AND SAUNDERS!
I CAN'T RISK LOSING SAUNDERS AGAIN.
YEOW!!
SPIDER SENSE BARELY WARNED ME IN TIME!
IRON MAN'S BEEN TOYING WITH ME... ANTICIPATING MY EVERY MOVE!
FACE IT, WEBHEAD...
...YOU'RE WAY OUT OF YOUR LEAGUE. WAIT-- BOBBY... HE'S...
...TAKEN A LOT OF FLYING GLASS...
...HURT BAD...
THAT SINKS IT.
ABSOLUTELY.

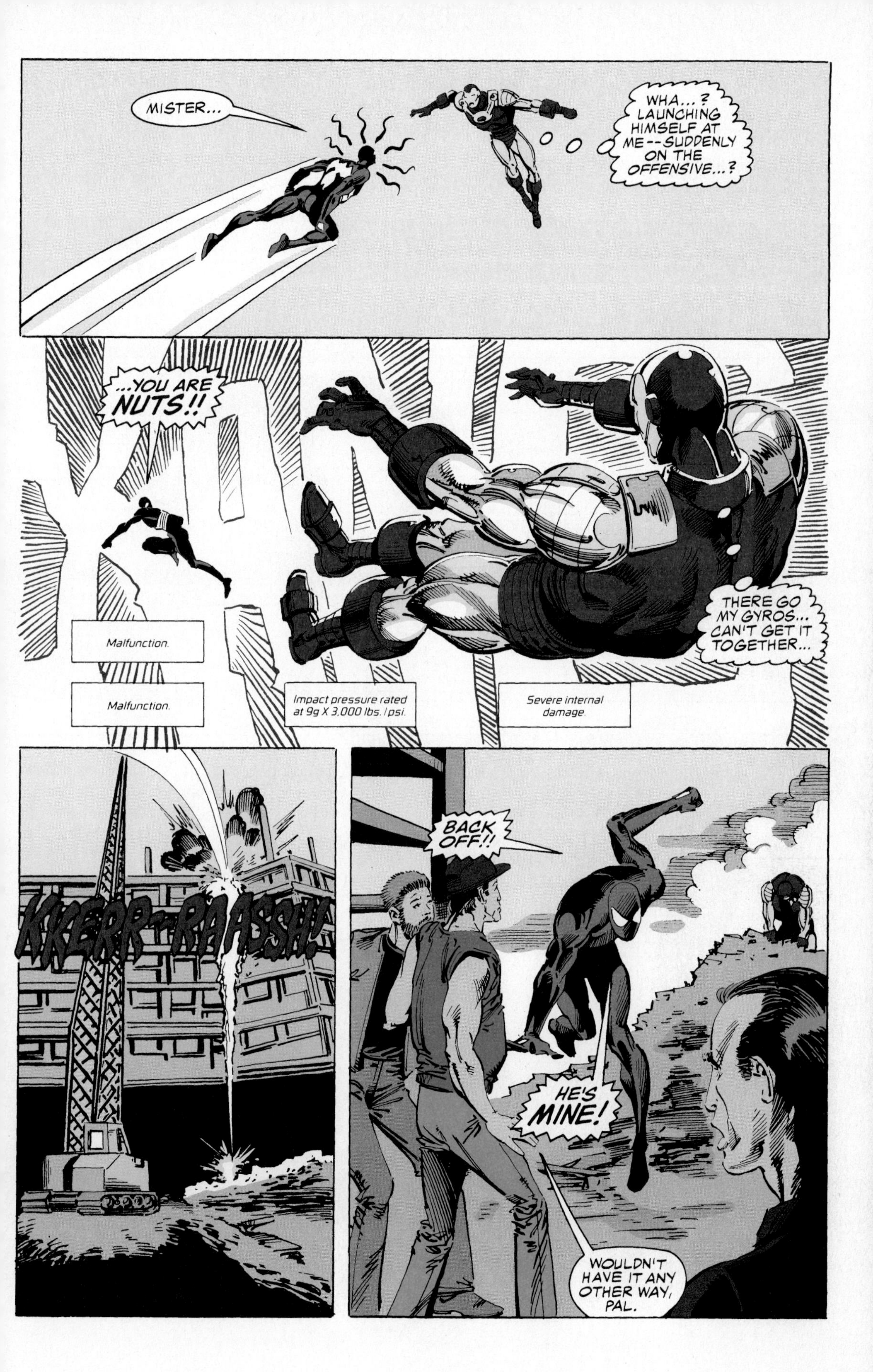
MISTER...
WHA...? LAUNCHING HIMSELF AT ME--SUDDENLY ON THE OFFENSIVE...?
...YOU ARE NUTS!!
THERE GO MY GYROS... CAN'T GET IT TOGETHER...
Malfunction.
Malfunction.
Impact pressure rated at 9g X 3,000 lbs./psi.
Severe internal damage.
KKERR-RAASSH!
BACK OFF!!
HE'S MINE!
WOULDN'T HAVE IT ANY OTHER WAY, PAL.

YOU HOLIER-THAN-THOU HYPOCRITE! YOU RUN AROUND WITH GUYS LIKE CAPTAIN AMERICA AND THOR--
--YOU CLAIM TO STAND FOR SOMETHING! TO REPRESENT AN IDEAL! AND THEN YOU GO AND TREAT PEOPLE LIKE DIRT!
Malfunction.
Housekeeping units responding.
YOU DON'T UNDERSTAND-- THERE'S SO LITTLE TIME--!!
WHERE ARE THOSE SYSTEMS?!
JUST 'CAUSE YOU'RE SO POWERFUL ...INVINCIBLE... YOU THINK YOU CAN DO WHATEVER YOU PLEASE!
15.627 seconds to Emergency Defense Condition 0.
I DON'T THINK I'M GOING TO HAVE FIFTEEN SECONDS...
System inoperative.
Malfunction.
WELL, I THINK THAT STINKS, PAL. MAYBE I CAN'T HURT YOU...
...MAYBE I CAN'T BEAT YOU...
...BUT MAYBE I CAN POUND SOME SENSE INTO YOU!!!
N...NO...HE'S ...SO STRONG... STABILIZERS SHORTING OUT...
Malfunction.
System inoperative.
System inoperative.
Sections B-19 through H-5 destroyed by impact.
Re-routing signal path around unavailable linkage.
37.552 seconds to linkage.
49.662 seconds to Emergency Defense Condition 0.
NO...NO TIME...
SPIDER-MAN'S BEYOND REASON...HIS RAGE DRIVING HIM ON...

HE'S... INCREDIBLY STRONG...
...LIGHTNING QUICK...
...CAN'T... CAN'T STAY OUT OF HIS WAY...
THE KID DID NOTHING TO YOU!! NOTHING!!
AND YOU'VE HURT HIM!! AND, IF I DON'T STOP YOU, YOU'LL PROBABLY KILL HIM!!
WELL, YOU'VE GOT ME OUT-GUNNED, MISTER, I'LL GIVE YOU THAT. I CAN'T TAKE YOU...

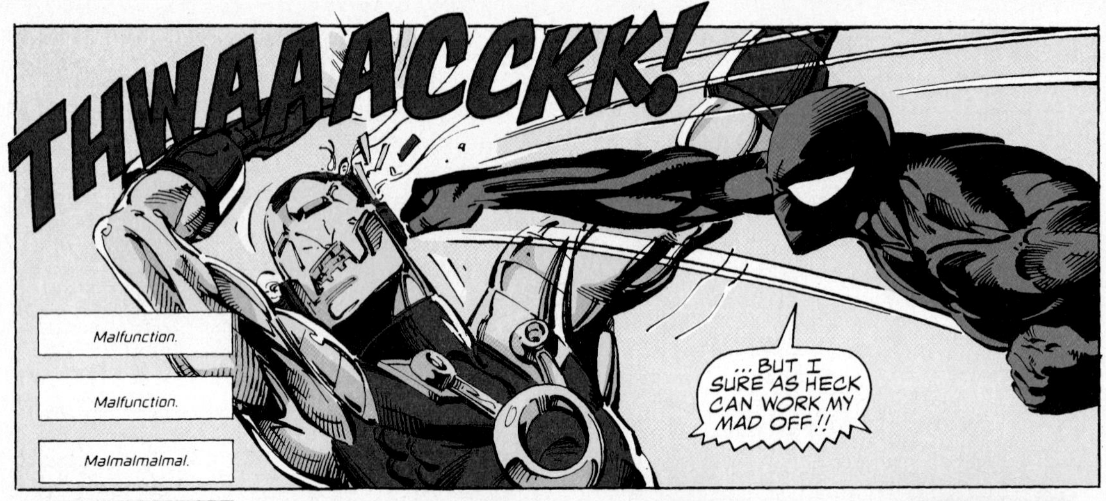
THWAAACCKK!
Malfunction.
Malfunction.
Malmalmalmal.
...BUT I SURE AS HECK CAN WORK MY MAD OFF!!

Engage inoperative malmal system A6.
IM6BP96201Q9M725452.
PP--KKOWW!

POW!

THAT'S IT, PAL.
I USED TO RESPECT YOU... ADMIRE YOU, ALMOST.
AND YOU... YOU...
CREEP!

WAIT... SPIDER-MAN ...YOU DON'T UNDERSTAND...
GOT THAT RIGHT.
I DON'T.
AND, NEVER WILL.

WAIT... THE TIME-SHIFT IS BEGINNING!! B..BUT ...I HAD MORE TIME...
I HAD MORE TIME!!!
VANISHED.
AND, I STILL DON'T QUITE KNOW...
...WHAT WE WERE FIGHTING ABOUT.

EMERGENCY
SEVERAL HOURS LATER...

THE SPIDER-MAN MENACE
12 YEAR-OLD HONOR STUDENT
INJURED IN SUPER-HERO SLUG-FEST
YOU MADE THE LATE EDITION, BOBBY.

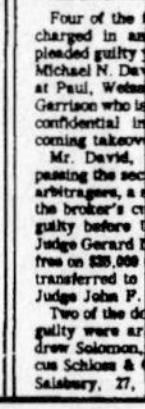

HAPPY?
YEAH, DAD.
THRILLED.
COME ON, BOBBY. SMILE A LITTLE, OKAY?
WHY BOTHER? YOU COULDN'T SEE IT.
RAP! RAP!

SPIDER-MAN!!
THAT POOR KID... DISFIGURED BY ALL THAT GLASS!

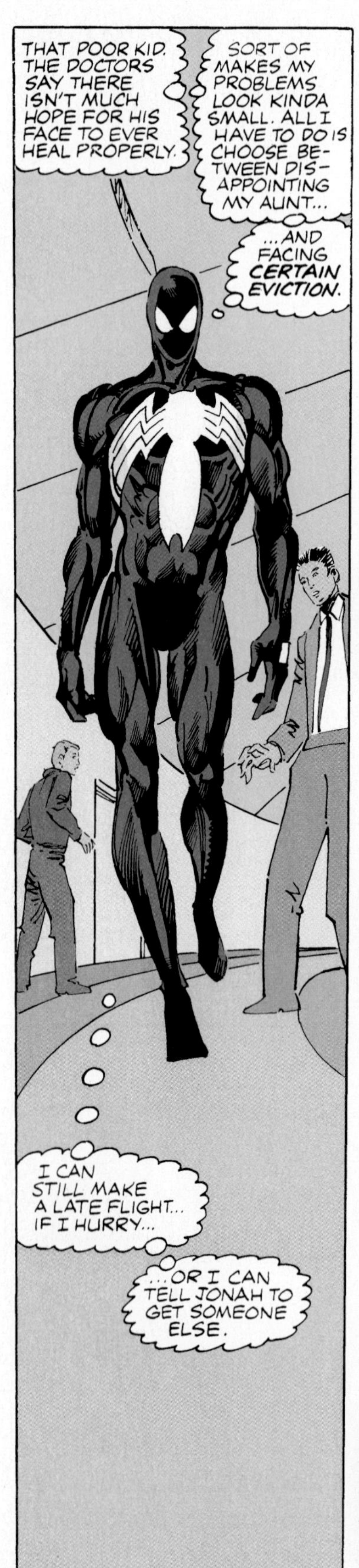
THAT POOR KID. THE DOCTORS SAY THERE ISN'T MUCH HOPE FOR HIS FACE TO EVER HEAL PROPERLY.
SORT OF MAKES MY PROBLEMS LOOK KINDA SMALL. ALL I HAVE TO DO IS CHOOSE BE-TWEEN DIS-APPOINTING MY AUNT...
...AND FACING CERTAIN EVICTION.
I CAN STILL MAKE A LATE FLIGHT... IF I HURRY...
...OR I CAN TELL JONAH TO GET SOMEONE ELSE.

SO, WHO DO I CALL... AUNT MAY OR JONAH?
EXCUSE ME...

OH GREAT. A COP.
I'M RICHARD SAUNDERS, BOBBY'S FATHER. I WANT TO THANK YOU FOR WHAT YOU DID FOR MY SON TODAY.
BOBBY'S A GOOD KID...A LITTLE AD-VENTUROUS, I GUESS. COMES FROM BEING LEFT ALONE SO MUCH.
MY BUSINESS INTERESTS TAKE ME OUT OF THE COUNTRY FREQUENTLY... OCCUPY A LOT OF MY TIME.
I'LL TELL YOU THOUGH, IT'S TIMES LIKE THESE THAT LET YOU KNOW...

...WHAT'S REALLY IMPORTANT IN LIFE.
KNOW WHAT I MEAN?

AH... YEAH.
LOOK, IF THERE'S ANYTHING I CAN DO FOR YOU...
AS A MATTER OF FACT, HOW ABOUT A LOAN...?
AH. OF COURSE.

HOW MUCH? TEN THOUSAND? FIFTEEN?
ACTUALLY... HOW ABOUT $275.36...?

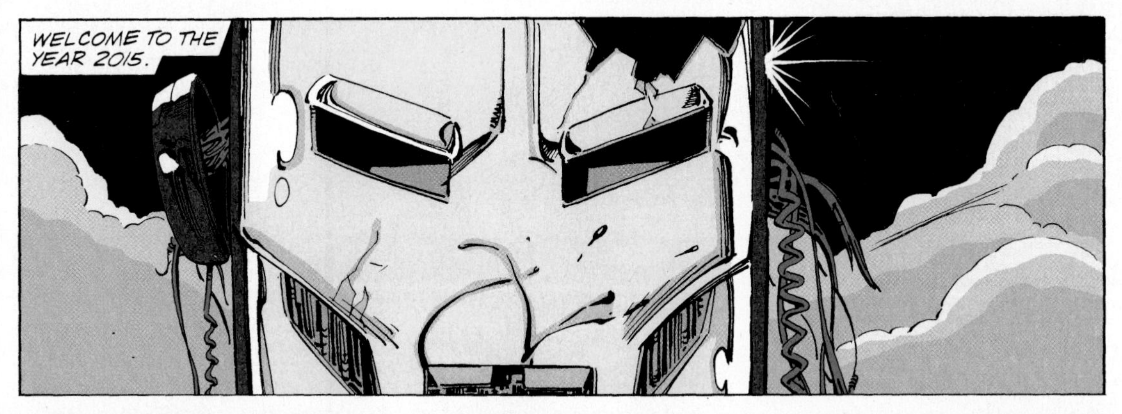
WELCOME TO THE YEAR 2015.

ARNO STARK, TIME MAGAZINE MAN OF THE YEAR, HAS JUST BEEN ABRUPTLY RETURNED FROM THE PAST.
HIS TIME MACHINE WAS AN UNQUALIFIED SUCCESS. IT OPERATED FLAWLESSLY.
STARK'S BOMB WAS LESS PERFECTED.

...NO...
THERE WAS A FATAL FLAW IN THE TIMING SEQUENCE.
AN ERROR IN LOGIC. ONE THAT WOULD HAVE EVENTUALLY BEEN DISCOVERED.

STARK
BUT ROBERT SAUNDERS ARMED THE BOMB.
...NO ...NO...
AND NO ONE COULD HAVE KNOWN. NO ONE COULD HAVE SUSPECTED.
STARK NEVER HAD A CHANCE.

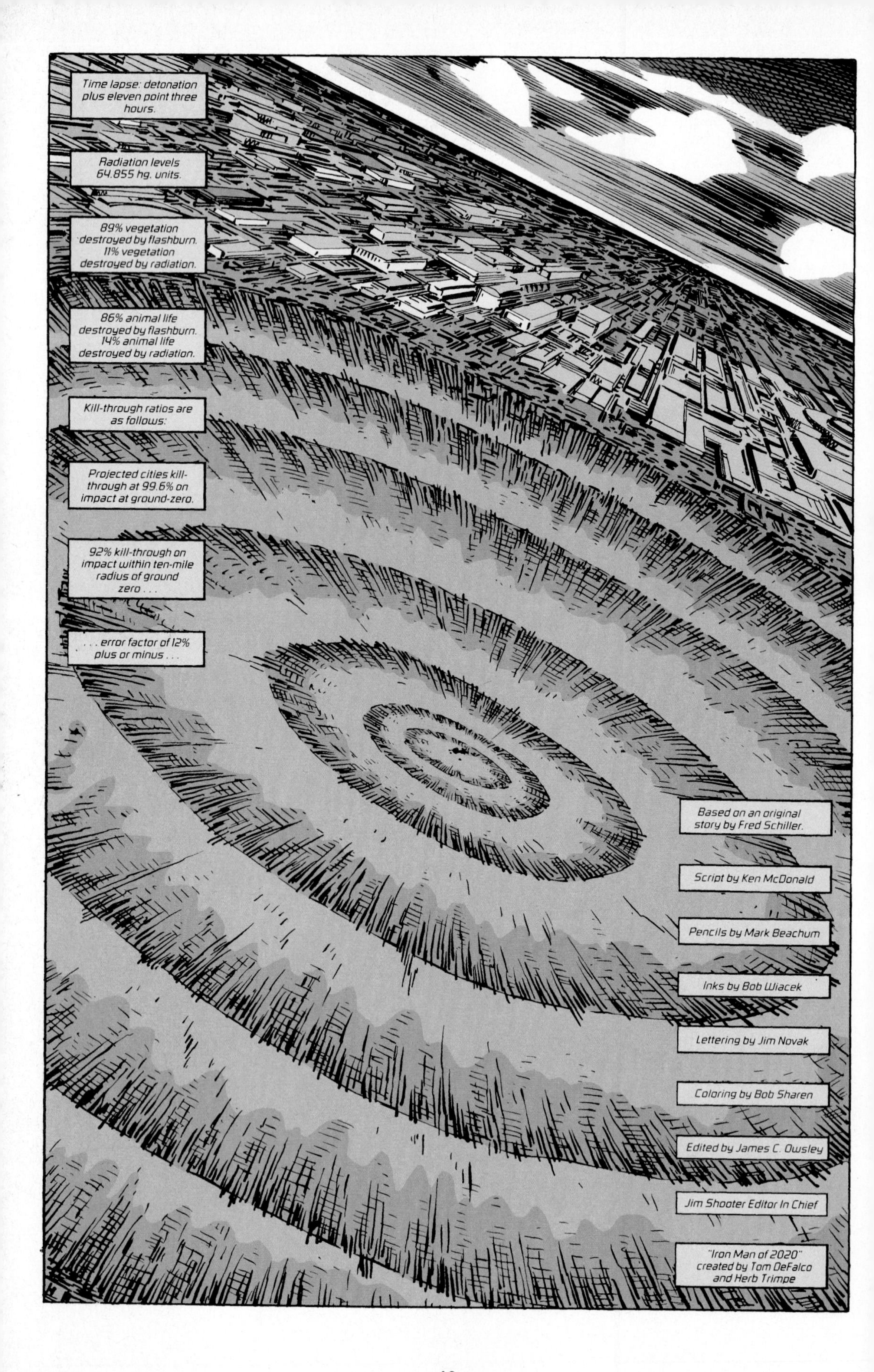
Time lapse: detonation plus eleven point three hours.
Radiation levels 64.855 hg. units.
89% vegetation destroyed by flashburn. 11% vegetation destroyed by radiation.
86% animal life destroyed by flashburn. 14% animal life destroyed by radiation.
Kill-through ratios are as follows:
Projected cities kill-through at 99.6% on impact at ground-zero.
92% kill-through on impact within ten-mile radius of ground zero . . .
. . . error factor of 12% plus or minus . . .
Based on an original story by Fred Schiller.
Script by Ken McDonald
Pencils by Mark Beachum
Inks by Bob Wiacek
Lettering by Jim Novak
Coloring by Bob Sharen
Edited by James C. Owsley
Jim Shooter Editor In Chief
"Iron Man of 2020" created by Tom DeFalco and Herb Trimpe

MARVEL®

#1 IN A FOUR-ISSUE LIMITED SERIES

# MACHINE MAN™



75¢
1
OCT
02977

APPROVED BY THE COMICS CODE AUTHORITY

ENTER THE TERRIFYING WORLD OF THE NEAR FUTURE! ENTER THE WORLD OF
MACHINE
"HE LIVES AGAIN!"
BAINTRONICS, INCORPORATED
STAN LEE PRESENTS:
TOM DeFALCO SCRIPT
HERB TRIMPE BREAKDOWNS
BARRY WINDSOR-SMITH FINISHES + COLOR
MICHAEL HIGGINS LETTERING
LARRY HAMA EDITOR
JIM SHOOTER EDITOR-IN-CHIEF

SEPTEMBER 23, 2020...
DEEP WITHIN BAINTRONICS STORAGE WAREHOUSE #5, A MASSIVE METAL CREATURE PROWLS THE FLOORS...
IT IS A MODEL IU-104/E...
...AN ELIMINATOR!

ITS PRIMARY FUNCTION IS TO REMOVE OBSOLETE MATERIALS FROM THIS WAREHOUSE COMPLEX...
EVERY STORAGE CONTAINER LOCATED WITHIN THIS SEVENTEEN MILE LONG BUILDING HAS BEEN BRANDED WITH A MAGNETIC TAPE WHICH IDENTIFIES ITS CONTENTS...
THE IU-104/E SCANS THESE TAPES--INSTANTLY CROSS-REFERENCING THEM WITH ITS PROGRAMMING FROM BAINTRONICS CENTRAL--AND ELIMINATES THOSE CONTAINERS WHICH ARE NO LONGER NEEDED...

THIS SYSTEM WAS IMPLEMENTED IN THE SPRING OF 2007, AND HAS BEEN UPGRADED EVERY SUCCEEDING FIVE YEARS...

OCCASIONALLY, IN THE DARKER RECESSES OF THE COMPLEX, THE IU-104/E STILL STUMBLES ACROSS AN OUTMODED CONTAINER--
DANGER
PRIORITY
RED
--WITH HAND-LETTERED INSTRUCTIONS INSTEAD OF A MAGNETIC TAPE...

SINCE THE IU-104/E CANNOT PROPERLY SCAN THESE CONTAINERS--
SIX
--IT IMMEDIATELY JUDGES THEM OBSOLETE!

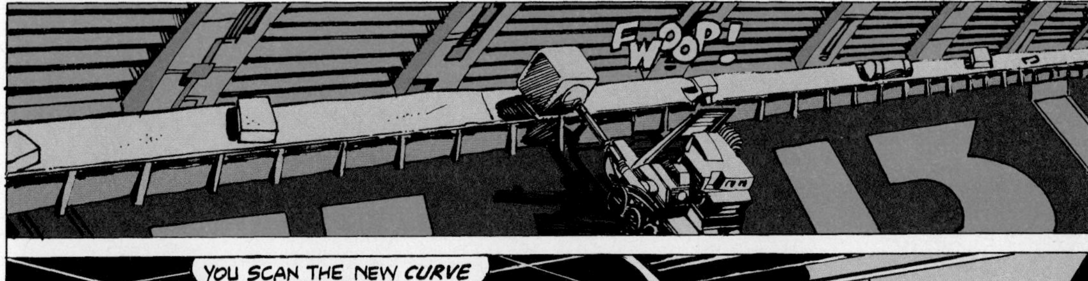
FWOOP!

YOU SCAN THE NEW CURVE IN SHIPPING?
DANGER
PRIORITY
RED
SIX
YEAH, BO' SHE'S TIGHT!

DANGER
PRIORITY
RED

PWOP!
BAINT
MIU 72

VRROAR!
BAINTRONICS
MIU 72RT
FWOOSH!
THUNDERING OVER THE NEW YORK CITY SKYLINE, THE IU-72RT MAKES THREE MORE STOPS IN ITS EARLY MORNING GARBAGE RUN--
--BEFORE PROCEEDING TO FIRE ISLAND, WHICH WAS CONVERTED TO A BAIN-TRONICS DUMPING GROUND DURING THE SUMMER RIOTS OF 1999...
BAINTRONICS
PRIVATE
PROPERTY!
ENTER AT RISK!
SMASH
MANY HOURS LATER, WHILE NIGHT DANCES ACROSS THE HORIZON, STRANGE, SILENT FIGURES BEGIN SHIFTING THROUGH THIS NEW MOUNTAIN OF DEBRIS...
DANGE
PRIORITY
RED
HEY! LOOK WHAT I'VE FOUND!

WAY TO SCAN, BRAIN!
YOU SCORED AN UNOPENED BAINY BOX! MAMA B MAY THINK IT'S FULL OF SKRAG BUT THERE'S ALWAYS A CHANCE WE'LL FIND SOMETHING USEFUL INSIDE!
BE CAREFUL, SLICK! THE BANNIES HAVE BEEN INCREASING SECURITY LATELY!
THAT BOX COULD BE WIRED...
OH, HASSLE, YOU WORRY ABOUT EVERY-THING!
I'M GLAD SOMEONE DOES, SWIFT! WE CAN'T ALL BE AS FEARLESS--OR AS WILD--AS YOU!
DANGER PRIORITY RED
THE BOX IS PRETTY OLD! I'VE SCANNED HER FOR ZAPPERS--BUT SHE LOOKS CLEAN...

THERE! I KNEW IT WOULDN'T TAKE LONG TO CRACK THEIR SEALS!
NOW, LET'S SEE JUST WHAT'S INSIDE...
XIS
DANGER PRIORITY RED
HOLY GOSH!

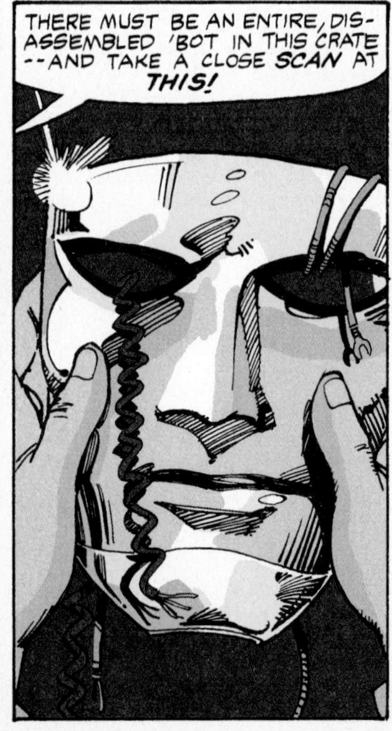
THERE MUST BE AN ENTIRE, DIS-ASSEMBLED 'BOT IN THIS CRATE --AND TAKE A CLOSE SCAN AT THIS!

I SURE WILL--
--JUST AS SOON AS I JOIN YOU!

WHAT EXACTLY IS IT, BRAIN?
I'VE NEVER SEEN ANYTHING LIKE IT BEFORE, SWIFT-- BUT I'D GUESS IT'S AN ARTIFICIAL FACE-- MEANT FOR A 'BOT.

A 'BOT WITH HUMAN FEATURES?!
GET STRAIGHT, BO'!
AW, SLICK, I THINK IT'S A REAL TIGHT IDEA!
THERE'S SOMETHING STRANGE ABOUT THIS RO! I WONDER WHY IT WAS DISASSEMBLED--?!

DO YOUR WONDERING LATER, BRAIN!
WE'VE WASTED ENOUGH TIME HERE! LET'S GET SKIPPIN' BEFORE--

TOO LATE! WE'VE ALREADY BEEN SCANNED!
HERE COME--

"--THE BAINIES!"
...WE HAVE FOUR DISTINCT HEAT PATTERNS-- TWO 'BOTS AND A PAIR OF CURVES!
ANOTHER PACK OF MIDNIGHT WRECKERS! WHY CAN'T THEY GET HONEST WORK-- INSTEAD OF RAIDING OUR DUMPS FOR DISCARDED TOOLS AND MATERIALS-- FOR THEIR ILLEGAL ROBOT TRADE?!
ACTIVATE THE KILLER-'BOTS! THE ONLY GOOD WRECKERS--

"--HAVE ALREADY STOPPED BREATHING!"
THEY'RE COMING IN TOO FAST!
WE'LL NEVER REACH OUR SKIPPERS IN TIME TO ESCAPE!

BLAST THEM!
IT'S OUR ONLY HOPE!

FWAM
FWAM
FWAM
FWAM

NICE SHOOTING, HASSLE! YOU MANAGED TO CRIPPLE THEIR COMMAND FLOATER!
HI, GUYS! MIND IF I DROP IN--?!
CLANG!

I DON'T BELIEVE SWIFT! SHE'S ACTUALLY ENJOYING THIS!
AND HASSLE IS AS CALM AND EMOTIONLESS AS EVER!

BA-DOOM!
SCREEN ME, SLICK! I'M GOING TO TRY TO LOAD THE CRATE ABOARD ONE OF OUR SKIPPERS!

I'LL TRY--BUT HURRY!
WE CAN'T KEEP THESE RO'S DISTRACTED FOREVER--AND THERE'S DEFINITELY NO PROFIT IN DYING!
TWOK!

DON'T BE A VIDIOT, SLICK!
SPWAM!
THESE COMBAT-DRONES ARE THE LEAST OF OUR PROBLEMS!

BDWAM!
IF THOSE TWO BAINIES HAD TIME TO TAG A CALL TO THEIR HOME BASE, WE MAY BE FACING A HORDE OF REINFORCEMENTS--
--OR EVEN WORSE... A C-28 BATTLE-'BOT!

HA! WE'RE NOT IMPORTANT ENOUGH FOR A DEATH-MACHINE LIKE THE C-28!
DANGER PRIORITY RED
ALL LOADED, SLICK!
THEN LET'S HIT THE SKIES, PACK!
YOU COMING, HASSLE?

NOT UNTIL I RELOAD!
I FEEL NAKED WITHOUT A FULL CHARGE!

SKRAG! THEY'VE FIRED THEIR SKIPPERS--AND THEY'RE ROCKETING TOWARD THE CITY!
THAT CURVE ZIGGED OUR TELE-SCREEN--

"--SO WE CAN'T EVEN SIGNAL A PASSING PATROL!"
NO SIGN OF PURSUIT!
JUST TO BE SAFE, LET'S BOUNCE BETWEEN A FEW MORE SCRAPERS --BEFORE WE HEAD HOME!
DANGER PRIORITY RED
DISTILLED LONDON DRY GIN

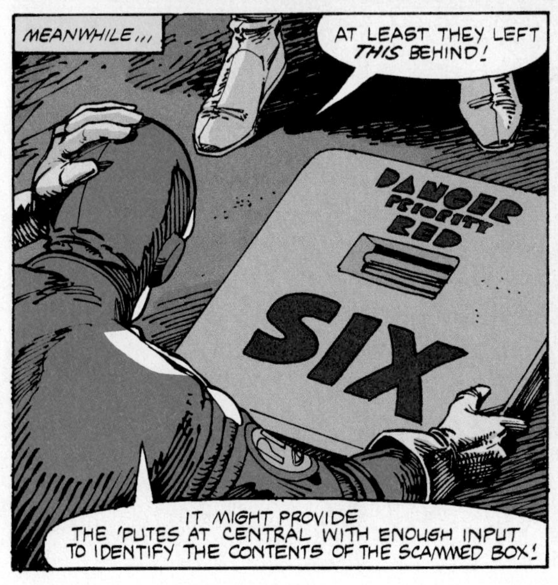
MEANWHILE...
AT LEAST THEY LEFT THIS BEHIND!
DANGER PRIORITY RED
SIX
IT MIGHT PROVIDE THE 'PUTES AT CENTRAL WITH ENOUGH INPUT TO IDENTIFY THE CONTENTS OF THE SCAMMED BOX!

EARLY THE NEXT MORNING AT BAINTRONICS CENTRAL...
I AM SURROUNDED BY MISFITS, INCOMPETENTS, AND ASSASSINS!
BAINTRONICS
BAINTRONICS

IN THE PRIVATE OFFICES OF SUNSET BAIN, THE PRINCIPLE OWNER OF BAINTRONICS, INC...
MEN LIKE YOU DISGUST ME! YOU WORK FOR THE RICHEST, MOST POWERFUL CORPORATION IN THE WORLD-- AND STILL YOU LET A BAND OF SCAVENGERS MAKE FOOLS OF YOU!
I USUALLY DON'T INVOLVE MYSELF IN THESE PETTY INCIDENTS-- BUT I WAS PARTICULARLY DISTURBED BY THE REPORT OF LAST NIGHT'S FIASCO!

BAINTRONICS MANUFACTURES ROBOTS. THESE GANGS OF "MIDNIGHT WRECKERS"-- AND THEIR HIGHLY ORGANIZED TRADE IN BLACKMARKET ROBOTICS--ARE A THREAT TO OUR FINANCIAL SECURITY.
I WANT THEM ELIMINATED-- NOW!

MADAM BAIN, ALL WRECKERS LIVE IN PACKS... LIKE ANIMALS... BUT I'VE NEVER SEEN A PACK LIKE THE ONE LAST NIGHT.
THERE WAS SOME THING REALLY SPECIAL ABOUT THE WAY THEY MOVED AND FOUGHT TOGETHER...

I WANT RESULTS--NOT EXCUSES!

WE MUST MAKE AN EXAMPLE OF THIS PACK! FIND THEM--AND THE CONTENTS OF THE BOX THEY STOLE! NOW!
YES, MADAM.
WILL YOU BE NEEDING US ANYMORE?

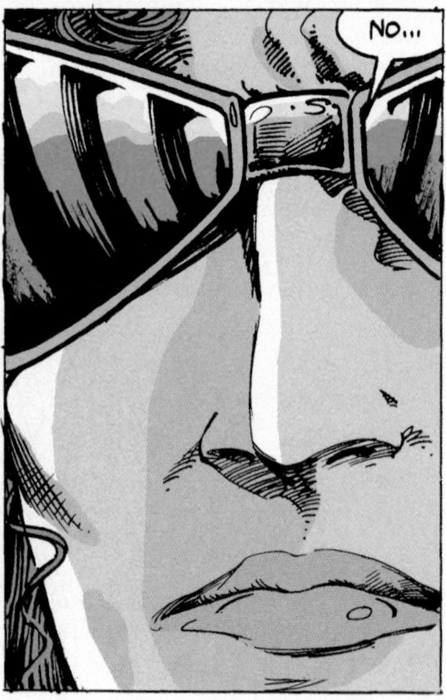
NO...

"...I WISH TO BE ALONE!"
FOOLS!
THEY'RE ALL FOOLS AND INCOMPETENTS!

EVEN MY PRIVATE BEAUTICIANS ARE FAILING ME!
FOR THE MONEY I PAY, YOU'D THINK THEY COULD MAKE ME LOOK YOUNGER, AND FAR MORE ATTRACTIVE...

I'M SURE THEY DO THEIR BEST... BUT, AFTER ALL, YOU ARE OVER SEVENTY YEARS OLD...
YOU--

--SPYING ON ME AGAIN?!
YOU KNOW BETTER THAN THAT!
WHAT'S WRONG, SUNSET? WE'VE BEEN TOGETHER A LONG TIME...
I CAN SENSE WHEN SOMETHING IS REALLY TROUBLING YOU...

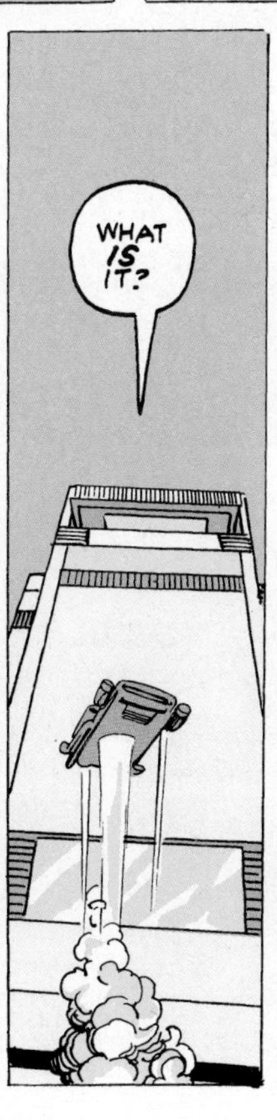
WHAT IS IT?

YOU'RE RIGHT. YOU'RE ALWAYS RIGHT...
THAT BOX--THE ONE WHICH WAS STOLEN --CONTAINED A MEMENTO FROM MY DISTANT PAST--

"--A MOMENTO WHICH I HAD HOPED WAS LOST AND GONE... FOREVER!"
WILL YOU PLEASE LOWER THE VOLUME ON THE QUADROSETTE--?!
Enter
$30 I KM
$10

C'MON, SLICK! I CAN'T CONCENTRATE ON MY DAILY EXERCISES WITH THAT THING BLASTING!
LUNCH
YOU HAVE NO APPRECIATION FOR THE FINER THINGS IN LIFE, SWIFT! THIS IS CLASSICAL MUSIC... THE PLASMATICS!
HOW'S THAT NEW 'BOT SCANNING, BRAIN?

IT'S ALL ASSEMBLED! I JUST WANTED TO GIVE IT SOME FRESH PAINT--AND A NEW LOOK!
YEAH, ITS OLD COLORS WERE A LITTLE DRAB!
THIS THING IS ANCIENT! MUST HAVE BEEN BUILT BEFORE THE ANTI-ROBOT RIOTS OF THE LATE 1990'S!

I DON'T KNOW IF ITS STORAGE BATTERIES CAN STILL HOLD A CHARGE--

--BUT I'M GOING TO TRY TO JUICE IT BACK INTO LIFE!
CLIK!

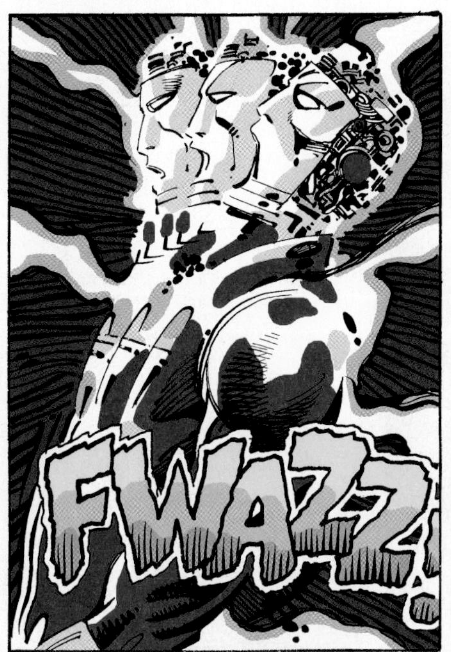
FWAZZ!

WHOA! HOPE I DIDN'T FUSE ALL OF ITS INTERNAL CIRCUITRY WITH THAT JOLT!
CLIK!

IT'S SHAKING LIKE A VIDEO ADDICT--A VIDIOT--WHO'S BEEN UNPLUGGED FROM HIS SCREEN!
GIVE IT A CHANCE! IT'S BEEN LYING DORMANT FOR A LOT OF YEARS!

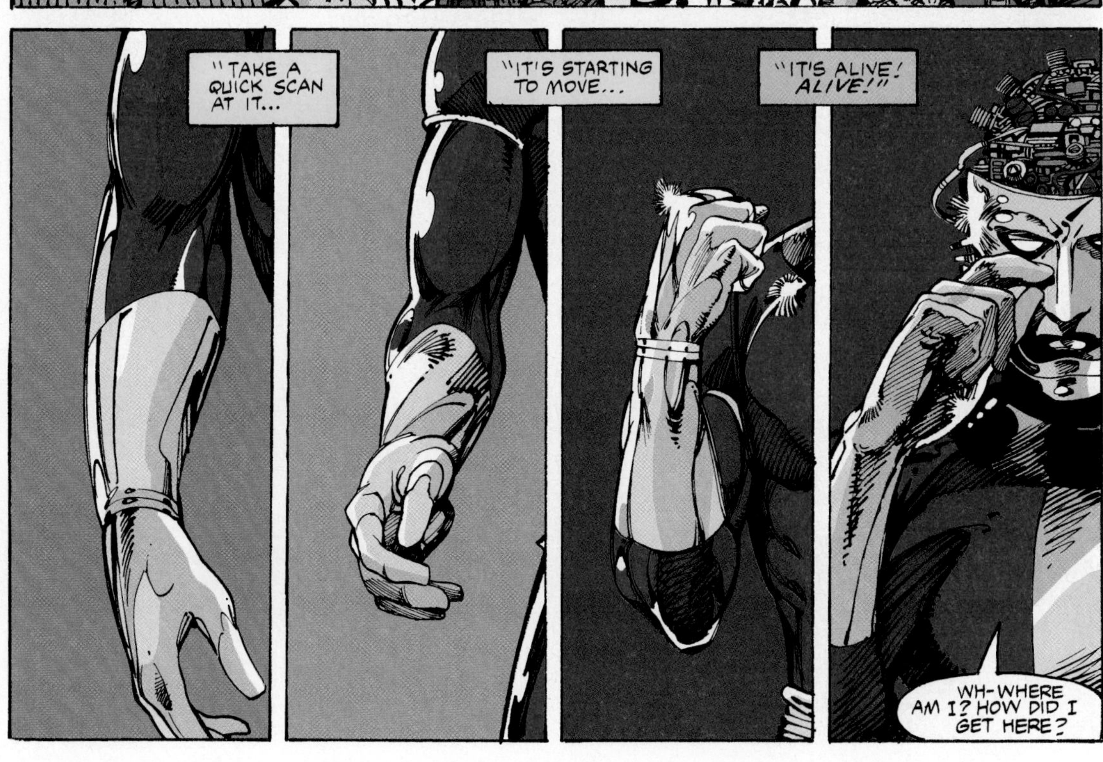
"TAKE A QUICK SCAN AT IT...
"IT'S STARTING TO MOVE...
"IT'S ALIVE! ALIVE!"
WH-WHERE AM I? HOW DID I GET HERE?

HOLY SKRAG! I KNEW IT WAS CAPABLE OF SPEECH--BUT IT SOUNDS ALMOST HUMAN!
WHO ARE YOU PEOPLE?
WE WERE JUST ABOUT TO ASK YOU THE SAME QUESTION.

I'VE HAD MANY NAMES IN MY TIME, BUT THE WORLD KNOWS ME BEST AS--

--MACHINE MAN!
SORRY, BUT THAT NAME DOESN'T LIGHT MY TELESCREEN!
YOUR WORDS ARE STRANGE... BUT YOUR MEANING IS CLEAR...

"PERHAPS, I SHOULD START AT THE BEGINNING. I WAS ORIGINALLY CREATED AS PART OF AN EXPERIMENT--TO DEVELOP A ROBOT--WHO WAS CAPABLE OF INDEPENDENT THOUGHT...
"MY PROGRAMMER, DR. ABEL STACK, TREATED ME LIKE I WAS HIS OWN SON.
SECRET DRAWER
Project X-51
TOP SECRET

"WHEN THE ORDER WAS GIVEN TO TERMINATE THE EXPERIMENT, DR. STACK SACRIFICED HIS OWN LIFE TO SAVE MINE...
"I NEVER RECOVERED FROM HIS DEATH
X-51

"I ALWAYS FELT LIKE AN OUTSIDER--EXCEPT WITH MY GOOD FRIENDS PETER SPAULDING AND GEARS GARVIN...
"THOSE TWO WERE ALWAYS BICKERING ABOUT SOMETHING...

"AND THEN, I MET JOCASTA--A FORMER MEMBER OF THE SUPER HERO TEAM KNOWN AS THE AVENGERS...
"WE MIGHT HAVE FOUND TRUE HAPPINESS TOGETHER, BUT HER ROBOT BODY WAS DESTROYED IN A TERRIBLE EXPLOSION...*
*IN MARVEL TWO-IN-ONE #93.

"OF COURSE, I HAD MY SHARE OF ENEMIES, LIKE SENATOR MILES BRICKMAN, A POLITICAL OPPORTUNIST--
"--AND MADAM MENACE, WHO DEALT IN ILLEGAL ARMAMENTS--AND WANTED TO MASS-PRODUCE ROBOTS LIKE ME FOR HER CLIENTS...

...I THINK HER REAL NAME WAS SUNSET BAIN!
"SUNSET BAIN"?!
I HOPE YOU DON'T MEAN THE SUNSET BAIN!
ER... DO YOU KNOW TODAY'S DATE?

NO, I'M NOT SURE... IT'S SO HARD TO THINK... MY MIND IS UNNN
WHAT'S WRONG WITH HIM, BRAIN?
I DON'T KNOW! GRAB HIM! DON'T LET HIM FALL!

MEANWHILE...
JUST THINK--TODAY WE MET THE LEGENDARY BOSS-LADY HERSELF!
MY MATING GROUP WILL NEVER BELIEVE ME!

I WOULDN'T DO ANY BRAGGING--UNTIL AFTER WE FIND THAT PACK OF WRECKERS!
GENTLE OUT, BO'! OUR 'PUTER RECORDED THEIR HEAT PATTERNS. IT'S ONLY A MATTER OF TIME BEFORE WE SCAN 'EM!
AND WE'LL BE READY FOR 'EM THIS TIME...
WE HAVE A FULL COMPLIMENT OF STANDARD-ISSUE COMBAT 'BOTS...

"...PLUS THE INVINCIBLE FIREPOWER OF A C-28 DEATH-DEALER!"

I STILL DON'T FLASH IT, BO'...
McDo

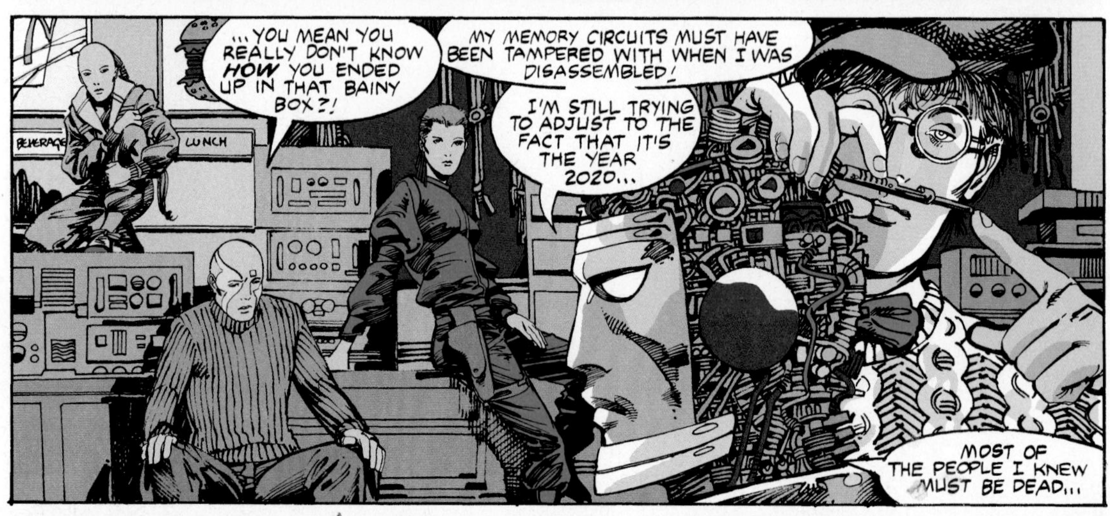
...YOU MEAN YOU REALLY DON'T KNOW HOW YOU ENDED UP IN THAT BAINY BOX?!
MY MEMORY CIRCUITS MUST HAVE BEEN TAMPERED WITH WHEN I WAS DISASSEMBLED!
I'M STILL TRYING TO ADJUST TO THE FACT THAT IT'S THE YEAR 2020...
MOST OF THE PEOPLE I KNEW MUST BE DEAD...
BEVERAGE
LUNCH

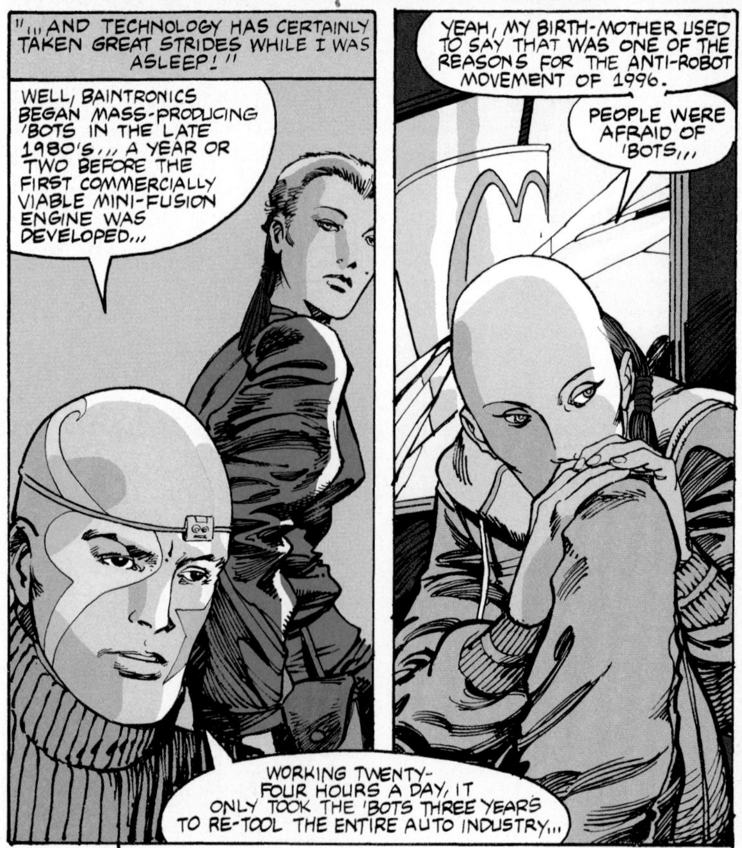
"...AND TECHNOLOGY HAS CERTAINLY TAKEN GREAT STRIDES WHILE I WAS ASLEEP!"
WELL, BAINTRONICS BEGAN MASS-PRODUCING 'BOTS IN THE LATE 1980'S... A YEAR OR TWO BEFORE THE FIRST COMMERCIALLY VIABLE MINI-FUSION ENGINE WAS DEVELOPED...
YEAH, MY BIRTH-MOTHER USED TO SAY THAT WAS ONE OF THE REASONS FOR THE ANTI-ROBOT MOVEMENT OF 1996.
PEOPLE WERE AFRAID OF 'BOTS...
WORKING TWENTY-FOUR HOURS A DAY, IT ONLY TOOK THE 'BOTS THREE YEARS TO RE-TOOL THE ENTIRE AUTO INDUSTRY...

THE GOVERNMENT ENDED THE RIOTS IN 2001-- WHEN IT BEGAN REGULATING THE SALE OF 'BOTS-- AND IT GRANTED BAINTRONICS A MONOPOLY ON THE TRADE!

BUT, PEOPLE WANT 'BOTS--SO PACKS LIKE OURS SUPPLY 'EM--FOR A PRICE!
HOLD STILL! I THINK I'VE FOUND YOUR PROBLEM...

YO!
THE SCANNER'S FLASHING!

THERE! YOU ONLY NEEDED A FEW MINOR ADJUSTMENTS. I GUESS I'M JUST NOT USED TO WORKING ON ANTIQUE MODELS LIKE YOU.
YES, I SUPPOSE I AM AN "ANTIQUE" TO YOU...

THAT'S GOING TO TAKE A LOT OF GETTING USED TO...
WHAT ARE WE GOING TO DO WITH HIM, SLICK?
HE ISN'T YOUR EVERYDAY INDUSTRIAL USE 'BOT!
WE CAN'T JUST SELL HIM TO THE HIGHEST BIDDER!
GIVE ME TIME TO THINK!

WAAAA!

YOU CAN THINK LATER!
SOMETHING'S PENETRATED OUR OUTER SECURITY SCREENS!
WE'VE GOT--

"--TROUBLE!"
FA-WAM!
DO NOT RUN! DO NOT MOVE!
DO NOT ATTEMPT TO ESCAPE!
I AM A LEGALLY-SANCTIONED C-28 DEATH-DEALER! AND I HAVE BEEN PROGRAMMED TO CRUSH ALL OPPOSITION!

IF YOU WISH TO LIVE, YOU WILL ALLOW MY NARCO-PELLETS TO RENDER YOU ALL UNCONSCIOUS!
THEY RELEASE A SLEEP-INDUCING CHEMICAL WHICH IS ABSORBED THROUGH THE SKIN!
FWIT!
FWIT!
FWIT!

GET DOWN!
FWAM
WE CAN'T LET THEM TAKE US!
HASSLE'S RIGHT! WE KNOW WHAT MAMA B HAS PLANNED FOR US!

YOU ARE ALL BEING VERY FOOLISH! I CAN WITHSTAND ANY ATTACK...

I CAN OBLITERATE ANY RESISTANCE...
BA-BAM

YOU SEEM TO HAVE A VERY INFLATED OPINION OF YOURSELF, FELLA!
I DON'T KNOW WHY YOU WANT THESE KIDS --BUT FATE SEEMS TO HAVE THROWN ME IN THEIR CORNER!
YOU CAN'T STOP ME!

MAYBE I CAN'T--
BUT I'M SURE
GOING TO TRY!
UNNN! YOU
ARE FAR
STRONGER THAN
I CALCULATED!
YOUR STRENGTH
ALMOST RIVALS
MY OWN!

BUT YOUR BODY IS
NOT EQUIPPED WITH
A PAIR OF ELECTRO-
BLASTERS!
UFFF
BWOOM!
I CAN SEE
THAT YOU DON'T SUBSCRIBE TO
THE CONCEPT OF "FAIR PLAY"!

BDAM!
BDAM!
I DON'T BELIEVE IT! MACHINE
MAN ACTUALLY SEEMS TO BE
HOLDING HIS OWN AGAINST
THAT C-28--
--BUT THAT'S
IMPOSSIBLE!

IMPOSSIBLE
OR NOT--
--I'M REAL GLAD
HE'S ON OUR
SIDE!

WOULD YOU
MIND TAKING
THIS FROM
ME?
I'M ALL THUMBS WHEN IT COMES
TO HEAVY OBJECTS!
KRASH!

YO, MACHINE MAN--ARE YOU STILL FUNCTIONAL?!
I THINK SO--BUT THAT C-28 PACKS ONE HECK OF A WALLOP!
SWIFT--BEHIND YOU! OTHERS ARE RUSHING FORWARD.

THANKS FOR THE SCAN, MM--BUT DON'T WORRY ABOUT ME!
I'LL JUST LEAP--FORWARD

--AND GIVE THESE PRETTY BO'S A GREETING--

--THEY'LL NEVER FORGET!
HOW? SHE MOVES LIKE A LIVING WHIRLWIND! :UNNN:
STOP HER!

UH-OH! THE COMBAT 'BOT IS MOVING IN FAST!
I HAVEN'T WORKED ON ONE OF THESE MODELS IN YEARS--

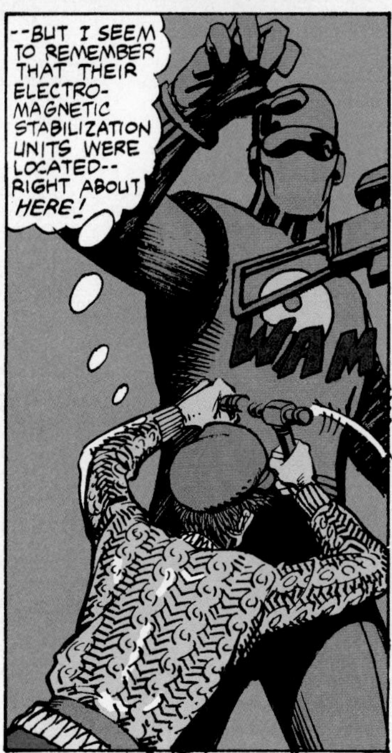
--BUT I SEEM TO REMEMBER THAT THEIR ELECTRO-MAGNETIC STABILIZATION UNITS WERE LOCATED--RIGHT ABOUT HERE!
WAM

YOU'D THINK SOMEONE WOULD CORRECT A DESIGN FLAW LIKE THAT!
SPROING!

I DON'T SUPPOSE YOU'D CARE TO POSTPONE THIS FIGHT! NEXT CENTURY WOULD BE FINE WITH ME!
WHAT KIND OF ROBOT ARE YOU? YOUR CLUMSY ATTEMPTS AT HUMOR SOUND ALMOST HUMAN!
I'LL TAKE THAT AS A COMPLIMENT!
I DONT CARE HOW YOU TAKE IT!

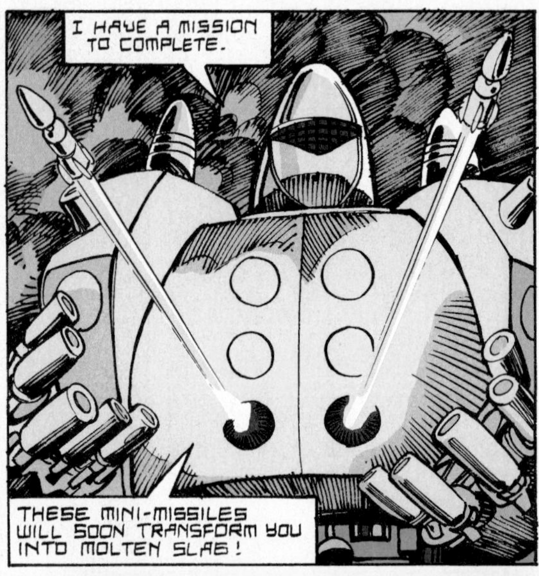
I HAVE A MISSION TO COMPLETE.
THESE MINI-MISSILES WILL SOON TRANSFORM YOU INTO MOLTEN SLAG!

NICE MISSILES!
CWOOM
CUTE--BUT DEADLY!
I'M SURE THEY WOULD HAVE DONE CONSIDERABLE DAMAGE--IF THEY HAD HIT ME BUT I CAME EQUIPPED WITH A FEW TRICKS OF MY OWN!

MY OLD FRIEND--GEARS GARVIN--EVEN INSTALLED A MODIFIED .357 MAGNUM IN MY RIGHT HAND!
PWAM

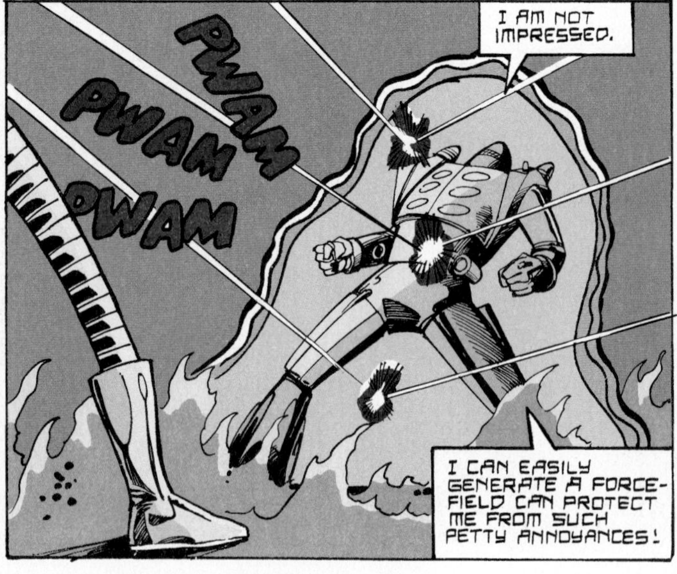
PWAM
PWAM
PWAM
I AM NOT IMPRESSED.
I CAN EASILY GENERATE A FORCE-FIELD CAN PROTECT ME FROM SUCH PETTY ANNOYANCES!

ALL RIGHT--MAYBE THE BULLETS WERE A BAD IDEA!
NOW THAT YOU'VE DROPPED YOUR FORCE-FIELD, I'LL TRY A MORE DIRECT APPROACH!

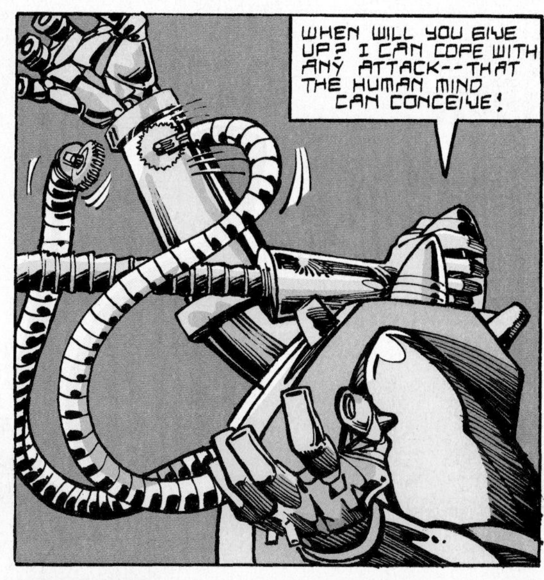
WHEN WILL YOU GIVE UP? I CAN COPE WITH ANY ATTACK--THAT THE HUMAN MIND CAN CONCEIVE!

YEOW!
RRRR

GO EASY ON THE MERCHANDISE, PAL!
I DON'T KNOW IF I CAN STILL GET REPLACEMENT PARTS!

I HAVE BEEN IN COUNTLESS BATTLES--BUT HAVE NEVER MET A FOE LIKE YOU. WHAT WILL IT TAKE TO DEFEAT YOU?
I REALLY DON'T KNOW.
NO ONE HAS EVER DONE IT!

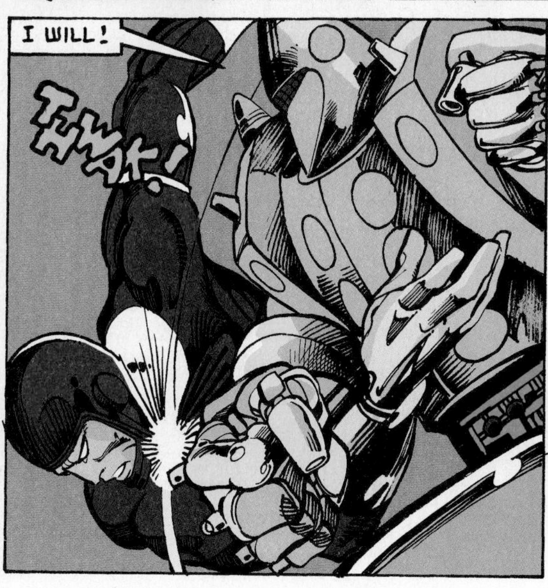
I WILL!
THWAK!

I INTEND TO BATHE YOU WITH A CONCENTRATED SPRAY OF ACID--
--STARTING WITH YOUR FACE!

NO!
YOU MIGHT NOT THINK MUCH OF MY FACE--BUT I'VE GROWN QUITE ACCUSTOMED TO IT!
RIP

ENOUGH!
I WILL KEEP HAMMERING AT YOU--UNTIL YOU HAVE THE GOOD SENSE TO SURRENDER!
SLAMM

BUT THAT COULD TAKE FOREVER-- AND I'VE ALREADY MADE DINNER PLANS!
IF MY FISTS WILL NOT CONVINCE YOU--PERHAPS MY LASER-BLAST WILL!

ANYTHING'S POSSIBLE...
HIGH VOLT OUTLET
Y'KNOW, PAL, I'M REAL GLAD YOU TOSSED ME IN THIS DIRECTION...

YOU SAID SOMETHING EARLIER-- ABOUT BEING ABLE TO COPE WITH ANY ATTACK-- THAT THE HUMAN MIND COULD CONCEIVE...

WELL, I DOUBT ANY HUMAN WOULD EVER CONSIDER USING HIS OWN BODY--

--TO COMPLETE AN ELECTRICAL CIRCUIT!
I WAS RIGHT! I CALCULATED THAT EVEN A POWER SYSTEM OF YOUR IMMENSE CAPABILITIES --COULDN'T HANDLE-- SUCH A MASSIVE OVERLOAD!
F-TOOM
ARRGGG!!

HE DID IT! MACHINE MAN BEAT THE C-28!
WE CAN CELEBRATE LATER! LET'S GET TO OUR SKIPPERS FIRST!
I'M COMING.
WHAT ARE YOU WAITING FOR, MM-- AN ENGRAVED INVITATION?!

YAH-ZOO! WE'LL BE SKIPPING ALONG THE OLD WESTSIDE HIGHWAY-- LONG BEFORE THOSE BAINIES HAVE A CHANCE TO REGROUP!
I DIDN'T KNOW YOU COULD FLY!
I CAN'T! I'M HITCHING A RIDE ON YOUR CRAFT-- BY NEGATING GRAVITY-- AND MAKING MYSELF WEIGHTLESS!

SO WHAT HAPPENS NOW?
HOW DO I FIT INTO THIS NEW WORLD?
DO I WANT TO?

CAN I TRUST THESE PEOPLE?
ARE ANY OF MY OLD FRIENDS STILL ALIVE?

QUESTIONS.
I HAVE TOO MANY QUESTIONS...

**Next Issue:** MACHINE MAN AND THE MIDNIGHT WRECKERS BEGIN THEIR SEARCH FOR-- **SANCTUARY!**

MARVEL®

#2 IN A FOUR-ISSUE LIMITED SERIES

75¢
2
NOV
02977



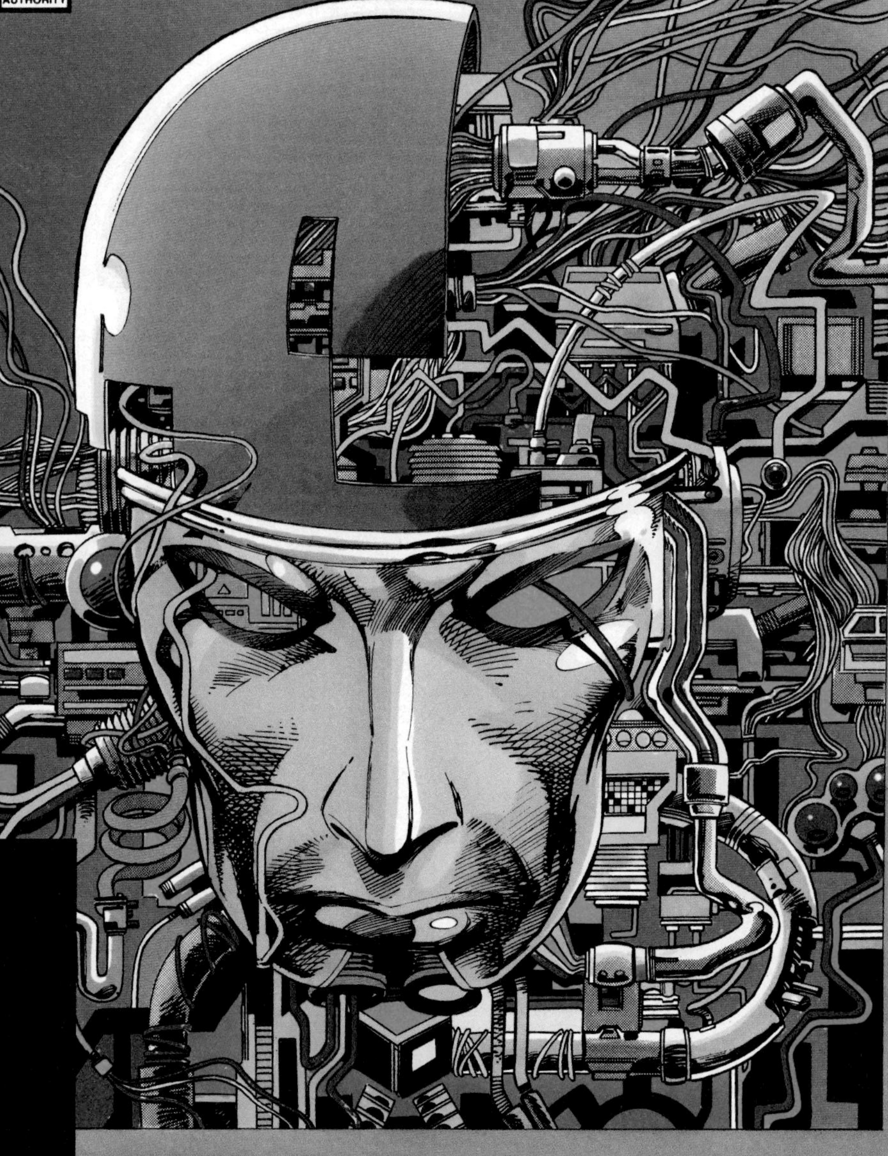

Enter the terrifying world of the near future! Enter the world of...
Machine Man
"If This Be Sanctuary?!"
Somewhere high above the streets of mid-town Manhattan, in the year 2020.
Juice it, Swift!
The Bainies have found us! We just picked up a pack of C-10 killer-bots!
I still don't scan it, Slick! We've been clipping spare robot parts from Bainy dumping grounds for years--and we've never made their hate parade!
But they've been on our tails ever since we found Machine Man in a discarded old storage container!
What's so special about him anyway?!
Stan Lee presents: Tom DeFalco script Herb Trimpe breakdowns Barry Windsor Smith finishes + colors Diana Albers letters Larry Hama editor Jim Shooter editor in chief

WE'LL FIND OUT SOON ENOU--
YEOW! WE'RE HIT!
CAN YOU KEEP US AIRBORNE, BRAIN?
BDAM
CRASH
I'LL TRY, HASSLE--BUT DON'T COUNT ON IT!

THOSE KIDS HAVEN'T GOT A CHANCE UNLESS...
SWIFT! BANK THIS SKIPPER TO THE RIGHT!
NOW!

WHAT'S THE SCAN, MACHINY?
THE ROBOTS OF THIS ERA MAY BE FAR MORE TECHNLOGICALLY ADVANCED THAN I--
--BUT I'M BETTING THAT EVEN THEY CAN'T REACT FAST ENOUGH--

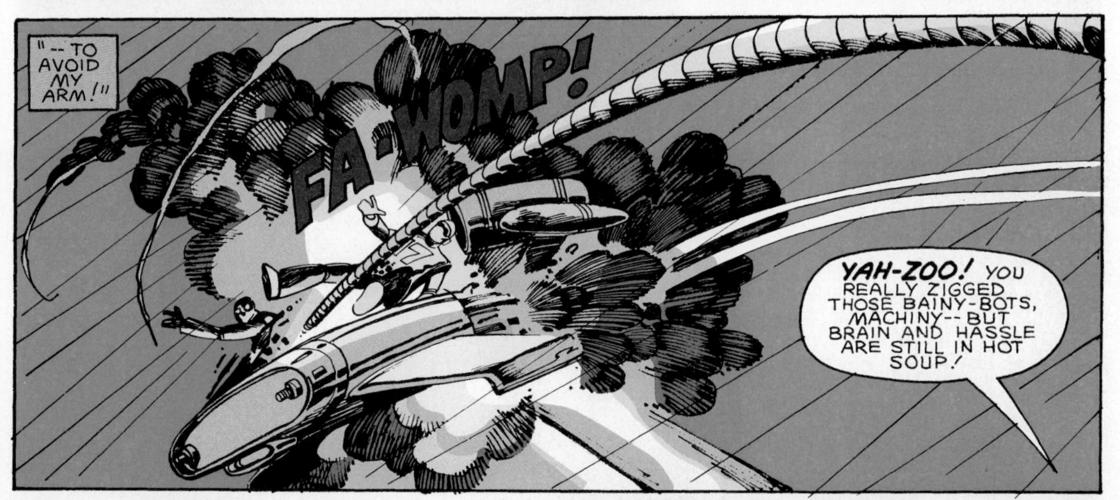
"--TO AVOID MY ARM!"
FA-WOMP!
YAH-ZOO! YOU REALLY ZIGGED THOSE BAINY-BOTS, MACHINY--BUT BRAIN AND HASSLE ARE STILL IN HOT SOUP!

I KNOW.
HURRY! LOCK US ON A COLLISION COURSE WITH THAT PURSUING CRAFT!
2

HEY! WHAT ARE YOU DOING--?!
RELAX.
MY LIMBS AND TORSO ARE EQUIPPED WITH TRANSISTORIZED ANTI-GRAVITY GENERATORS! WE'RE GOING TO SACRIFICE YOUR SKIPPER--

"FOR THE LIVES OF YOUR FRIENDS!"
KA WHAMM

HANG TIGHT, HASSLE! NOW THAT THE BAINIES ARE OFF OUR BACKS, I CAN TRY TO BRING US DOWN... IN ONE PIECE!
SCREEEE

NOT BAD, BRAIN! YOU ALWAYS DID HAVE A GENTLE TOUCH!
ARE YOU TWO ALL RIGHT?
SURE, WHY NOT?
THOSE C-10s MIGHT'VE TELESCREENED OUR LOCATION! WE'D BETTER GET MOVING!

DON'T FRET, IT, HASSLE! WE'LL BE LONG GONE BEFORE ANY-ONE CAN SCAN US!
HOW? YOU'VE LOST BOTH OF YOUR SKIPPERS!

HAVEN'T YOU EVER HEARD OF THE NEW YORK SUBWAY SYSTEM?!
DIG DEEP, PACK! WE NEED $14.37 IN EXACT CHANGE FOR EACH OF US!
SUBWAY
UPTOWN

BAINTRONICS CENTRAL...
I DON'T BELIEVE IT! ONE OF MY PATROLS REPORTED SIGHTING MACHINE MAN--

--BUT HE MANAGED TO ESCAPE AGAIN!
LET HIM GO, SUNSET! LEAVE HIM ALONE, AND FORGET ALL ABOUT HIM! HASN'T HE ALREADY SUFFERED ENOUGH AT YOUR HANDS?
DON'T TALK NONSENSE, JOCASTA! YOU KNOW VERY WELL THAT MY LIFE IS IN DANGER AS LONG AS MACHINE MAN LIVES!
BY NOW HE MUST REALIZE THAT I'M THE ONE WHO HAD HIM DEACTIVATED OVER THIRTY YEARS AGO.

SUNSET!
I MUST SPEAK WITH YOU-- IMMEDIATELY!
I'M SORRY, MADAM BAIN. HE INSISTED!
NO HARM DONE. I WAS EXPECTING AMBASSADOR BRICKMAN!
HOW ARE YOU, MILES?

LET'S NOT WASTE TIME WITH INSINCERE PLEASANTRIES! I JUST SCANNED THOSE TAPES YOU TELESCREENED ME! ARE THEY TRUE?
HAS MACHINE MAN REALLY RETURNED FROM THE GRAVE?!

I WOULD HAVE THOUGHT THAT A FORMER AMBASSADOR TO THE UNITED NATIONS COULD CONDUCT HIMSELF WITH GREATER DIGNITY.
WHAT'S JOCASTA DOING HERE? WASN'T SHE ONCE INVOLVED WITH MACHINE MAN?
YOU NEEDN'T CONCERN YOURSELF WITH JOCASTA--

--OR MACHINE MAN! I HAVE ALREADY ACQUIRED THE SERVICES OF AN EXPENSIVE, BUT HIGHLY EFFICIENT, "SPECIALIST" WHO WILL ATTEND TO HIM
I HOPE I'M NOT DISTURBING YOU, ARNO.
CLIK
NOT AT ALL, MADAM BAIN. IN FACT, I WAS ABOUT TO CALL YOU...
4

...AS YOU KNOW, MACHINE MAN IS TRAVELING WITH A PACK OF MIDNIGHT WRECKERS--A SMALL BAND OF CRIMINALS WHO DEAL IN ILLEGAL ROBOTICS!

THEY'RE SPOOKED--AND ON THE RUN--BUT I BELIEVE THAT I KNOW THEIR FINAL DESTINATION...


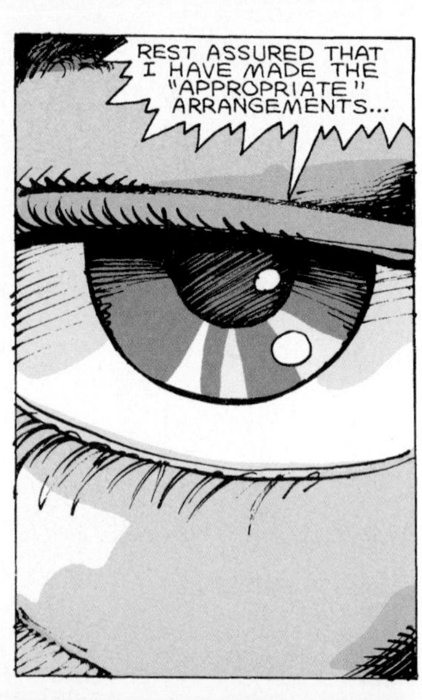

REST ASSURED THAT I HAVE MADE THE "APPROPRIATE" ARRANGEMENTS...

FOREST HILLS, QUEENS...

ENJOY THE HAT AND COAT, MM! GIFTS FROM A PROFESSIONAL MUGGER I MET ON THE SUBWAY LAST NIGHT!
WHAT DID YOU GIVE HIM, HASSLE?
HIS LIFE.
STEP IT UP, PACK! BROADONI IS EXPECTING US--AND YOU KNOW HOW HE HATES TO BE KEPT WAITING!

ASTRO
VID PARLOUR
ALL DAYS
WE'RE HERE.
SKRAG! A WORTHLESS SLIME-SUCKER LIKE BROADONI WOULD OWN A VID-PARLOR!

GO EASY, HASSLE!
WHY SHOULD I, SLICK?
THESE VIDOTS CAN'T HEAR ME! THEY'RE ALL IN THEIR OWN PRIVATE UNIVERSES!
5

LITE-BITE
Bongoloids
KILL YOUR NEIGHBOR
THEY'VE ALL BEEN SURGICALLY IMPLANTED WITH SPECIAL TERMINALS--WHICH LINK THEIR MINDS DIRECTLY TO THEIR MACHINES!
I KNOW ALL ABOUT THESE USELESS FREAKS!
MY OWN PARENTS WERE VIDEO ADDICTS!

YOU ARE LATE... BY FIVE FULL MINUTES!
I EXPECT TO BE COMPENSATED FOR MY LOST TIME.
YOU WILL BE.
LET'S NOT WASTE ANYMORE OF IT, FAT MAN! YOU KNOW WHY WE'RE HERE!
WE NEED SAFE TRANSPORT OUT OF TOWN!

WORD IS THAT THE BAINIES THINK YOU ARE ONE HOT PACK OF WRECKERS!
THAT'S TROUBLE--BAD TROUBLE--AND I AVOID TROUBLE--

--UNLESS THE PRICE IS RIGHT!
HOW MUCH DO YOU WANT?
MAKE ME AN OFFER!

WHAT IS HE--?!

FREEZE IT, FAT MAN!
MAKE ANOTHER MOVE--AND YOU'RE A PILE OF CHARRED MEAT
HASSLE! HAVE YOU GONE ZONKERS? WHAT ARE YOU--?!
I'M JUST TAKING PRECAUTIONS, SLICK! I THINK THIS WEASEL'S SOLD US OUT!

THERE! SOMETHING MOVING BEHIND THE CURTAIN!
BDOOM!

I WAS RIGHT.
WE WERE SET UP!
A PITY YOU DIDN'T REALIZE THAT EARLIER, MY DEAR--
--YOU MIGHT HAVE SAVED ME THE EXPENSE OF REPLACING THAT FINE EXAMPLE OF CHINESE VEILING!
TAKE THEM!

DON'T SHOOT! I WANT NO GUNPLAY HERE!
MY PERSIAN RUGS MUSN'T BE STAINED WITH BLOOD!

HMMM!
NO BLOOD, HUH?
WHIRRR
CLIK!
7

HOW DO YOU FEEL ABOUT OIL?!
WAY TO GO, MACHINE MAN!
LET'S RACK'EM, WRECKERS!
PWAM! PWAM!
NO! NO! YOU'RE NOT SUPPOSED TO FIGHT BACK!

MIDNIGHT WRECKERS DON'T PLAY BY ANYONE ELSE'S RULES, BROADONI!
WE MAKE UP OUR OWN!
TAKE THIS ANCIENT PIECE OF POTTERY FOR EXAMPLE...

I'M SURE ITS ORIGINAL DESIGNER NEVER INTENDED FOR IT TO BE USED AS A BATTERING RAM!
FWAM!

WELL, WELL! I MANAGED TO BUST THROUGH THE WALL!
OF COURSE, VIDIOTS WOULDN'T EVEN NOTICE IF WE SET FIRE TO THE PLACE--
--WHICH WE STILL MIGHT DO TO COVER OUR ESCAPE!
8

HERE'S MY CHANCE TO TEST THIS LITTLE GIZMO!
HOPE IT'S WORTH THE EFFORT--

"--I INVESTED IN BUILDING IT!"
BZITT

FWAK!

IT'S WORKING! MY ELECTRONIC IMPULSE DISTORTER IS PLAYING HAVOC WITH THAT 'BOT'S INTERNAL COMMAND CIRCUITRY!

WHOOPS!
HI THERE! I DIDN'T HEAR YOU COMING UP BEHIND ME!
REMEMBER NOW: NO BLOOD! NO BLOOD!

UGNN Y'KNOW, I USUALLY LIKE TO THINK MY WAY OUT OF PROBLEMS!

BUT SOMETIMES ALL THE CLEVERNESS IN THE WORLD CAN'T EQUAL A SINGLE, WELL-PLACED--
DA-WAM!
--SHOT BETWEEN THE EYES!
9

NICE MOVE BRAIN!
WISH I COULD HANDLE A BLASTER AS WELL AS YOU OR HASSLE--

FWIK!
BUT I'M ALL *THUMBS* WHEN IT COMES TO WEAPONS!


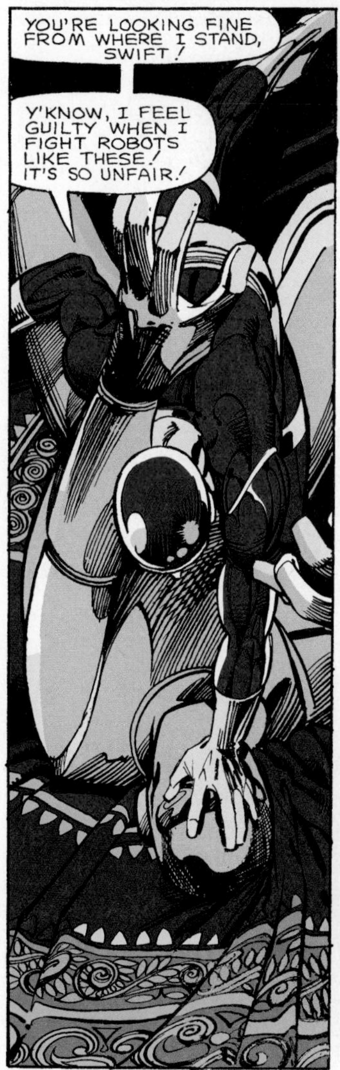

YOU'RE LOOKING FINE FROM WHERE I STAND, SWIFT!
Y'KNOW, I FEEL GUILTY WHEN I FIGHT ROBOTS LIKE THESE! IT'S SO UNFAIR!


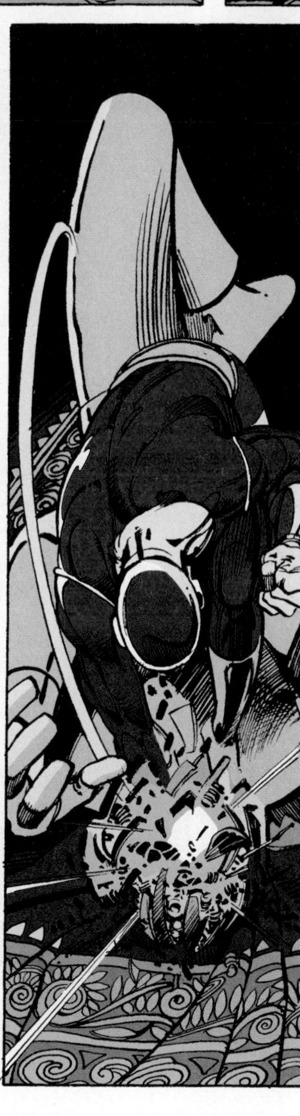

SAVE YOUR PITY FOR YOURSELF, METAL MAN! YOU AND YOUR FRIENDS ARE DOOMED!
*BAINTRONICS* HAS OFFERED A SMALL FORTUNE FOR YOUR CAPTURE!
YOU'LL NEVER BE SAFE!

HEADS UP, WRECKERS! BROADONI'S JUST SHOWN US THE WAY OUT!

WEEEEEE
SIRENS! RE-ENFORCEMENTS MUST BE ARRIVING!
GET IN THE CHUTE! HURRY!

YAH-ZOO!
MACHINE MAN! I WANT YOU TO FOLLOW ME!

MOVE IT, BO!
TIME IS RACING AWAY!

COME ON, HASSLE!
WHAT ARE YOU WAITING FOR?
SOMEONE HAS TO COVER THE RETREAT!

ME!
SAY GOOD-BYE TO THE OTHERS FOR ME!
UFF

UNNN TOO MANY OF THEM...CAN'T HOLD'EM ALL BACK...
BUT I GOTTA KEEP FIGHTING! GOTTA BUY THE PACK ENOUGH TIME--
11

"--TO ESCAPE!"
I HEAR TURBINES HUMMING UP AHEAD!
LOOK! BROADONI'S ENTERING A JET-FLYER!
HE'LL BE LONG GONE BEFORE WE CAN REACH HIM!
MAYBE NOT, SWIFT!
MY ARM MAY NOT HAVE STRENGTH WHEN IT'S COMPLETELY EXTENDED--

--BUT I CAN STILL USE IT'S INTERNAL COOLING SYSTEM!

YOU DID IT, MACHINY! YOU MANAGED TO FREEZE BROADONI IN PLACE.
DON'T YOU REALIZE HOW FUTILE THIS IS?
YOU MAY HAVE BEATEN ME--BUT BAINTRONICS WILL CRUSH YOU!

IT'S THE RICHEST, MOST POWERFUL INDUSTRIAL POWER IN THE ENTIRE WORLD!
YOU DON'T HAVE A CHANCE!
CAN YOU SWIM?
SWIM--?! WHAT WHAT HAS THAT TO DO WITH ANYTHING?!

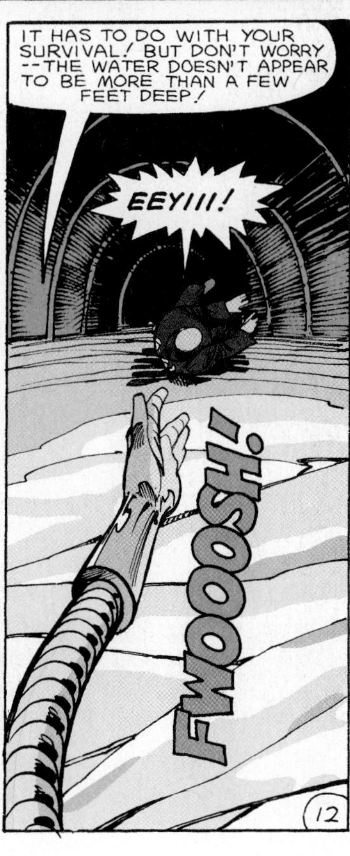
IT HAS TO DO WITH YOUR SURVIVAL! BUT DON'T WORRY --THE WATER DOESN'T APPEAR TO BE MORE THAN A FEW FEET DEEP!
EEYIIII!
FWOOOSH!
12

GET ON BOARD! I'LL HAVE THE ICE MELTED WITHIN SECONDS...
HEY! WHERE'S HASSLE?
SHE STAYED BEHIND TO COVER OUR ESCAPE!
WHAT--?!

I'M GOING BACK FOR HER.
NO! SHE KNEW WHAT SHE WAS DOING!
THIS ISN'T THE TIME FOR ANY STUPID MACHO HEROICS!

HERE COME THE BAINIES! THAT MEANS THEY'VE ALREADY CAPTURED HASSLE-- OR KILLED HER!
WE'VE GOTTA GO--NOW!

FORGET IT, BRAIN! I'VE PLAYED THE GOOD LITTLE SOLDIER UNTIL NOW! I'VE FOLLOWED ORDERS AND GONE ALONG WITH YOU KIDS-- BUT I DON'T LEAVE FRIENDS BEHIND!
NOT NOW-- NOT EVER!

I'M SORRY YOU FEEL THAT WAY, MACHINE MAN! REAL SORRY!
WHAT THE--?!
CLICK

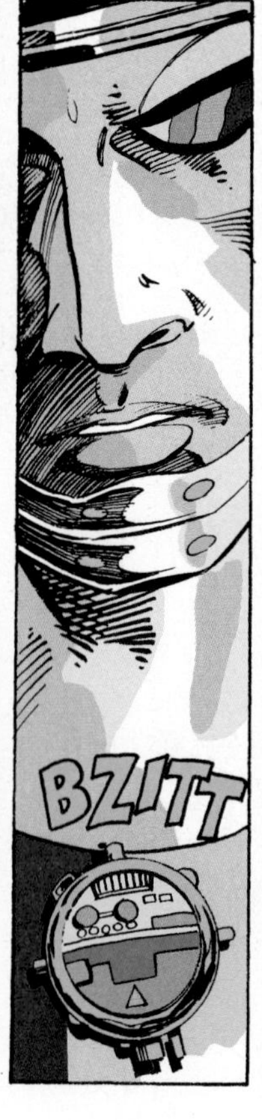
BZITT

OHHH, MY GOSHHH
HELP ME SLICK--

"--WE'VE GOT TO GET HIM ON BOARD BEFORE THE BAINIES CLOSE IN!"
PWAM PWAM
VROOM
13

RING AROUND THE COLLAR...
RING AROUND THE COLLAR...
WHAT'D YOU DO TO MACHINE MAN, BRAIN?
I ZAPPED HIM WITH ONE OF MY ELECTRONIC IMPULSE DISRUPTORS!
THERE'S THE EXIT!
SO...WHERE DO WE GO FROM HERE?!
IF BAINTRONICS REALLY IS HOT FOR US, THERE'S ONLY ONE PLACE WE CAN GO--

--TO SANCTUARY
KEEP OUT TOXIC WASTE

YES, I SAID "SANCTUARY"... I WANT ITS PRECISE LOCATION!
BAINTRONICS

YOU NEEDN'T BE SO SURPRISED, MY DEAR. I'VE KNOWN ABOUT THIS LEGENDARY HOME OF ALL MIDNIGHT WRECKERS FOR YEARS.
I JUST NEVER TROUBLED MYSELF ABOUT IT UNTIL NOW.
YOU'RE WASTING YOUR TIME,

AM I?
YOU'RE SUCH A PRETTY LITTLE THING. I DO HOPE DR. CYCLOBE WON'T SCAR YOU TOO HORRIBLY.
DROP DEAD.
14

DON'T WORRY, MADAM BAIN...
I DO NOT LEAVE VISIBLE SCARS!
PROCEED, DOCTOR.
THIS ONE IS FULL OF SPIRIT.
I SHALL SO ENJOY QUESTIONING HER.
ARE YOU READY TO BEGIN, MY SWEET?
WHY DON'T YOU JUST KISS MY--
FWEEESK
ARGGH!
A PROPER LADY DOESN'T USE SUCH LANGUAGE.
SHALL WE TRY AGAIN?
FWOOSK
AAAAA
15

I BELIEVE THE TOPIC IS... "SANCTUARY"

YOU FILTHY SON OF A--

FWAASK!

ENOUGH!
THIS IS GETTING NOWHERE! CAN'T YOU SEE THAT YOU'RE KILLING HER?!

JOCASTA MAY HAVE A POINT. PERHAPS, WE ARE BEING A BIT TOO PERSISTENT.
A SMALL RECESS IS IN ORDER.
SNAP

TAKE HER AWAY! SHE MAY RESPOND DIFFERENTLY--AFTER SHE'S HAD TIME TO CONSIDER THE DISADVANTAGES OF CONTINUED STUBBORNESS!

16

A PISTOL?! THAT'S ODD!

PWAM!

PWOOM!

EXPRESS TO SKY DECK

THIS IS TOO EASY...
17

KRAKK!
WAY TOO EASY...

BRMMMMMM

VWAMM!

EXCELLENT!

EVERYTHING IS GOING ACCORDING TO ARNO'S PLAN!
HE'LL BE SO PLEASED!
18

SOMEWHERE IN THE CANADIAN NORTH WOODS...

ARE YOU SURE THIS IS THE RIGHT AREA?
I'VE NEVER BEEN TO SANCTUARY!
THEN, YOU'RE IN FOR A TREAT!
SANCTUARY IS WHERE MOST WRECKERS LEARN THEIR TRADE. IT'S ALSO THE HOME OF THE ANCIENT WRECKER HIMSELF-- THE MAN WHO STARTED IT ALL!

BRAIN, I'M REAL SORRY ABOUT HASSLE! I KNOW HOW MUCH YOU--
YEAH... SURE! BUT DON'T YOU WORRY ABOUT HASSLE! SHE'LL KNOW WHERE TO FIND US IF... WHEN SHE GETS FREE!
YOU OKAY, MACHINE MAN?
I'M THE REAL THING... A REGULAR TASTE SENSATION...

COME ON! LET'S SCAN THE TERRAIN. MAYBE WE CAN SPOT A FAMILIAR LANDMARK OR TWO.
AFTER ALL, WE HAVEN'T BEEN HERE IN A LOOOONG TIME!
WHEN ITS TIME TO RELAX... ONE BEER STANDS TRUE...

HEY! WHAT'S THAT--?!
SWIK!
19

FWOOMP!

VISIT OKLAHOMA
"THAT, MY GOOD FRIEND, IS TROUBLE...
...WITH A CAPITAL "T"!
HERE'S TO GOOD FRIENDS... SOMETHING KIND OF SPECIAL...
AND AWAY GOES TROUBLE... DOWN THE DRAIN...
20

ELSEWHERE, AT THAT VERY MOMENT...
THANK YOU FOR CALLING, MADAM BAIN...

YES, I SHALL PERSONALLY TAKE CHARGE OF MATTERS FROM THIS POINT FORWARD... GOOD DAY, MY LADY!
STARK
ENTERPRISES

≥SIGH≤ I SUPPOSE I REALLY SHOULD GET READY...
IF ALL GOES ACCORDING TO PLAN--AND THERE'S NO REASON WHY IT SHOULDN'T--THE GIRL WILL SOON LEAD ME TO MACHINE MAN AND SANCTUARY!

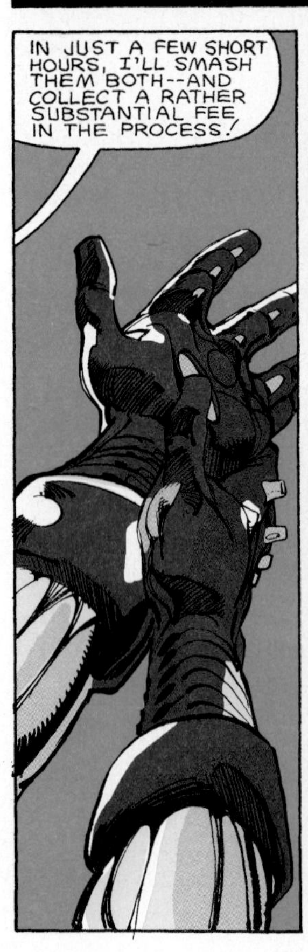
IN JUST A FEW SHORT HOURS, I'LL SMASH THEM BOTH--AND COLLECT A RATHER SUBSTANTIAL FEE IN THE PROCESS!

HOWEVER, I MUST CONFESS THAT I'M QUITE TAKEN WITH THE IDEA OF MEETING THIS MACHINE MAN...

FROM ALL REPORTS, HE APPEARS TO BE EXTREMELY RESOURCEFUL, AND INCREDIBLY POWERFUL.
PERHAPS A FOE TRULY WORTHY OF ME.

YES, I'M ANXIOUS TO SEE HOW HE'LL FARE AGAINST ARNO STARK--
21

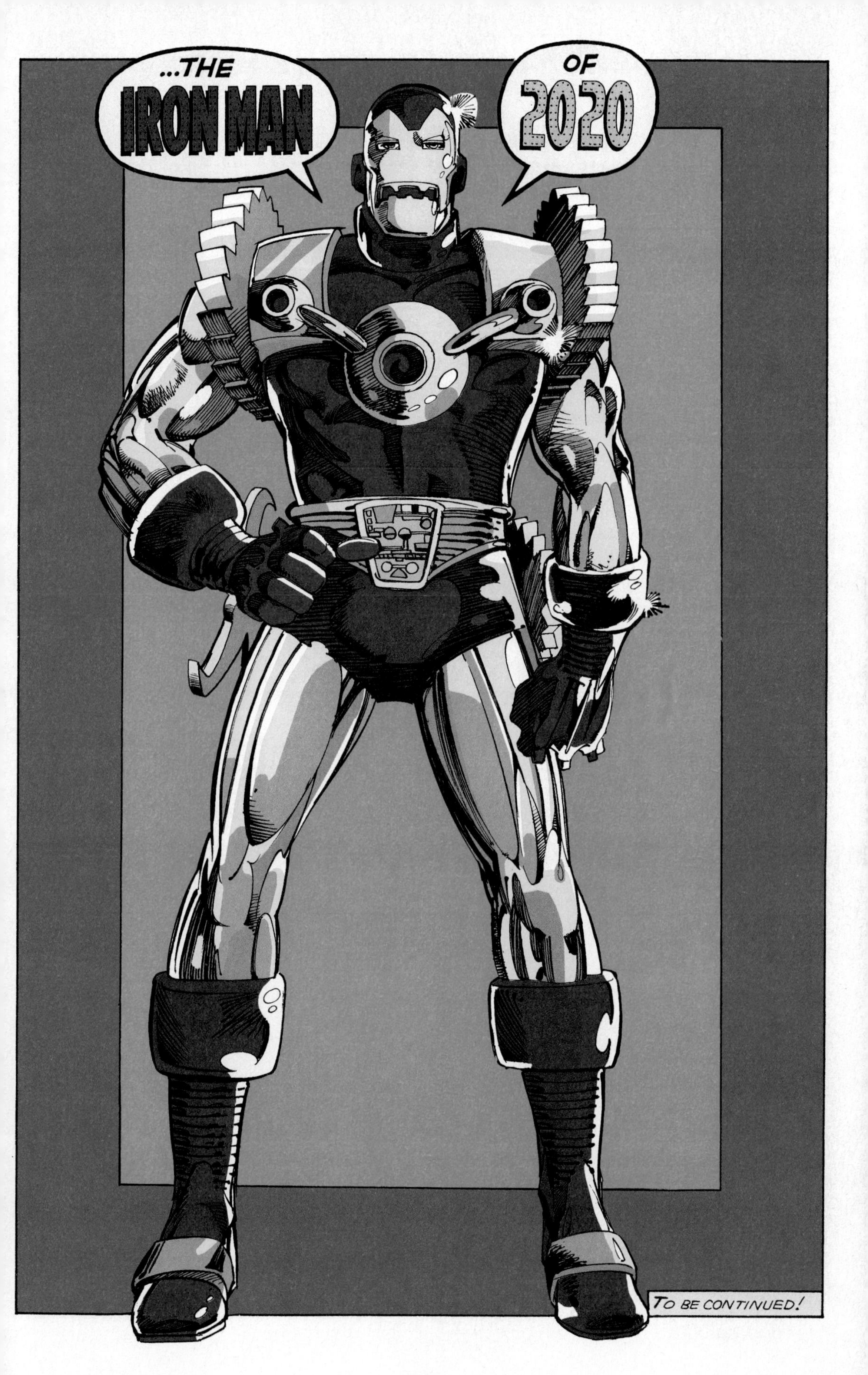
...THE
IRON MAN
OF
2020
TO BE CONTINUED!

MARVEL®

TM

75¢
3
DEC
02977

APPROVED BY THE COMICS CODE AUTHORITY

#3 IN A FOUR-ISSUE LIMITED SERIES

MACHINE MAN

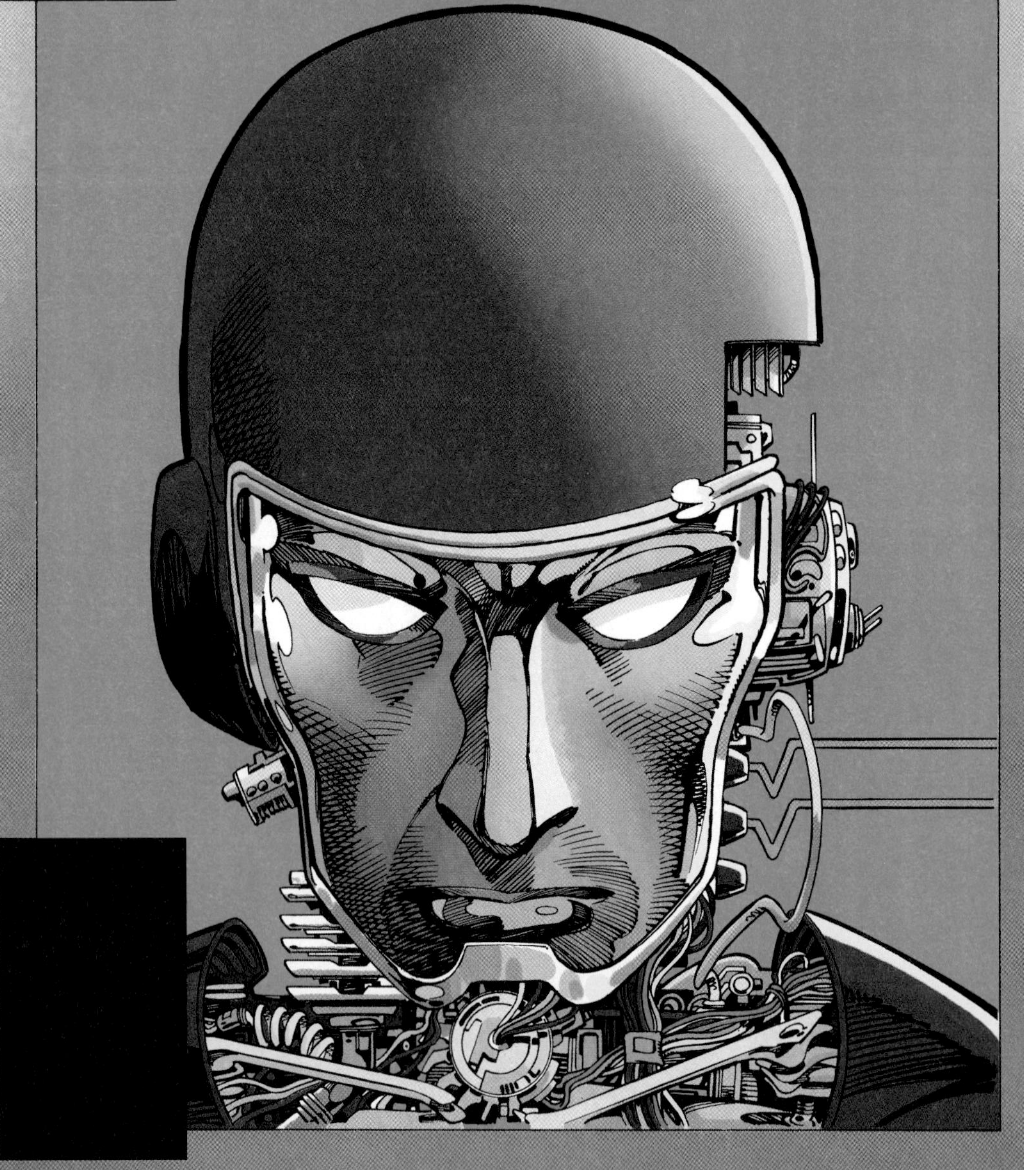

ENTER THE TERRIFYING WORLD OF THE NEAR FUTURE. ENTER THE WORLD OF...
MACHINE MAN
RIME OF THE ANCIENT WRECKER!
SEPTEMBER 25, 2020...
C'MON, HASSLE... HOLD IT TOGETHER! DON'T LET THOSE BAINIES ON YOUR TAIL SEE YOUR TEETH CHATTERING!
I KNEW ESCAPING FROM SUNSET BAIN'S HQ COULDN'T HAVE BEEN THAT SIMPLE... THE 'BOT WITH THE PISTOL HOLSTER... THE FLOATER JUST SITTING THERE?! GIVE ME A BREAK!*
I'M POSITIVE THE FLOATER I STOLE HAD SOME SORT OF TRACKING DEVICE ON BOARD... IF NOT A SELF-DESTRUCT RELAY. LUCKILY, I RAN UP ON THIS FLOATER... BUT HOT-WIRING THE STUPID THING COST ME OVER AN HOUR!
AND NOW I'VE GOT COMPANY! A C-10 KILLER 'BOT ON MY TAIL, AND A SECOND ONE--
BWAK! BWAK! BWAK!
FWAM!
FWAM!
STAN LEE PRESENTS: TOM DEFALCO SCRIPT HERB TRIMPE BREAKDOWNS BARRY WINDSOR-SMITH FINISHES & COLORS JANICE CHIANG LETTERS LARRY HAMA EDITOR JIM SHOOTER CHIEF
*SEE LAST ISSUE!

--IN MY SIGHTS!
KA-WAM!

STILL CAN'T BELIEVE THAT MY INTERROGATION WAS PERSONALLY SUPERVISED BY MAMA B HERSELF-- SUNSET BAIN!
SHE PRACTICALLY OWNS BAINTRONICS--THE RICHEST CORPORATION IN THE WORLD! WHAT WAS HER INTEREST IN ME?!
BWAK! BWAK!
BWAK!
UH-OH. BETTER CONCENTRATE ON THE BUSINESS AT HAND!

VROOMMM!

I HOPE MACHINE MAN AND MY FELLOW MIDNIGHT WRECKERS MADE IT TO SANCTUARY OKAY...

...'CAUSE MY CHANCES DON'T LOOK TOO GOOD RIGHT NOW...
...AND I HATE IT WHEN THE BAD GUYS WIN!

SCREEEE
-WHEW- I CUT THAT A LITTLE TOO CLOSE!
ALMOST STALLED MY ENGINES!
GOT TO HUG THE EARTH NOW-- AND PRAY FOR THE BEST!

MY PLAN WORKED! HE LOST ME IN THE GROUND DETAIL. HE'S OVERSHOOTING ME!
CARELESS...
2

BARROOM!
VERY CARELESS!

NO OTHER SIGNS OF PURSUIT! GUESS THEY DIDN'T TELESCREEN FOR REINFORCEMENTS!
I'M SAFE--

--FOR NOW!
YES...

...EVERYTHING IS GOING ACCORDING TO PLAN! I AM CERTAIN THAT THE WOMAN--I BELIEVE HER NAME IS, "HASSLE"--STILL DOESN'T REALIZE THAT WE ENGINEERED HER ESCAPE...

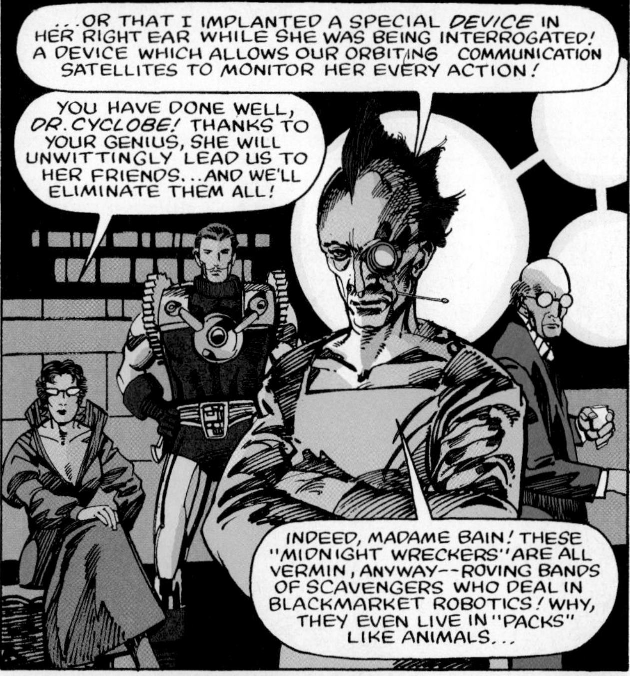
...OR THAT I IMPLANTED A SPECIAL DEVICE IN HER RIGHT EAR WHILE SHE WAS BEING INTERROGATED! A DEVICE WHICH ALLOWS OUR ORBITING COMMUNICATION SATELLITES TO MONITOR HER EVERY ACTION!
YOU HAVE DONE WELL, DR. CYCLOBE! THANKS TO YOUR GENIUS, SHE WILL UNWITTINGLY LEAD US TO HER FRIENDS...AND WE'LL ELIMINATE THEM ALL!
INDEED, MADAME BAIN! THESE "MIDNIGHT WRECKERS" ARE ALL VERMIN, ANYWAY--ROVING BANDS OF SCAVENGERS WHO DEAL IN BLACKMARKET ROBOTICS! WHY, THEY EVEN LIVE IN "PACKS" LIKE ANIMALS...

BAH! THESE "WRECKERS" HAVE NEVER BEEN OUR MAIN CONCERN!
MACHINE MAN IS THE REAL PROBLEM!
3

AFTER FORTY YEARS, HE'S RETURNED-- TO PLAGUE US AGAIN!

WHAT ARE YOU DOING ABOUT HIM?! WE'LL NEVER BE SAFE WHILE HE LIVES!
AMBASSADOR BRICKMAN, YOU NEEDN'T WORRY ABOUT MACHINE MAN ANY LONGER!

I AM ARNO STARK--THE IRON MAN OF 2020! YOU MAY HAVE HEARD OF ME... I PURCHASED THE EXCLUSIVE RIGHTS TO THE NAME AND THIS ARMOR AFTER THE ORIGINAL IRON MAN'S TRAGIC DEATH!
IN ANY EVENT, MADAM BAIN HAS RETAINED ME FOR THE EXPRESS PURPOSE OF ATTENDING TO THIS MACHINE MAN!

I'VE HEARD QUITE A BIT ABOUT HIM--AND I MUST CONFESS THAT I LOOK FORWARD TO MEETING HIM!
STARK
ENTERPRISES
ACCORDING TO THE INFORMATION I'VE RECEIVED, HE IS CURRENTLY TRAVELING WITH THE REMAINING MEMBERS OF HASSLE'S PACK!

THEY ARE HEADED FOR SANCTUARY--THE LEGENDARY STRONGHOLD OF THE MIDNIGHT WRECKERS!

IN A FEW SHORT HOURS, AFTER HASSLE HAS REJOINED THEM, I SHALL EAGERLY RID THE WORLD OF BOTH THE WRECKERS... AND MACHINE MAN!
NOW, ISN'T THAT CAUSE FOR CELEBRATION--?
TINK!
THE ROBOT CALLED JOCASTA DOES NOT JOIN IN THE FESTIVITIES!

ONCE, LONG AGO, SHE HAD CARED FOR MACHINE MAN... AS DEEPLY AS A ROBOT COULD...
AND NOW--?!
SHE DARES NOT FACE THAT QUESTION!
4

MEANWHILE, SOMEWHERE HIGH ABOVE THE CANADIAN NORTH WOODS...
IF YOU'VE GOT THE TIME...

...WE'VE GOT THE BEER...
HEY, BRAIN, YOU'VE REALLY GOT TO DO SOMETHING ABOUT MACHINE MAN! HE'S STARTING TO ZIG ME OUT WITH HIS MOLDY-OLD COMMERCIAL JINGLES!
HE CAN'T HELP HIMSELF, SWIFT! YOU KNOW I HAD TO ZAP HIM WITH ONE OF MY ELECTRONIC IMPULSE DISRUPTERS!
SHUT UP--THE BOTH OF YOU! I'M GOING TO TRY TO WEASLE US OUT OF HERE!

HEY, BO'! HOW MUCH LONGER YOU GONNA KEEP US TRUSSED UP LIKE THIS?!
GIVE TO US THE BREAK! CAN'T YOU SCAN THAT WE'RE BROTHER WRECKERS?!

MAYBE SO--BUT YOU COULD ALSO BE A PACK OF BAINIES IN DISGUISE!
OUR LEADER--THE ANCIENT WRECKER HIMSELF--WILL DECIDE WHAT'S TO BE DONE WITH YOU!

JUST EASE BACK INTO THE NET--AND PUT A CLAMP ON YOUR JAW!
ONCE WE'RE THROUGH THESE ARTIFICIAL CLOUDS, OUR NEXT STOP WILL BE--
5

"--SANCTUARY!"

YAH-ZOO!
BRAIN! SLICK! THE PLACE IS EVEN WIGGIER THAN THE TWO OF YOU EVER DESCRIBED!

MOMENTS LATER...
I'VE GOTTA REPORT TO THE ANCIENT WRECKER! WHY DON'T YOU BOYS ESCORT OUR GUESTS TO THEIR QUARTERS?
WILL DO, BONES!

"GUESTS"?!
DON'T PUSH IT, SWIFT!

BESIDES, THESE ACCOMODATIONS AREN'T HALF BAD!
ME FOR THE FIRST SONIC-SHOWER!
...I HOPE YOUR SAFEGUARD HOLDS UP...
HOW YOU FLYING, BRAIN? YOU GONNA MAKE IT?
I'M...FINE, SWIFT! WHY DO YOU ASK?
7

HEY, I KNOW THAT I USUALLY ACT LIKE MY FUSE BOX IS MISSING A FEW CIRCUITS--BUT IT DOESN'T TAKE ANY GREAT INTELLECT TO SCAN YOUR FEELINGS FOR HASSLE!
YOU'RE PUTTING UP A GOOD FRONT, BUT YOU MUST BE WORRIED SICK ABOUT HER! WANT TO TALK--?
NO!

HASSLE KNEW THE RISKS WHEN SHE JOINED THIS PACK--AND SHE TOOK THE SAME CHANCES AS EVERYONE ELSE! I JUST WISH YOU'D LEARN TO MIND YOUR OWN BUSINESS!

EXCUUUSE ME! I DIDN'T MEAN TO INTRUDE INTO MACHO-LAND!
DO YOURSELF A FAVOR, SMART GUY! IF YOU EVER DO GET ANOTHER OPPORTUNITY, TELL HER HOW YOU FEEL--
--BEFORE IT'S TOO LATE!

...OOH, THE PICTURES YOU MISSED... BEFORE THE KODAK DISC...
YOU KNOW SOMETHING, MACHINY?
YOU'RE NOT THE ONLY MEMBER OF THIS TEAM--

--WHO IS TALKING NONSENSE!

AH! THAT WAS MOST REFRESHING!
NOTHING LIKE A FEW GOOD BLASTS OF SONIC ENERGY--TO CLEAR THE PORES--AND GET THE HEART PUMPING!

I FEEL ALMOST HUMAN AGAIN!
I'LL BE READY TO TAKE ON THE WORLD--JUST AS SOON AS I FINISH PUTTING ON MY FACE!
I'VE OFTEN WONDERED WHY YOU WEAR THAT MAKE-UP, SLICK!
IMAGE, MY DEAR SWIFT! IMAGE!
8

IF YOU SCAN AS BEING IMPRESSIVE, PEOPLE WILL THINK YOU ARE!
...I'M IMPRESSED!
BEAUTIFUL! A TRUE WORK OF ART!
IF YOU SAY SO! GIGGLE
I DO! I MOST CERTAINLY DO!

NOW THEN, BRAIN, I THINK IT'S HIGH TIME YOU BROUGHT MACHINE MAN BACK INTO THE REALM OF THE CONSCIOUS!
THAT COULD BE DANGER-OUS!

I DON'T THINK HE'LL APPRECIATE OUR REASONS FOR PUTTING HIM UNDER!
UNFORTUNATELY, THAT CAN'T BE HELPED! WE JUST MIGHT NEED HIM LATER!
WOW--
KUNG!
--I COULD'VE HAD A V8...

...THERE'S A FORD IN YOUR FUTURE...
ALL RIGHT, SLICK! YOU'RE THE LEADER OF THE PACK...

...WE'RE GOING TO MAKE A HOT CEREAL LOVER OUT OF YOU...
GET READY! I AM GOING TO DISENGAGE THE DISRUPTER...

"NOW!"
KAR-ZKK!
...A HOT CEREAL LOVERARGHHH!
9

EASY! TAKE IT EASY!
DON'T MAKE ANY SUDDEN MOVES UNTIL YOUR CIRCUITRY HAS HAD TIME TO STABILIZE ITSELF!
WH-WHAT... DID YOU DO TO ME?!
YOU REFUSED TO OBEY ORDERS, SO I WAS FORCED TO... SEDATE YOU!

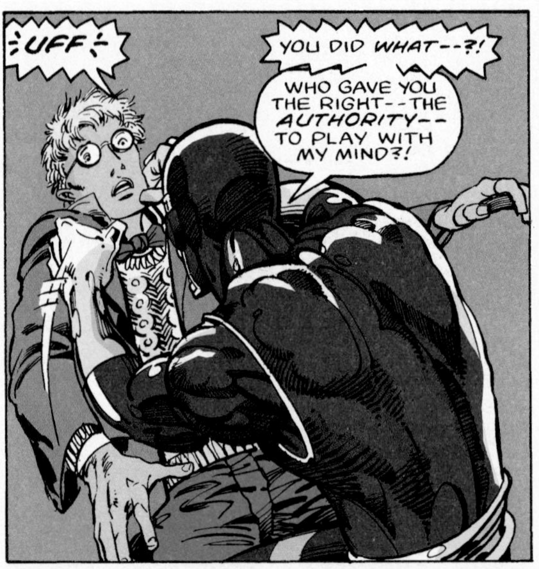
UFF
YOU DID WHAT--?!
WHO GAVE YOU THE RIGHT--THE AUTHORITY--TO PLAY WITH MY MIND?!

DOWNSHIFT, FRIEND! I KNOW YOU'RE UPSET... I'D FEEL THE SAME WAY IF I WERE IN YOUR POSITION... BUT I WANT YOU TO UNDERSTAND THAT BRAIN WAS ONLY ACTING IN YOUR BEST INTERESTS!
SAVE THE SNAKE OIL, SLICK! I'M NOT BUYING IT!
YOU DON'T CARE ABOUT ME!

YOU NEVER DID!
YOU THINK THAT I'M JUST ANOTHER BLACKMARKET ROBOT--FOR YOU TO USE--AND THEN SELL TO THE HIGHEST BIDDER! YOU'RE WRONG!

MY BODY MAY BE COMPOSED OF CIRCUITS AND STEEL--BUT I HAVE FEELINGS, TOO... REAL HONEST-TO-GOD HUMAN EMOTIONS!
I'M REAL TIRED OF BEING TREATED LIKE AN UNTHINKING INANIMATE OBJECT.
I GUESS WE OWE YOU AN APOLOGY OR TWO...
Y'KNOW, SOMEWHERE ALONG THE LINE YOU STOPPED BEING JUST ANOTHER 'BOT TO US...

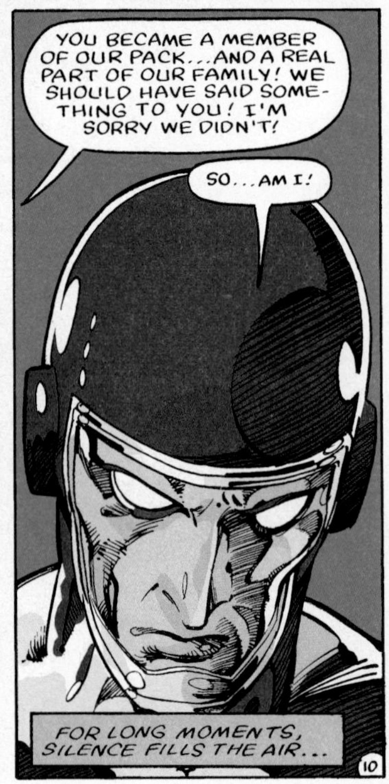
YOU BECAME A MEMBER OF OUR PACK... AND A REAL PART OF OUR FAMILY! WE SHOULD HAVE SAID SOMETHING TO YOU! I'M SORRY WE DIDN'T!
SO... AM I!
FOR LONG MOMENTS, SILENCE FILLS THE AIR...
10

AND THEN...
WHY ALL THE LONG FACES?!
IT'S PARTY TIME!

HOWDY, FOLKS! I'M THE CHIEF HONCHO IN THESE PARTS! THE LOCALS CALL ME THE ANCIENT WRECKER!
HATE TO BUST IN ON YOU FOLKS LIKE THIS-- BUT I HEARD AN OLD PAL OF MINE WAS STAYING HERE!
YOU!
I CAN'T BELIEVE IT'S REALLY YOU!

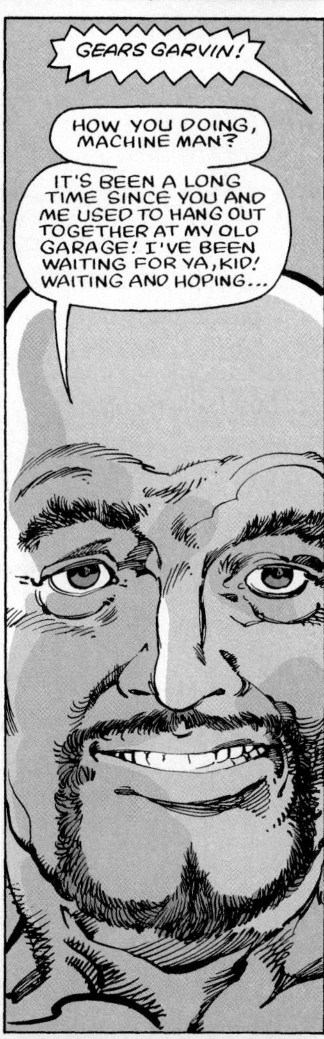
GEARS GARVIN!
HOW YOU DOING, MACHINE MAN?
IT'S BEEN A LONG TIME SINCE YOU AND ME USED TO HANG OUT TOGETHER AT MY OLD GARAGE! I'VE BEEN WAITING FOR YA, KID! WAITING AND HOPING...

MEANWHILE...
IT'S OVER, SUNSET! ALL OF IT!
STARK
ENTERPRISES
11

WE HAVE BEEN LIVING A LIE FOR THE PAST FORTY YEARS-- AND IT HAS FINALLY CAUGHT UP WITH US!
WE PRETENDED THAT MACHINE MAN WAS DEAD... THAT WE WERE SAFE... HA!
YOU'RE DRUNK, AMBASSADOR!

PERHAPS, BUT THAT DOESN'T CHANGE THE FACT THAT WE'RE BOTH GOING TO DIE!
MACHINE MAN WILL FIND A WAY TO REACH US!
HE ALWAYS FINDS A WAY...

FOLLOWING A TRAIL OF EMPTY BOTTLES, NO DOUBT.

SUNSET! I DON'T MEAN TO INTRUDE-- BUT MR. STARK HAS JUST FINISHED ASSEMBLING HIS ASSAULT TEAM!
HE INTENDS TO LAUNCH MOMENTARILY!
THANK YOU, JOCASTA!

YOUR FEARS APPEAR TO BE GROUNDLESS, AMBASSADOR.
EVERYTHING IS PROCEEDING NICELY.

THAT IS ONLY AN ILLUSION, SUNSET!
YOUR HIRED THUG HASN'T GOT A CHANCE AGAINST MACHINE MAN! NOTHING CAN STOP HIM! NOTHING!
JOCASTA, AMBASSADOR BRICKMAN IS NOT WELL...

"...SEE THAT HE IS SAFELY ESCORTED TO HIS HOME!"
YAH-ZOO!
12

GONNA WRECK 'EM! GONNA RACK 'EM! GONNA BEAT THEM BAINIES BAD!
HI-HO, BONES! YOU THROW ONE MIGHTY MEAN BASH!
ONLY THE VERY FINEST TO WELCOME A PACK OF BROTHER-WRECKERS!
I'M, UH, SORRY ABOUT EARLIER!
DON'T SCAN IT!
ZOWEEE! WE'RE BEING TREATED LIKE ROYALTY OR SOMETHING! I STILL CAN'T BELIEVE THAT MACHINY USE TO KNOW THE ANCIENT ONE--THE MAN WHO FIRST ORGANIZED THE WRECKERS--AND RAISED SCAVENGERY INTO AN ART FORM!
CARE TO GIVE YOUR ASSETS A SHAKE?
YEA, BO'... T'WOULD BE MY...
...PLEASURE.
SOMETHING WRONG, LADY?
NO, THERE'S NOTHING WRONG...
...WITH ME!
13

MEANWHILE...
I ALMOST CAN'T BELIEVE IT, KID.
YOU'RE BACK. YOU'RE FINALLY BACK.
WHAT HAPPENED, GEARS? WHERE DID ALL THE YEARS GO? HOW DID THIS MADNESS BEGIN?!

AW, GEE... IT MUST HAVE STARTED THIRTY-FIVE, MAYBE FORTY YEARS AGO.
DO YOU REMEMBER HOW IT USED TO BE? YOU, ME AND PETER SPAULDING-- THE THREE OF US ALWAYS HANGING OUT TOGETHER IN MY OLD GARAGE...

"I THINK OUR BIGGEST WORRY AT THAT TIME WAS JOCASTA... SHE HAD BEEN BLOWN APART BY YOUR ENEMY ULTRON*... AND WE WERE TRYING TO COME UP WITH A WAY TO REVIVE HER ROBOT BRAIN!
*SEE MARVEL TWO-IN-ONE #93!

"ANYWAY, I HAD TO GO OUT FOR SOME PARTS, OR SOMETHING... AND WHEN I RETURNED..."
OH, NO! NO!

"YOU AND JOCASTA WERE GONE, AND SPAULDING WAS DEAD...
"I HAD NEVER REALLY LIKED PETER. ALWAYS THOUGHT HE WAS A STUCK-UP WIMP.
"I WAS WRONG.
"THE PLACE WAS IN SHAMBLES. HE MUST HAVE PUT UP ONE HECK OF A FIGHT. YEAH, GOOD OLD PETER..."

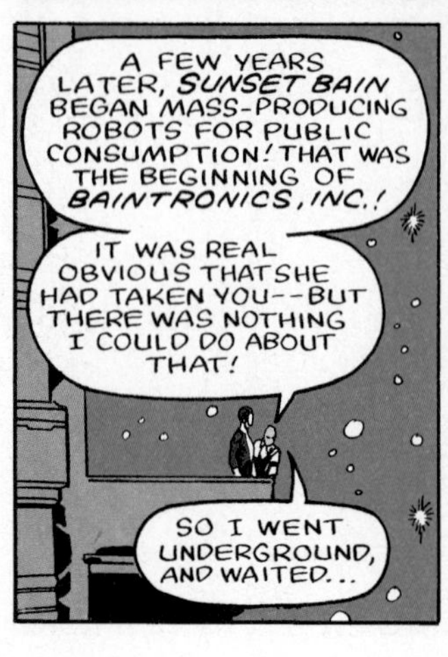
A FEW YEARS LATER, SUNSET BAIN BEGAN MASS-PRODUCING ROBOTS FOR PUBLIC CONSUMPTION! THAT WAS THE BEGINNING OF BAINTRONICS, INC.!
IT WAS REAL OBVIOUS THAT SHE HAD TAKEN YOU--BUT THERE WAS NOTHING I COULD DO ABOUT THAT!
SO I WENT UNDERGROUND, AND WAITED...

YOU'VE BEEN WAITING ALL THESE YEARS FOR ME--?!
YEAH, I NEVER GAVE UP HOPE. I KNEW YOU'D FIND A WAY TO COME BACK TO ME, KID.
IT HASN'T BEEN A BAD LIFE. OF COURSE, I CAN'T GET DECENT PIZZA THESE DAYS...

...AND IT'S BEEN SO BLASTED LONELY AT TIMES!
WELCOME HOME, KID! I'VE MISSED YOU!
14

AT THAT VERY INSTANT...
LOWER THE SHIELDS!
WE'VE CAPTURED ANOTHER INTRUDER!

WE CAUGHT THIS ONE PILOTING A BAINY FLOATER!

SHE CLAIMS TO BELONG TO THE PACK WE FOUND EARLIER!

HASSLE--?!
HASSLE!

HASSLE!
GET OUT OF MY WAY!
LET ME THROUGH!

CLEAR A PATH! THIS BO'S GONE ZONKO!
HASSLE!
15

HI, BRAIN.

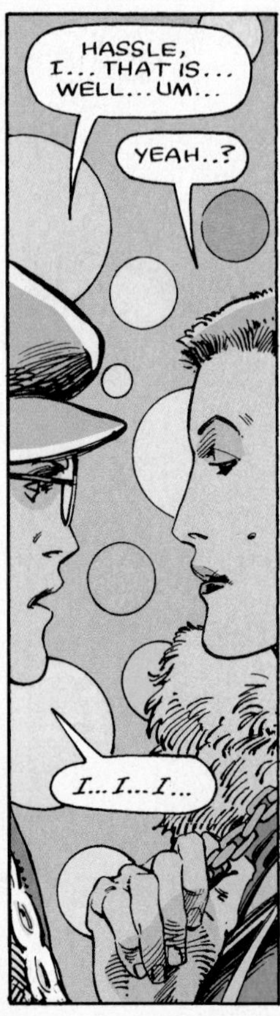
HASSLE, I... THAT IS... WELL... UM...
YEAH..?
I... I... I...

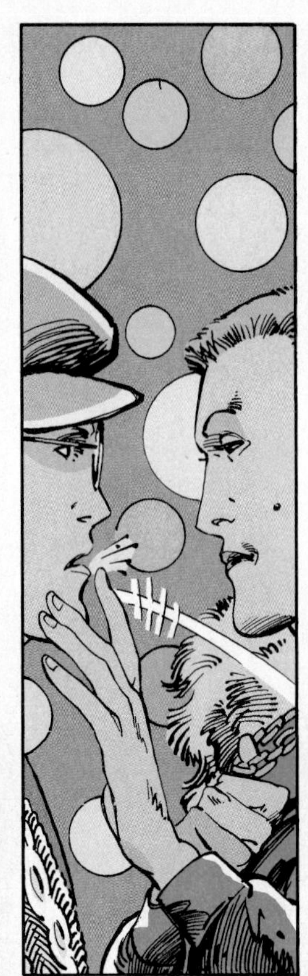

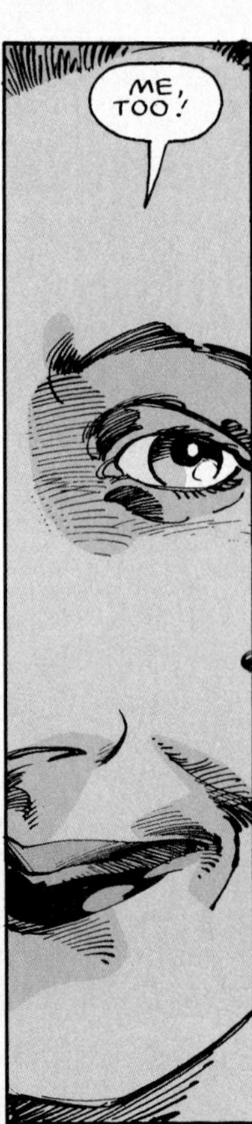
ME, TOO!

SUDDENLY...
SECURE THE COMPOUND-- NOW!
THIS IS NOT A TEST! I REPEAT...

"THIS IS NOT A TEST!"
WHAT IS IT, SLICK?
WHAT'S HAPPENING?
SOMETHING MUST HAVE BREACHED THE OUTER PERIMETERS--
16

"--SANCTUARY IS UNDER ATTACK!
ATTENTION, ALL YOU MEN! ACTIVATE FULL ASSAULT MODE!
TAKE NO PRISONERS!

HOW DID THEY FIND US? OUR ARTIFICIAL CLOUD COVER IS EQUIPPED WITH ENOUGH BAFFLES TO SCRAMBLE ANY SCANNER!
WE CAN'T WORRY ABOUT THAT NOW--

WE HAVE A FULL-SCALE WAR ON OUR HANDSSSYYIII
GNAMM!
SID! THEY GOT SID!
17

HEY, BONES! CAN ME AND MY PACK BORROW A FEW SKY-CYKES?
SURE... IF YOU'RE FAST ENOUGH! YOU KNOW THERE'S NO PRIVATE OWNERSHIP IN SANCTUARY!
THE FIRST WRECKERS SEATED-- ARE THE ONES WHO FLY!

HOW?! HOW DID THEY FIND ME?! I'M SURE I LOST THEM!

SKRAG! THIS IS MY FAULT!
SORRY, BO! I REALLY BLEW IT BY COMING HERE AT ALL...
UFF
...I'VE GOT TO MAKE AMMENDS FOR THIS MESS!

LET'S RACK 'EM, WRECKERS!
VRRRRRRRMMMMMMMM

GEARS! WE'VE GOT TO STOP THIS INSANITY! MOST OF THESE KIDS ARE STILL IN THEIR TEENS! THEY COULD ALL BE KILLED!
YEAH, I KNOW! THE WHOLE SYSTEM STINKS!
RRRUUM
NOBODY CARES IF THE BAINIES BLOW US AWAY!
MOST PEOPLE TODAY ARE LIVING IN REAL COMFORT! ROBOTS DO THEIR WORK-- AND VIDEO BOXES KEEP 'EM AMUSED!

THESE KIDS WANTED MORE OUT OF LIFE!
WELL, THEY GOT IT-- IN SPADES!
18

FORWARD! FORWARD!
BLAMM!
WHOMM!
WE MUST SECURE THIS FORTRESS!

THEY'RE LANDING TOO FAST! CAN'T HOLD THEM BACK!
FWAM!
SORRY, BOYS! NO TRESPASSING!
WE'RE OUTGUNNED-- AND OUTMANNED!

THE WRECKERS ARE IN TOTAL DISARRAY! MY SUDDEN ONSLAUGHT HAS TAKEN THEM COMPLETELY BY SURPRISE, AS I KNEW IT WOULD...
THAT ROBOT! HE FITS THE DESCRIPTION I WAS GIVEN OF MACHINE MAN!

FWANG!
ARRG

THAT WAS ALMOST TOO EASY!
HE NEVER HAD A CHANCE!
19

HOW DISAPPOINTING! I HAD HOPED THAT HE WOULD PROVE TO BE MORE OF A CHALLENGE!
-UNNN- I'M SORRY I DIDN'T LIVE UP TO YOUR EXPECTATIONS!
BOOM!

THWAM!
HOW'S THIS?!

"--BAH! YOU ARE HARDLY A MOMENT'S DISTRACTION TO SOMEONE WITH MY POWER!"
FWAM!
-ARGG-

MY CHEST BEAM WILL PULVERIZE YOUR INTERNAL CIRCUITRY!
WITHIN SECONDS, YOU'LL BE A LIFELESS HULK!

DON'T YOU BELIEVE IT!
BWAM!

FWOOM!
THAT BLAST SHATTERED THE OUTCROPPING ABOVE ME!

HOWEVER, MY ARMOR CAN EASILY PROTECT ME--BY GENERATING AN ELECTRO-MAGNETIC FORCE-FIELD!
20

MEANWHILE, NOT FAR AWAY, ONE OF THE IRON-BOTS REACHES SANCTUARY'S BULKHEAD, AND THEN--
BWOOM!

WITHIN MOMENTS, A RAPID SERIES OF MASSIVE EXPLOSIONS ERUPT FROM WITHIN...
BWAM!
BWAM!
BWAM!

INSTANTLY, SANCTUARY BEGINS TO SHAKE VIOLENTLY--
YIII!
--CONVULSING LIKE SOME GREAT, DYING BEAST!

WHAT IS IT? WHAT'S HAPPENING?!
SOMEONE MUST HAVE HIT THE ANTI-GRAVITY GENERATORS!
SANCTUARY'S GOING DOWN!

WE'VE GOT TO REACH THE CENTRAL COMPUTER! GOT TO CHANNEL ALL AVAILABLE POWER INTO THE STABILIZATION UNITS--
--OR WE'LL CRASH INTO THE EARTH!

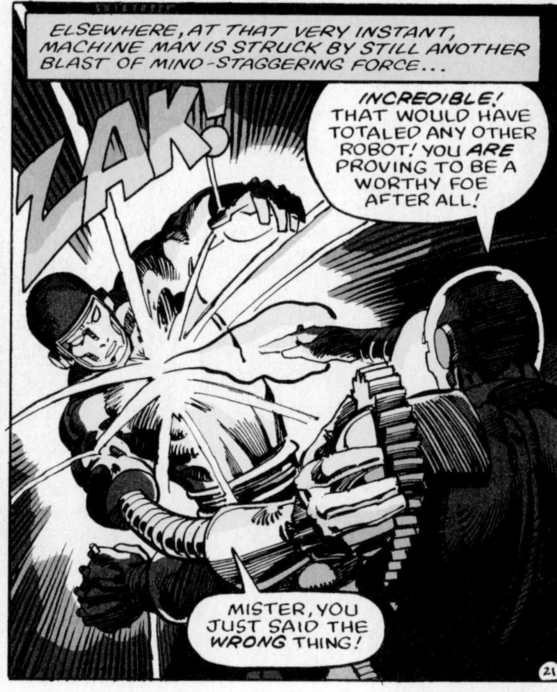
ELSEWHERE, AT THAT VERY INSTANT, MACHINE MAN IS STRUCK BY STILL ANOTHER BLAST OF MIND-STAGGERING FORCE...
ZAK!
INCREDIBLE! THAT WOULD HAVE TOTALED ANY OTHER ROBOT! YOU ARE PROVING TO BE A WORTHY FOE AFTER ALL!
MISTER, YOU JUST SAID THE WRONG THING!
21

I WASN'T PLACED ON THIS EARTH TO AMUSE YOU-- OR ANYONE ELSE!
YOUR HAND--!
FWOOM
I'M A ROBOT, REMEMBER? EVERY ONE OF MY LIMBS IS A TOOL WHICH CAN BE PRE-PROGRAMMED WITH A SPECIFIC FUNCTION.

AN ANTI-MAGNETIC NULL FIELD!
YOU FOOL! MY ARMOR WILL EASILY OVERWHELM THIS PATHETIC ATTEMPT TO IMPRISON ME!

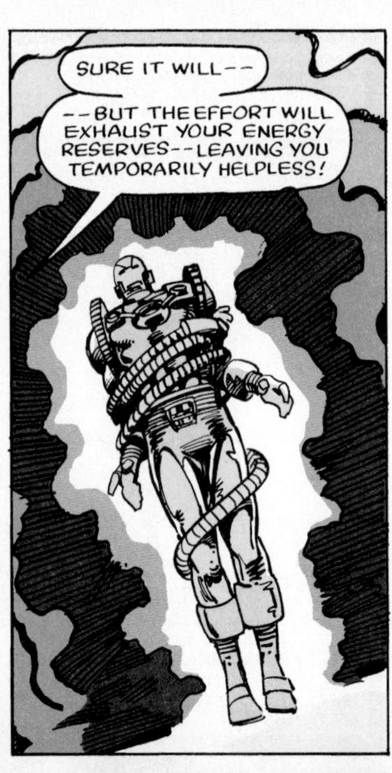
SURE IT WILL--
--BUT THE EFFORT WILL EXHAUST YOUR ENERGY RESERVES--LEAVING YOU TEMPORARILY HELPLESS!

I KNOW WE'LL MEET AGAIN--TO CONTINUE THIS BATTLE--BUT I'M AFRAID THAT I MUST LEAVE YOU NOW--

"--I'M NEEDED ELSEWHERE!"
BRAIN! THE SITUATION--

--WHAT IS IT?!
IT'S BAD! REAL BAD!

WE'RE LOSING POWER AT A PHENOMENAL RATE--AND THE CENTRAL COMPUTER WON'T RESPOND TO MY COMMANDS!
THE MAIN INPUT TERMINAL'S BEEN SABOTAGED!
IT DOESN'T MATTER!
MY FINGERS ARE EQUIPPED WITH COUPLINGS WHICH CAN LINK MY MIND DIRECTLY WITH THE COMPUTER'S CORE!
22

IT'S WORKING! THE STABILIZERS JUST KICKED IN!

ARGH
ENERGY BACKLASH! THE STRAIN ON MY INTERNAL CIRCUITRY IS INCREDIBLE...

FIGHT IT! YOU CAN'T STOP NOW!

NEVER KNEW ANYTHING COULD HURT... SO MUCH... BUT I CAN'T LET GO... CAN'T FAIL... NOT NOW... NOT NOW...

EVEN THOUGH HIS METAL BODY IS BATTERED BY FORCES VIOLENT ENOUGH TO SHATTER A CONCRETE FORTRESS, MACHINE MAN IS FILLED WITH A SPIRIT THAT CANNOT BE CRUSHED, AND SO...
IT'S OVER! YOU DID IT! YOU...
...WON.

MINUTES LATER.....
WE'RE ALL SECURE!
HOWEVER, THE BAINIES MANAGED TO RESCUE THEIR LEADER--

--AND GET AWAY!
NO SWEAT! WE'LL HAVE TO CHANGE SANCTUARY'S LOCATION TO AVOID ANOTHER ATTACK--
--BUT I THINK WE GOT OFF EASY!
YOU'RE WRONG, GEARS!
OUR TROUBLES ARE JUST STARTING!

IF WE WANT TO END THIS WAR, WE'LL HAVE TO TAKE IT TO SUNSET BAIN HERSELF!
TAKE ON BAINTRONICS, INC.? ARE YOU CRAZY?!
MAYBE, BUT I'VE BEEN ON THE DEFENSIVE EVER SINCE I WAS RESURRECTED...
...NOW IT'S MY TURN!
TO BE CONCLUDED--!
23

MARVEL®

#4 IN A FOUR-ISSUE LIMITED SERIES

# MACHINE MAN™

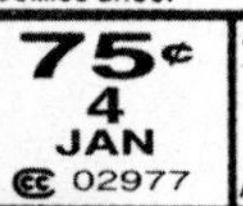

75¢
4
JAN
02977

APPROVED BY THE COMICS CODE AUTHORITY

VICTORY
SEPTEMBER 27, 2020: HOVERING FIVE THOUSAND FEET ABOVE THE CANADIAN NORTH WOODS IS SANCTUARY, THE MOBILE HEAD-QUARTERS OF THE MIDNIGHT WRECKERS, AND THE SITE OF A HIGHLY SPIRITED DEBATE...
ARE YOU CRAZY?! WE JUST FINISHED FIGHTING OFF AN INVASION BY IRON MAN AND HIS BAND OF MERCENARIES*-- AND NOW YOU WANNA TAKE ON SUNSET BAIN?!
IT'S SUICIDE!
YAH-ZOO! YOU MUST HAVE LOST YOUR MIND--ALONG WITH YOUR RIGHT HAND--IF YOU THINK YOU'D HAVE A CHANCE AGAINST BAIN!
THAT WOMAN CONTROLS BAINTRONICS INC, ONE OF THE WORLD'S RICHEST CORPORATIONS!
KLIK
STAN LEE PRESENTS:
TOM DEFALCO--PLOT/SCRIPT
BARRY WINDSOR-SMITH--PLOT/ART/COLOR
JIM NOVAK--LETTERS
LARRY HAMA--EDITOR
JIM SHOOTER--EDITOR-IN-CHIEF
*SEE LAST ISSUE!

I KNOW THE ODDS ARE AGAINST ME, GEARS-- BUT SUNSET HAS BEEN HOUNDING ME EVER SINCE THE WRECKERS FOUND MY BODY IN A DISCARDED STORAGE CONTAINER--AND REBUILT ME!
KID, YOU GOTTA LISTEN TO REASON--!

NO!
MACHINE MAN'S RIGHT! IT'S TIME WE ACED THE OLD BROAD!
HOLD ON, HASSLE! I'M NOT PLANNING TO COMMIT MURDER!
I AM.
THAT WOMAN HELD ME PRISONER! TORTURED ME REAL BAD! MIGHT HAVE EVEN KILLED ME IF IT WASN'T FOR HER 'BOT, JOCASTA...

JOCASTA--?!
OH, BOY!
WHAT DO YOU KNOW OF JOCASTA?
SHE WAS WITH MAMA B! A SILVER-TONED FEMININE MODE! I COULDN'T TELL IF SHE WAS PROGRAMMED AS A MAID, OR A BODYGUARD...
YOU KNEW ABOUT THIS?!
YEAH, YEAH, BUT IT AIN'T HOW YOU'RE THINKING, KID!

I DIDN'T WANNA SAY ANYTHING TILL I HAD ME SOME CONCRETE PROOF THAT BAIN HAD RESURRECTED YOUR OLD GIRLFRIEND! I JUST COULDN'T GET YOUR HOPES UP!
HEY, KID! WAIT--!
ENOUGH TALK!

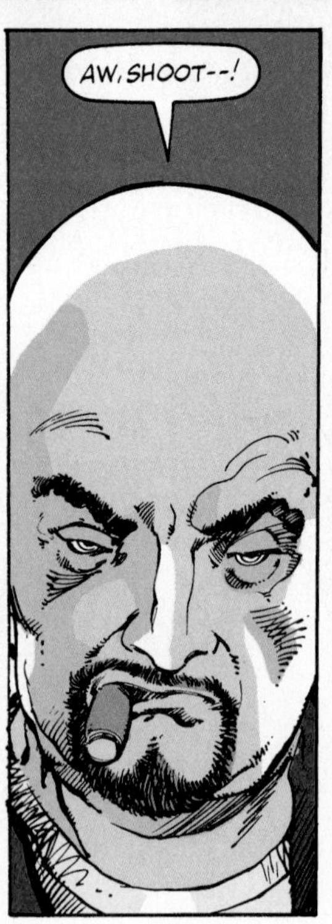
AW, SHOOT--!

WELL??!
ARE YOU ALL JUST GOING TO STAND THERE?!

MACHINE MAN BEFRIENDED US ALL! HE BECAME A MEMBER OF OUR PACK--OUR FAMILY!

HOW COULD YOU THINK OF DESERTING HIM NOW?

ALONE, SAVE FOR THE PLAINTIVE CRY OF A FALLEN BAINTONICS FLYER WHICH STILL CALLS TO ITS DEAD MASTER, MACHINE MAN PONDERS THE COST OF HIS WAR WITH SUNSET BAIN...
SKAHK ALL UNITS REPORT SKAHK
HE IS SICKENED BY THE WASTE--THE TRAGEDY--OF IT ALL!

UMM... I'D LIKE TO POINT OUT THAT THE SITUATION ISN'T AS DIRE AS IT SEEMS! AFTER ALL, MACHINE MAN DOESN'T EVEN KNOW WHERE BAINTRONICS CENTRAL IS LOCATED--

"--AND WE'RE CERTAINLY NOT GOING TO TELL HIM!"
SKAHK RETURN TO CENTRAL HEADQUARTERS SKAHK SECTOR SEVEN BAINTRONICS SKAHK
AMID THE RUBBLE, HE SPIES THE HAND HE LOST WHILE BATTLING ARNO STARK, THE IRON MAN OF 2020...

UNBIDDEN, THOUGHTS OF JOCASTA BEGIN TO FLOOD HIS MIND...
SKAHK LONGITUDE 73°50 WEST SKAHK

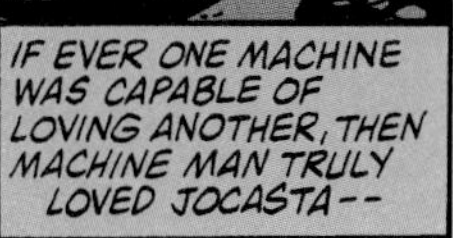
IF EVER ONE MACHINE WAS CAPABLE OF LOVING ANOTHER, THEN MACHINE MAN TRULY LOVED JOCASTA--

--BUT THAT WAS LONG... SO VERY LONG AGO!
SKAHK LATITUDE 40°40 NORTH SKAHK
CHIK-
HE DOESN'T KNOW HOW HE FEELS ABOUT HER NOW! YET, HE IS FILLED WITH RAGE AT THE THOUGHT OF HER IN THE HANDS OF HIS GREATEST ENEMY...

SKAHK
IN THAT INSTANT, A PLAN IS FORMED--
--AND A DECISION MADE!

WHAT TH--?!
IT'S THE BAINIES! THEY'RE BACK!
NAH! THAT'S ONLY A SKY-CYCLE REVVING--
OUTSIDE--! QUICK--!

WE'RE TOO LATE!
I CAN SEE THAT, SLICK!
BUT, WHERE'S HE GOING?
LISTEN--!
SKAHK LONGITUDE 73°50 WEST SKAHK LATITUDE SKAHK
OH, NO!
HE KNOWS! NOW, ARE YOU WITH HIM, OR NOT?!?
LADY, I WAS NEVER NOT WITH HIM! I JUST DIDN'T BELIEVE HE'D REALLY TAKE OFF ON US!
C'MON! WE GOTTA FIND US SOME CYKES!
NOW YOU'RE TALKING, MR. GARVIN!

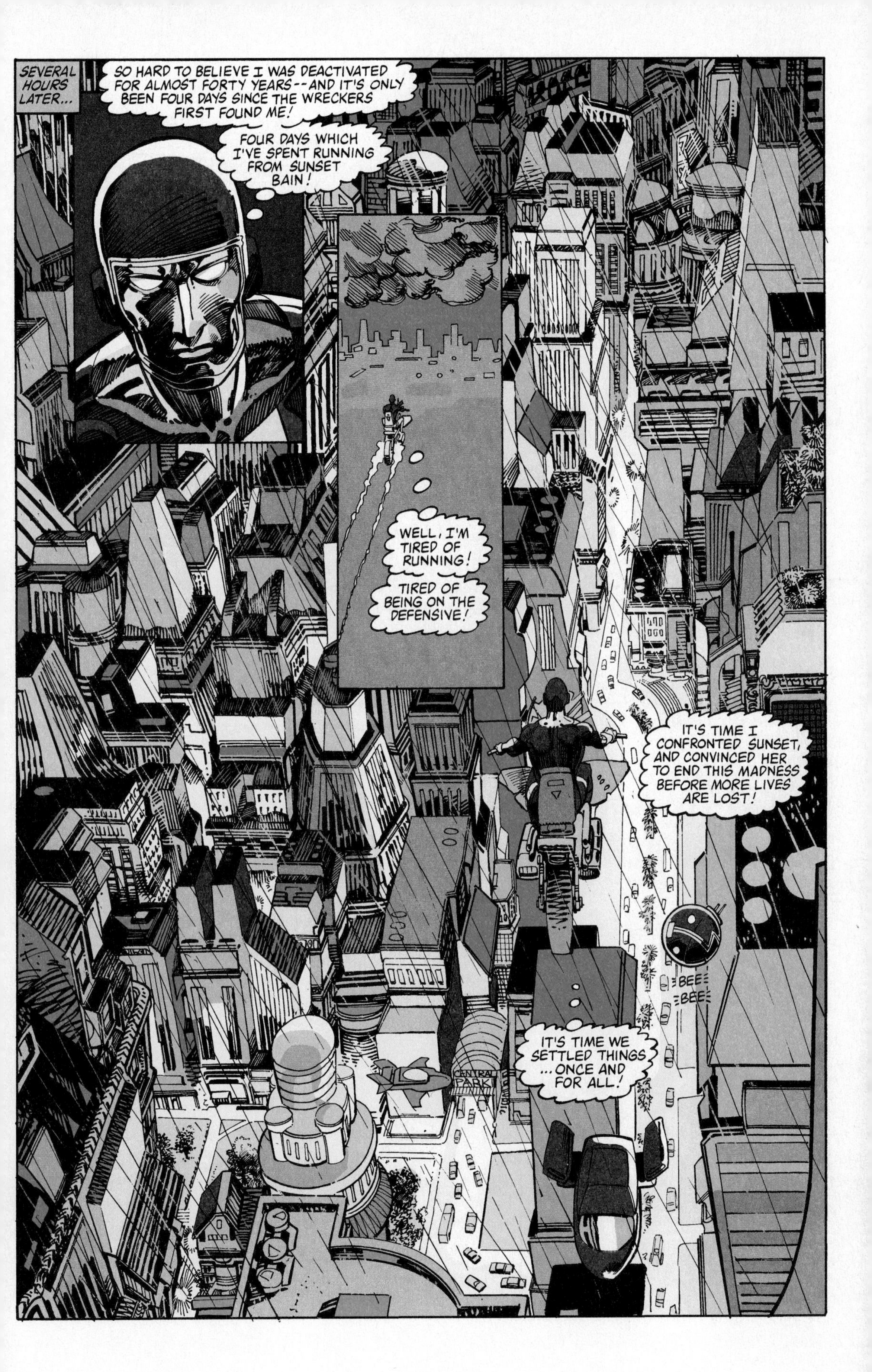
SEVERAL HOURS LATER...
SO HARD TO BELIEVE I WAS DEACTIVATED FOR ALMOST FORTY YEARS--AND IT'S ONLY BEEN FOUR DAYS SINCE THE WRECKERS FIRST FOUND ME!
FOUR DAYS WHICH I'VE SPENT RUNNING FROM SUNSET BAIN!
WELL, I'M TIRED OF RUNNING!
TIRED OF BEING ON THE DEFENSIVE!
IT'S TIME I CONFRONTED SUNSET, AND CONVINCED HER TO END THIS MADNESS BEFORE MORE LIVES ARE LOST!
BEE BEE
IT'S TIME WE SETTLED THINGS ...ONCE AND FOR ALL!
CENTRAL PARK

MEANWHILE, DEEP WITHIN BAINTRONICS CENTRAL...
AOOOGAA
AOOOGAA

AOOGAA
KLIK

SUNSET! I HEARD THE SIRENS--! WHAT'S HAPPENING?
ARNO, IT APPEARS THAT YOUR BUNGLED INVASION OF SANCTUARY HAS BROUGHT A REPRISAL!
INCREDIBLE! I DIDN'T THINK EVEN THE MIDNIGHT WRECKERS WERE STUPID ENOUGH TO ATTACK THIS STRONGHOLD!
I'LL BE WITH YOU AS SOON AS I FINISH RECHARGING MY BATTLE ARMOR!


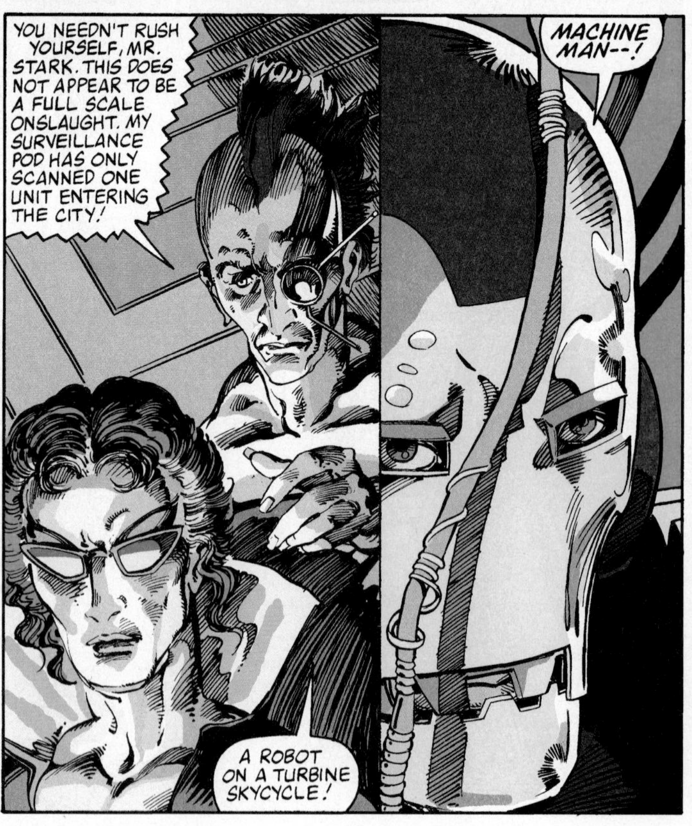

YOU NEEDN'T RUSH YOURSELF, MR. STARK. THIS DOES NOT APPEAR TO BE A FULL SCALE ONSLAUGHT. MY SURVEILLANCE POD HAS ONLY SCANNED ONE UNIT ENTERING THE CITY!
A ROBOT ON A TURBINE SKYCYCLE!
MACHINE MAN--!

YES... MACHINE MAN!
DR. CYCLOBE, ORDER AN ASSAULT TEAM UP TO THE LANDING PAD!
BUT THAT'S ONLY THIRTY MEN, MADAM BAIN! FROM WHAT I'VE HEARD YOU'LL NEED A LOT MORE TO STOP THAT ROBOT!
JUST DO IT!
AS YOU WISH...

"ATTENTION, TROOPERS! TAKE YOUR POSITIONS ON THE ROOF!"

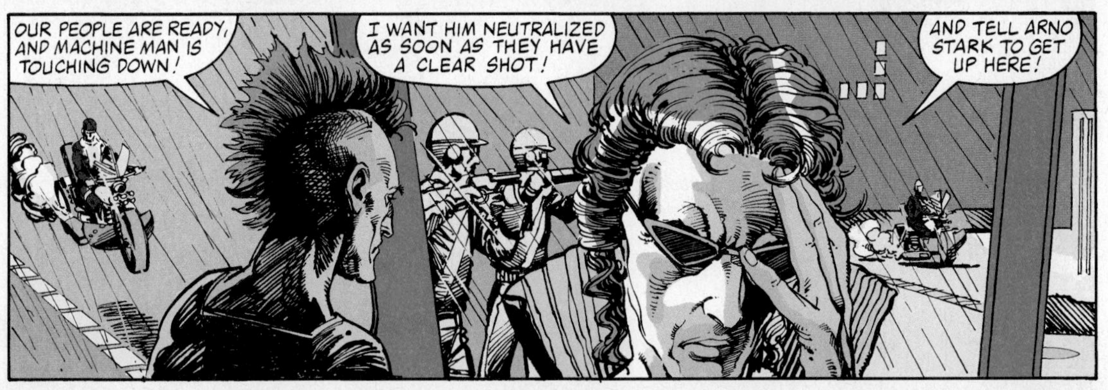
OUR PEOPLE ARE READY, AND MACHINE MAN IS TOUCHING DOWN!
I WANT HIM NEUTRALIZED AS SOON AS THEY HAVE A CLEAR SHOT!
AND TELL ARNO STARK TO GET UP HERE!

EASY... EASY...

NOW--!
PEOW
BUDDADUDDA
CHING
TWANG
VEOW
PEOW
UHN

STOP SHOOTING! I JUST CAME TO TALK!
TO END THIS NEEDLESS VIOLENCE--!
TEOW!

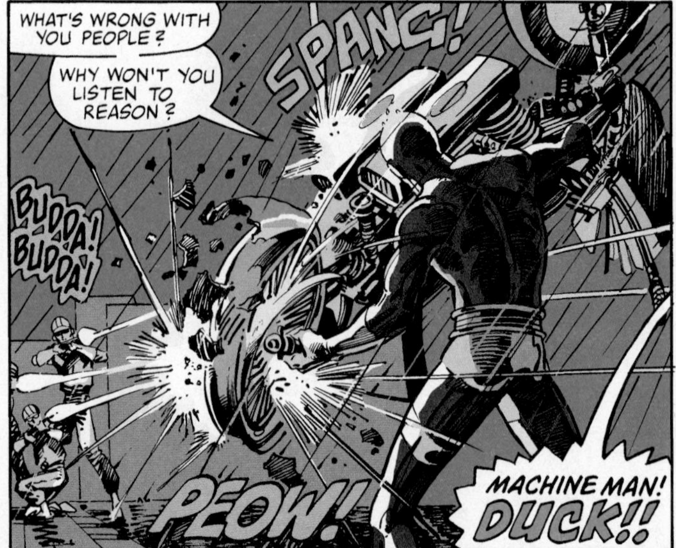
WHAT'S WRONG WITH YOU PEOPLE?
WHY WON'T YOU LISTEN TO REASON?
SPANG!
BUDDA! BUDDA!
PEOW!
MACHINE MAN! DUCK!!

AND CATCH ME!
SCATTER! THE SKY-CYKE'S COMING DOWN--!
SLICK--!

UFFF
BLOOOM!

THOSE MEN--! THEY DIDN'T HAVE A CHANCE!
COULDN'T BE HELPED, OL' BUDDY!
THEY WERE ABOUT TO FRY YOUR DIODES!

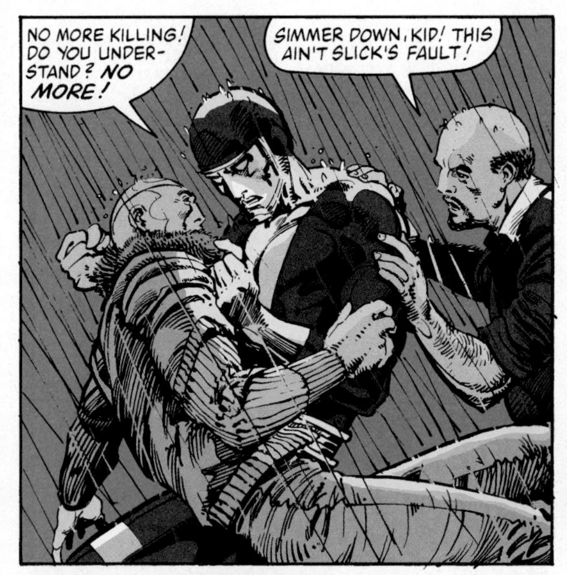
NO MORE KILLING! DO YOU UNDERSTAND? NO MORE!
SIMMER DOWN, KID! THIS AIN'T SLICK'S FAULT!

BAH! YOU ALWAYS WAS TOO MUCH OF A BLASTED IDEALIST!
DID YA THINK SUNSET BAIN WAS GOING TO WELCOME YOU WITH OPEN ARMS? THIS IS WAR! IF YOU CAN'T STAND THE KILLING, YOU SHOULDN'T HAVE STARTED THIS--!
WE TRIED TO TALK YOU OUT OF IT!

BUDDA BUDDA
REINFORCEMENTS! COMING FROM BELOW--!
GET DOWN!

I STARTED THIS, EH? WELL, THEN, I'LL PUT AND END TO IT...
NOW!

WHERE'S HE GOING, GEARS?
YOUR GUESS IS AS GOOD AS MINE!

ZOOOOOOM!
BAINTRONICS

HM..
BEEE
BEEE

UNLESS I'M VERY MUCH MISTAKEN...

...MY INSTRUMENTS INDICATE THAT OUR QUARRY IS HOVERING RIGHT OUTSIDE OUR WINDOW!
WHAT--?!

OH, MY GOD!

SUNSET!

ORDER YOUR MEN OFF THE ROOF! THE KILLING HAS GOT TO STOP! IT'S ALREADY GONE TOO FAR!

I KNEW THAT YOU WERE MONITORING ME ALL ALONG-- BUT I THOUGHT YOU'D GIVE ME A CHANCE TO EXPLAIN WHY I CAME-- IF I APPROACHED IN PEACE!
THIRTY MEN JUST DIED BECAUSE OF YOUR TREACHERY! ISN'T THAT ENOUGH?!

YOU'RE INSANE, SUNSET!
AND YOUR INSANITY JUST MIGHT COST ME THE LIVES OF MY FRIENDS--
--AND BRING THIS BUILDING DOWN IN A PILE OF RUBBLE!

THIS WAR IS STRICTLY BETWEEN YOU AND ME! WHY SHOULD OTHERS DIE?
ALL RIGHT! I HAVE NOTHING TO GAIN BY HAVING BAINTRONICS RAZED TO THE GROUND!

DR. CYCLOBE, CALL A CEASEFIRE ON THE ROOF!
WILL THAT BE ALL, MADAM?
YES! GET OUT OF HERE! LOCK THE DOOR--
--AND DON'T COME BACK!

NOW THEN, MR. STARK, I BELIEVE YOU STILL HAVE A CONTRACT TO HONOR...
KILL HIM!

WITH PLEASURE!
SHA-BWAM!
TASH!

GET UP!
YOU MIGHT HAVE BEATEN ME THE LAST TIME WE FOUGHT--
BZ-ZIT

--BUT YOU HAD TO RESORT TO YOUR LOUSY ROBOT TRICKS TO DO IT!
DO YOU HAVE THE COURAGE TO FACE ME ON EQUAL TERMS THIS TIME?
CAN YOU FIGHT ME LIKE A MAN?!

KA-CHOK!

I HOPE THEY KILL EACH OTHER!
JOCASTA! DO YOU READ ME?
I'M HERE IN THE CONTROL ANNEX, AND AM MONITORING ALL FRONTS!
CAN THE FIRE ON THE ROOF BE CONTAINED?!

YES, BUT IT'S ONLY A MATTER OF TIME BEFORE THE AUTHORITIES GET HERE!
THEN, RESUME THE OFFENSIVE! I WANT THOSE WRECKERS WIPED OUT BEFORE THE LAW TURNS UP!
BUT, SUNSET--!
YOU HAVE YOUR ORDERS, JOCASTA!
IS SENATOR BRICKMAN WITH YOU?

THIS IS OUR NIGHT, MILES! ALL OUR ENEMIES DESTROYED IN ONE SWOOP!
WHAT IF IRON MAN LOSES, SUNSET?! THEN WE'RE ALL DEAD!
WHY DON'T YOU LAY OFF THE BOOZE, SENATOR? IT GIVES YOU SUCH A NEGATIVE OUTLOOK.

SHE IS RIGHT, YOU KNOW. YOU'RE NOT HELPING...
YOU'RE JUST A BLASTED ROBOT! HOW CAN YOU KNOW WHAT IT'S LIKE TO BE ON THE VERGE OF LOSING EVERYTHING YOU EVER HAD?!

I THINK I KNOW, SENATOR.

KUNCH!

WHERE'S ALL YOUR SNAPPY PATTER NOW, MACHINE MAN?
BOK!
WHAT HAPPENED TO THE CUTE REMARKS AND FALSE BRAVADO?

MANKIND MADE A SERIOUS MISTAKE WHEN IT FIRST BEGAN DESIGNING YOU METAL MONSTERS IN ITS OWN IMAGE!
SOMEHOW YOU GOT THE WRONG IDEA!
YOU BEGAN THINKING YOU WERE AS GOOD AS MEN!

YOU'RE NOT-- AND I'M GOING TO PROVE THAT TO YOU!

KNOW SOMETHING, STARK?
YOU'RE A BIGOT!
KRASH!

I DIDN'T WANT TO FIGHT YOU! I CAME HERE TO TALK--! TO END THIS MADNESS!
CHUNCK

BUT YOU HAD TO PROVE THAT YOU WERE SUPERIOR--! THAT YOU COULD BEAT ME JUST BECAUSE YOU'RE HUMAN!
YOU CAN'T!
YOU'RE JUST NOT GOOD ENOUGH!

NO! I'LL LOSE EVERYTHING IF MACHINE MAN WINS!
ZZZZZ

THESE HIGH POWER CABLES WERE SEVERED DURING THE FIGHT!
THEY'RE MY ONLY HOPE!
SSKK

ZZOT
AAARRGH!

THAT WAS A CRAZY STUNT, SUNSET! YOU COULD HAVE KILLED ME, TOO!
I HAD TO TAKE THAT CHANCE, HERO! I COULDN'T AFFORD TO LET YOU LOSE!
NOW, GET YOURSELF TOGETHER, AND REPORT TO THE ROOF!

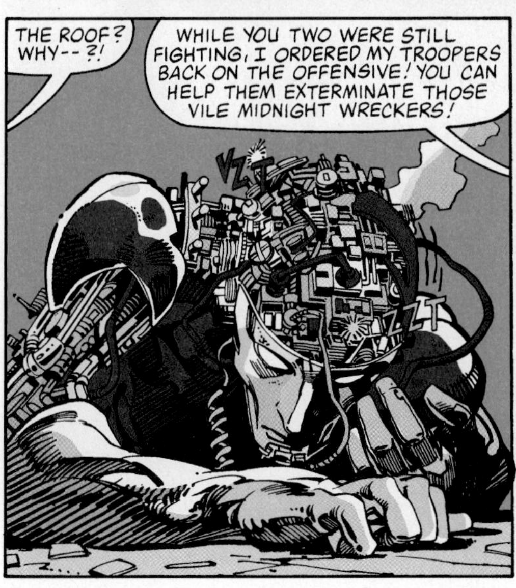
THE ROOF? WHY-- ?!
WHILE YOU TWO WERE STILL FIGHTING, I ORDERED MY TROOPERS BACK ON THE OFFENSIVE! YOU CAN HELP THEM EXTERMINATE THOSE VILE MIDNIGHT WRECKERS!

FZT
I SHOULD HAVE KNOWN THAT YOU WOULDN'T HONOR THE CEASEFIRE!
GOOD LORD! HE'S STILL ALIVE!
DON'T WORRY, SUNSET! I CAN HANDLE HIM NOW!

INCREDIBLE--! THAT ELECTRICAL JOLT WOULD HAVE TOTALLED ANY OTHER ROBOT!
WHAT'S KEEPING MACHINE MAN ON HIS FEET?!
DON'T YOU SEE? HE'S UNSTOPPABLE! UNSTOPPABLE!
HE'LL NEVER ADMIT DEFEAT! HE'LL NEVER GIVE UP! HE'LL JUST KEEP COMING BACK, AGAIN AND AGAIN...

"...UNTIL HE FINDS A WAY TO DESTROY US!"
K-TCHUNK!
UGNN

I'VE LIVED IN FEAR FOR ALMOST FORTY YEARS, BECAUSE I KNEW THIS DAY WOULD COME!
COME ON, STARK! STAND UP--! FACE ME LIKE A MAN!
SHOW ME HOW TOUGH YOU ARE!
IT'S OVER.
AT LONG LAST, IT'S ALL OVER...

YOU'RE NOTHING, STARK! NOTHING!
YOU'RE JUST A MAN PRETENDING TO BE A ROBOT! FRAGILE FLESH DRESSED IN AN ARMOR-PLATED SUIT!
WUD!
THE FACT THAT YOU WERE BORN HUMAN DOESN'T MAKE YOU SUPERIOR TO ME!
I COULD EASILY KILL YOU NOW, BUT I WON'T...

...BECAUSE I'M A BETTER MAN THAN YOU ARE!
KRUNCH!!
UNNN
I HOPE YOU WERE PAYING ATTENTION, SUNSET!
I COULD EASILY DO THE SAME THING TO YOU!
B-BUT YOU WOULDN'T DARE--!
WOULDN'T I?
KLIK
ATTENTION ALL UNITS! CEASE FIRE! RETREAT, AND AWAIT MY FURTHER ORDERS!

THERE! I ONLY HOPE I'VE STOPPED THE FIGHTING IN TIME--!
FOLLOW ME, SENATOR! WE'VE GOT TO HELP, SUNSET!
NO.
IT'S ALREADY TOO LATE FOR HER...FOR US...
ABOUT FORTY YEARS TOO LATE...
NOTHING CAN SAVE US NOW. WE'RE ALL GOING TO DIE...AT THE HANDS OF A MACHINE...
A MACHINE THAT THINKS IT'S A *MAN*!
HOWEVER...
...I DO HAVE AN ALTERNATIVE.

YOU THINK I WON'T SMASH YOU LIKE I SMASHED HIM?
YOU'RE THE ONE WHO HAD ME DEACTIVATED!
CRASH!
AAARGHH!
YOU BUILT AN EMPIRE ON THE TECHNOLOGY YOU STOLE FROM ME!
WHEN YOU LEFT ME TO ROT!
WHY SHOULDN'T I TAKE REVENGE?!

ENOUGH! I'VE HAD ENOUGH! DON'T HURT ME! PLEASE--!
MACHINE MAN, STOP--!
JOCASTA--?!

YOU NEEDN'T TERROR-IZE HER ANYMORE, MACHINE MAN! YOU'VE WON!
I'VE ALREADY ORDERED OUR TROOPERS OFF THE ROOF...

"...THE WAR IS OVER!"
HEY! THEY WERE WINNING! WHY'D THEY QUIT--?!
WHO CARES, SLICK...JUST AS LONG AS THEY KEEP RUNNING!

ATTENTION, BELOW! THIS IS THE METROPOLITAN PEACE AUTHORITY! YOU ARE ALL UNDER ARREST!
UH-OH.
SPLIT UP!
HASSLE'S RIGHT! WE CAN'T LET THEM TAKE US! WE'RE STILL CRIMINALS IN THE EYES OF THE LAW!

STAND TO! YOU HAVE BEEN ORDERED TO SURRENDER! IT IS FUTILE TO ATTEMPT ESCAPE!
MACHINEMAN'S SOME-WHERE BELOW!
WE GOTTA FIND HIM, AND GET OUT OF HERE!

I... CAN'T FIGHT YOU ANYMORE!
YOU'VE GOT TO STOP HOUNDING ME AND MY FRIENDS! SWEAR THAT YOU'LL LEAVE US ALONE!
WH-WHAT DO YOU WANT?
GIVE ME YOUR WORD THAT BAIN-TRONICS INC WILL STOP MAKING WAR ON THE MIDNIGHT WRECKERS!

I... SWEAR IT!
HE'S CHANGED, JOCASTA! THE MACHINE MAN I USED TO KNOW WASN'T SO RUTHLESS, SO BRUTAL... BUT THIS ONE WOULD HAVE KILLED ME IF NOT FOR YOU!
IS THIS TRUE, MACHINE MAN?

NO!
I HAD NO INTENTION TO HARM HER! BUT I HAD TO CONVINCE HER THAT I WAS SERIOUS...

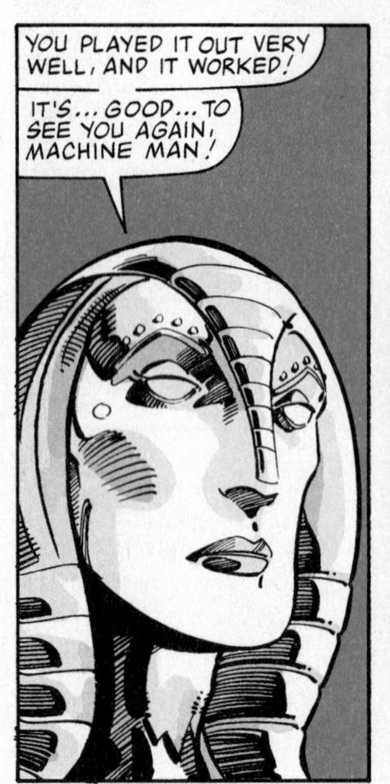
YOU PLAYED IT OUT VERY WELL, AND IT WORKED!
IT'S... GOOD... TO SEE YOU AGAIN, MACHINE MAN!

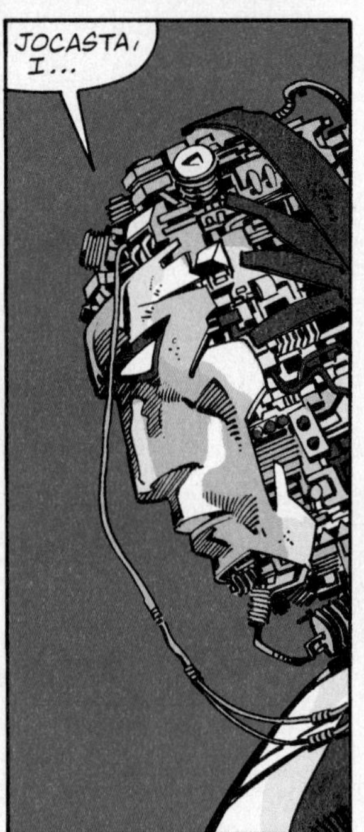
JOCASTA, I...

YO, MACHINE MAN!
THE POLICE HAVE THE PLACE SURROUNDED!
HEY! WHAT'S GOING ON HERE?

YOU ALL RIGHT, KID?
I'M FINE! SUNSET AND I WERE JUST COMING TO TERMS! SHE'S AGREED TO A PERMANENT TRUCE!
THE WAR BETWEEN BAINTRONICS AND THE WRECKERS IS OVER!
NOT YET, IT ISN'T...
I STILL HAVE A PERSONAL SCORE TO SETTLE WITH MAMA B!

NO! SHE'S ALREADY SUFFERED ENOUGH FOR ONE DAY! I WON'T LET YOU HURT HER!
WHAT MAKES YOU THINK I WOULDN'T PUT A HOLE IN YOU, TOO?

EASE UP, HASSLE! THE FIGHTING'S OVER! SUNSET GAVE ME HER WORD!
HOW CAN YOU TRUST THAT MURDERING WITCH? HER WHOLE LIFE HAS BEEN BUILT ON LIES!

WHAT ABOUT IT, SUNSET? HASSLE DOES HAVE A POINT, YOU KNOW!
YOU HAVEN'T EXACTLY BEEN THE MOST HONORABLE PERSON I'VE EVER MET!

BUT, OF COURSE, YOU MUST REALIZE WHAT WILL HAPPEN IF YOU DO GO BACK ON YOUR WORD...
BELIEVE ME, SUNSET, YOU DON'T WANT ME COMING BACK HERE!

DO YOU--?
NO...

...I DON'T.

YOU NEEDN'T WORRY ANYMORE! I'LL SEE THAT SHE KEEPS HER WORD!
YOU'RE GOING TO STAY WITH HER? BUT, I THOUGHT...

TRUST ME, IT WOULDN'T HAVE WORKED OUT! I'VE SPENT THE LAST FORTY YEARS OF MY LIFE WITH SUNSET! SHE'S BECOME TOO MUCH A PART OF ME! AND, SHE NEEDS ME...
I COULD NEVER LEAVE HER NOW...

ATTENTION! YOU ARE ALL UNDER ARREST!
I THINK I UNDERSTAND!..
POLICE
LAY DOWN YOUR WEAPONS!
HEY, KID! I THINK IT'S TIME WE WERE GOING!
I HOPE YOU DO!

MOVE IT, MACHINE MAN! WE'VE GOT TO HIT THE SKIES!
PERHAPS, WE'LL MEET AGAIN...
DO NOT ATTEMPT TO ESCAPE!
POLICE
I'D LIKE THAT! THERE'S SO MUCH YOU COULD TELL ME ABOUT THE PAST FORTY YEARS!
C'MON, YOU BIG DUMMY! GET ON THE BACK OF MY BIKE!
BRM BRM
BRMM
BR

GOODBYE, MACHINE MAN! HAVE A GOOD LIFE!
POLICE
THIS IS GONNA BE TIGHT! OUR ONLY HOPE IS TO DIP UNDER'EM... AND HOPE WE CAN OUTMANEUVER THEM IN THE SIDE STREETS!
BRM RRM
VRM RM

JOCASTA, WHAT ARE YOU DOING?
KLIK
KLIK
KLIK
I'M HELPING...
...HELPING MY FRIEND!

SIR! OUR TELESCREENS JUST WENT OUT!
SOME OUTSIDE SIGNAL IS JAMMING US!
BBBAAVROOOOOOOOMMM
POL
76

WE'VE LOST OUR TARGETS! THEY'RE GETTING AWAY!
YAH-ZOO! LOOKS LIKE MACHINE MAN'S GIRLFRIEND REALLY CAME THROUGH FOR US!
BAINTRONIC
VROOOMM!!
POLICE
WRMM
MMM
FAREWELL, JOCASTA! I'LL NEVER FORGET YOU...

HEY! WHAT'S GOING TO HAPPEN TO US WRECKERS, NOW THAT WE DON'T HAVE THE BAINIES ON OUR BACKS ANYMORE?
YOUR GUESS IS AS GOOD AS MINE!

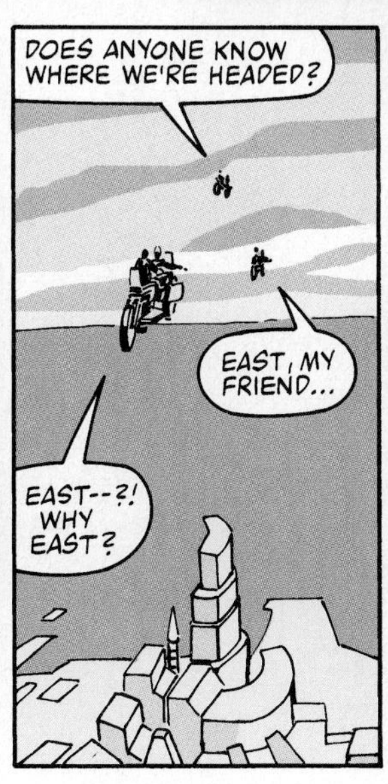
DOES ANYONE KNOW WHERE WE'RE HEADED?
EAST, MY FRIEND...
EAST--?! WHY EAST?

WHY NOT?
THE END!

MARVEL
DEATH'S HEAD
UK 65P
US $1.75
CAN $2.25
10
SEPT
THERE'S ONLY ONE IRON MAN...
AND I'M IT, YES?

Stan Lee presents:

# DEATH'S HEAD™

Writer SIMON FURMAN · Art BRYAN HITCH · Letterer ANNIE H · Colourist EVAN PETERS · Editor STEVE WHITE · Managing Editor JENNY O'CONNOR

YOU SEE, I GET THE DISTINCT IMPRESSION YOU MEAN TO HARM THE PEOPLE I'VE BEEN HIRED TO PROTECT...
AND WE CAN'T HAVE THAT, CAN WE?
AWW, SHOOT! I AIN'T EVEN SLOWIN' HIM DOWN! HE-HE AIN'T HUMAN—

GHAKK!
KRUD

AND THESE ARE JUST MY WARM-UP EXERCISES! IF YOU BOYS WANT TO SURRENDER BEFORE WE GET TO THE WORKOUT PROPER... I'LL UNDERSTAND!
DON' LISTEN TO HIM!

HE'S JUST FLESH 'N' BLOOD INSIDE THAT TIN SUIT! JUST A LITTLE MAN WHO THINKS SOME ARMOUR AND A FANCY NAME MAKES HIM A BIG MAN!
C'MON, LET'S SHOW MISTER IRON MAN HERE...EXACTLY HOW IMPRESSED WE ARE!

WUDDA
BLAM
BRUDA

UNF! OKAY, BOYS...

IF YOU WANT TO PLAY ROUGH...

THAT SUITS ME JUST FINE!
CHUD
"OH, HE'S WONDERFUL! WHERE EVER DID YOU FIND HIM, ATHEY?"

"IN THE OFFICES OF STARK ENTERPRISES, SIR."
KLICK

"THE GENTLEMAN IN THE ARMOUR IS NONE OTHER THAN ITS CHAIRMAN ARNO STARK."
WHUD
BRRRAT
"I UNDERSTAND HE INHERITED THE ARMOUR FROM HIS PREDECESSOR AND... AH, UPDATED IT."

HE'S TEARIN' US APART! LET'S MOVE!
SECURI-CARRY
"BUT SURELY, ATHEY, A MAN LIKE STARK DOESN'T NEED THE MONEY. SO WHY THE MERCENARY BIT?"

"I BELIEVE, SIR, IT'S HOW HE GETS HIS **KICKS**."
SORRY, BOYS— BUT WHEN THEY HIRED ME...
"AH YES. I CAN **UNDERSTAND** THAT."

WHOOM!
...THEY DID SAY SOMETHING ABOUT **NO PRISONERS!**
"I THOUGHT YOU MIGHT, SIR."

WHO **ARE** YOU?! WE ARE MEN OF **PEACE**. WE WANT NO VIOLENCE, NO KILLING!
STAY IN YOUR CAR. THERE MAY BE OTHERS!
**OTHERS?** THERE MUST BE SOME MISTAKE. WHY WOULD ANYONE WANT TO HARM US?

WE COME HERE AS EMISSARIES OF OUR COUNTRY, BEARING ONLY FRIENDSHIP AND GOODWILL TO YOUR NATION.
SALE
WAY I HEAR IT, THERE'S SOME GUYS BACK HOME WANT TO SEE YOU FAIL, WANT TO SEE YOUR BLOOD SPILT ON FOREIGN SOIL!

**MADNESS!** WHO TOLD YOU THIS **FICTION?** DRIVER— **GO!**
"I TAKE IT THIS WAS YOUR CONCOCTION, WAS IT? YES, ASSASSINATION PLOTS, POTENTIAL COUPS —IT SOUNDS LIKE YOU, ATHEY."

"AH HA. THANK YOU, SIR. OF COURSE, IT WOULDN'T BEAR UP TO **CLOSE** INSPECTION..."
PLEASE, NO! **NOT AGAIN!** LET THIS ONE BE **RIGHT!**

...BUT THEN THAT'S REALLY WHY MISTER STARK WAS SUCH AN IDEAL SELECTION!

AFTER HIS LAST TWO SPECTACULAR FAILURES, MERCENARY WORK WAS IN SOMEWHAT SHORT SUPPLY FOR OUR ERSTWHILE IRON MAN OF 2020. HE JUMPED AT THE --
AHEM. ANOTHER BRANDY, SIR?

CALL ME, CHANCE, ATHEY. AFTER ALL, THAT WAS WHAT THE DICEMEN COUNCIL DUBBED ME WHEN I JOINED.
AS YOU WISH... SIR.

NOW WHERE WAS I? AH, YES. STARK, LIKE THE GUNMEN I HIRED, TOOK THE JOB WITHOUT PROBING TOO DEEPLY INTO THE WHYS AND WHEREFORES OF THE COVER STORY.

YES, YES. THIS IS ALL VERY INTERESTING, ATHEY... BUT CAN WE USE HIM AGAIN?

AGAIN?

MAY I REMIND YOU... CHANCE, THAT THE DICEMEN HAVE A STRICT RULE ABOUT REPETITION. WE INVOLVE PLAYERS ONLY ONCE!
CONTINUING GAMES COULD BE TRACED BACK TO THE INSTIGATORS, AND NO ONE DICEMAN IS ALLOWED TO COMPROMISE THE OTHERS' SECURITY.
YOUR CONTINUED MEMBERSHIP OF THIS ELITE GROUP DEPENDS ON YOU OBEYING THE RULES. RICH AND INFLUENTIAL AS YOU ARE, I DOUBT YOU COULD STAGE THESE LITTLE ...INDULGENCES UNAIDED.
DON'T GO ON, ATHEY. I KNOW THE RULES... AND THEY'RE JUST PLAIN UNREASONABLE!
LOOK, I'M IN CHARGE HERE, AND I'M TELLING YOU TO ARRANGE A SECOND GAME FOR THIS IRON MAN.
:SIGH: VERY WELL, SIR. I BELIEVE I HAVE AN OPPONENT WHO'LL GIVE HIM A RUN FOR HIS MONEY; A BOUNTY-HUNTER WHO GOES BY THE SOMEWHAT TACKY NAME OF DEATH'S HEAD.
IF YOU'LL KINDLY TURN TO THE SCREEN...
SO, DEATH'S HEAD, HOW ABOUT TELLING THE VIEWERS WHY YOU WENT AFTER THE LEADER OF THE WARLORDS. WAS IT OUT OF CIVIC DUTY, OR DID YOU JUST WANT THE REWARD?
THE REWARD MONEY OF COURSE. BEEN HERE TWO DAYS NOW... AND I'M NOT ON HOLIDAY YES?
HE'S MAGNIFICENT! GET HIM FOR ME... IMMEDIATELY!
VERY WELL...
ON YOUR OWN HEAD BE IT!

FIVE MINUTES TO THE DEADLINE... FIVE MINUTES FOR THEM TO CALL AND AGREE TO OUR DEMANDS!

CHRIST, WHY DID WE HAVE TO HOLE UP HERE? HELL'S KITCHEN THEY USED TO CALL THIS PLACE... NOW THEY JUST CALL IT HELL!

WHEN WE WERE KIDS WE THOUGHT THESE BUILDINGS BELONGED TO THE DEVIL. USED TO DARE EACH OTHER TO GO INSIDE.

KRATCH!
GNNK!
WRONG NUMBER. YES?

HOLY SPIT! BLAST IT, HECTOR— MOVE YOURSELF! THEY'VE FOUND US!
Nuh-NO... NO! CARLOS WAS RIGHT... EES HIM!

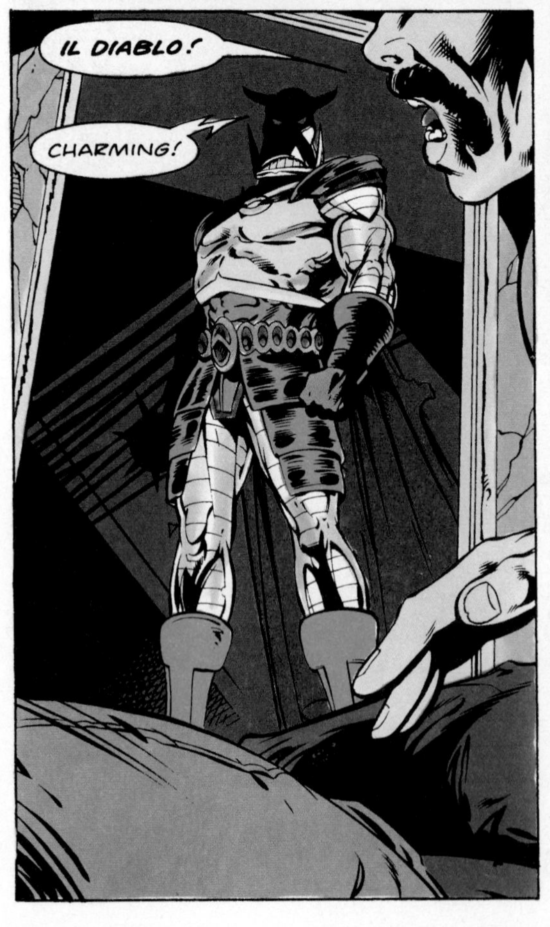
IL DIABLO!
CHARMING!

BEEN CALLED SOME THINGS IN MY TIME, HUH? BUT NOT THE DEVIL! CAN'T SEE THE RESEMBLENCE MYSELF!
STILL, ONE THING'S FOR SURE...

...I AM YOUR WORST NIGHTMARE, YES?

IS THAT SO? WELL, DEVIL OR NOT, YOU'D BETTER START SAYING YOUR PRAYERS!
AH.

HRM.
WELL SOMEONE UP THERE LIKES ME, YES?

C'MON, KID. DON'T BE AFRAID, HUH? YOU'RE GOING HOME!

NO...NO...EL DIABLO...COME TO CLAIM ME...
Sigh... JUST DON'T MAKE 'EM LIKE THEY USED TO, EH?

OKAY, KID— YOU'VE A DATE WITH DAD, AND I'VE A DATE WITH THE MONEY HE OFFERED TO ANYONE WHO COULD FIND AND SAVE YOU!
LET'S NOT KEEP EITHER OF THEM WAITING, HUH?
NOT STAND
JODE
JUDE

SOON. ACROSS TOWN...
VERY NICE, YES? A FEW MORE LIKE THAT AND I'LL BE ABLE TO GET MY SPACECRAFT REBUILT... AGAIN!
THOUGHT I'D BEEN STITCHED UP ROYALLY— DUMPED IN 2020 BY REED RICHARDS* —BUT QUITE THE OPPOSITE IS TRUE, RIGHT?
*OF THE FANTASTIC FOUR —LAST ISSUE.

NOT ONLY IS 2020 MORE CRIME RIDDEN THAN 8162, BUT I'M FINALLY RID OF THAT PEST OF A PARTNER, SPRATT, YES?

PITY ABOUT THE VULTURE, HUH?
DEATH'S HEAD
AHEM.

DEATH'S HEAD?
SEEMS LIKELY, HUH?
DEATH'S HEAD
UM. YES. WELL, IF YOU'RE INTERESTED, I HAVE SOME BUSINESS I CAN THROW YOUR WAY.

THESE TWO ARE INTERNATIONAL TERRORISTS, CURRENTLY IN NEW YORK. THE PEOPLE I REPRESENT CAN'T TOUCH THEM BECAUSE OF THEIR DIPLOMATIC IMMUNITY. BUT YOU... YOU COULD!

SEEMS STRAIGHTFORWARD ENOUGH, YES? HOW MUCH?
TWENTY THOUSAND DOLLARS. HALF NOW, HALF ON COMPLETION.

HRM. TOO EAGER? TOO MUCH? SEEMS RIGHT, BUT GUT FEELING SEEMS WRONG.
I'LL TAKE THE JOB...
...BUT NOT YOUR WORD, YES?

LATER...
OKAY, IT SEEMS TO BE CLEAR. IN YOU GO... HURRY!
WILL YOU PLEASE LEAVE US ALONE! GO AWAY!

WE DON'T KNOW YOU, AND DON'T KNOW WHY ANYONE WOULD HAVE HIRED YOU TO PROTECT US. THIS IS ALL A DREADFUL MISTAKE!
YOU'RE WRONG...
...I HOPE!

I'M STICKING WITH YOU EVERY STEP OF THE WAY. THIS IS ONE JOB I'M GOING TO SEE GOES RIGHT--UH?
SORRY, FULL UP. PLEASE TAKE THE NEXT LIFT, YES?

BUT--
THIS IS ONLY FOR PEOPLE GOING UP...

...IN SMOKE, RIGHT?
A·LEVEL

KRETHUNG
UNF!
SHUM

I THINK, MISTER... THIS IS YOUR FLOOR!

GHAA!
SHRAM!

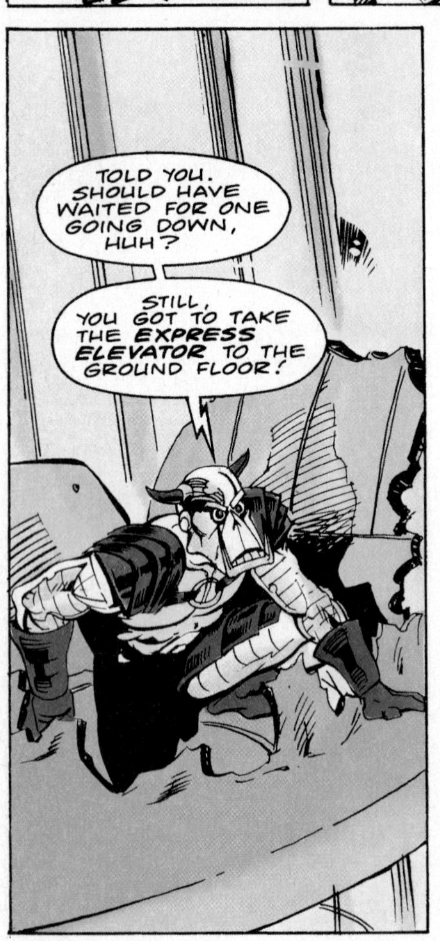
TOLD YOU. SHOULD HAVE WAITED FOR ONE GOING DOWN, HUH?
STILL, YOU GOT TO TAKE THE EXPRESS ELEVATOR TO THE GROUND FLOOR!

ON THE OTHER HAND... MAYBE NOT!
TSK. BOOT JETS. SHOULD HAVE PATENTED MINE, YES?

AHK!

MY GOD! THE ELEVATOR! IT'S GONNA' FALL!
UUUH!

DOING MY JOB FOR ME, EH? WELL DON'T GET ANY IDEAS, HUH? THIS IS THE ONLY CUT YOU CAN EXPECT...

NO!
WHUUF!
CHASSHH

I WON'T LET YOU BUTCHER INNOCENT PEOPLE. YOU HAVE TO BE STOPPED...

...AND STOPPED HARD!
RUNCH

URR... DEAD MAN, YES? IT'S HUMANS LIKE YOU WHO GIVE MECHANOIDS A BAD NAME... UNH...
UH UH, FELLA...

I LET YOU KILL THOSE GUYS AND ANY CHANCE OF PEACE BETWEEN OUR COUNTRIES WILL BE GONE! BESIDES, THERE'S ONLY ROOM FOR ONE IRON MAN IN THIS CITY...

AND IT'S ME!
RATCH

HE DID IT! HE BEAT HIM!
PERHAPS...
BLAST IT! I WAS BETTING ON THE BOUNTY-HUNTER!

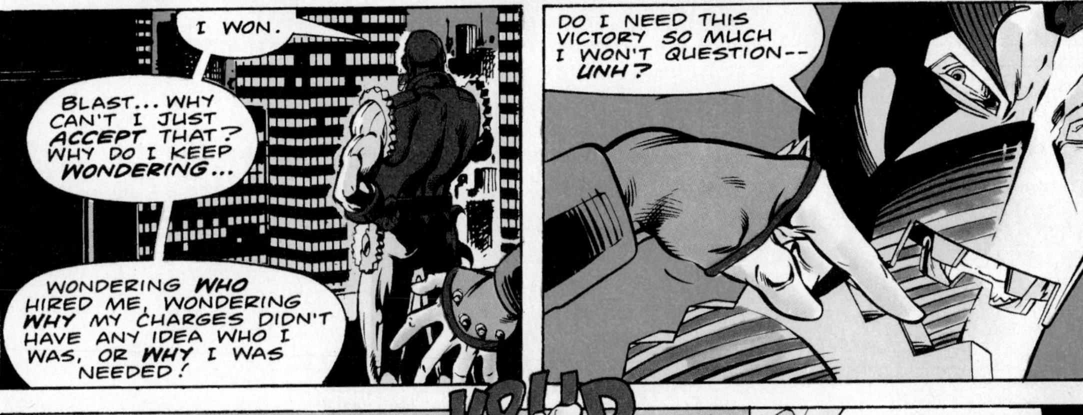
I WON.
BLAST... WHY CAN'T I JUST ACCEPT THAT? WHY DO I KEEP WONDERING...
WONDERING WHO HIRED ME, WONDERING WHY MY CHARGES DIDN'T HAVE ANY IDEA WHO I WAS, OR WHY I WAS NEEDED!
DO I NEED THIS VICTORY SO MUCH I WON'T QUESTION-- UNH?

KRUD
NO-GNNNK!

SORRY TO INTERRUPT THAT RATHER INTRIGUING MONOLOGUE. GET BACK TO THAT IN A MOMENT, HUH?
RIGHT NOW, THOUGH... I NEED TO HIT SOMETHING, YES?

EVER HAD YOUR HEAD RIPPED OFF, HUH? HRM... SILLY QUESTION, YES?
WHUD!

BWUNG!
ANYWAY, IT HURTS! DOES NOTHING FOR ONE'S SENSE OF HUMOUR.

SO JUST GIVE ME A WHILE TO GET THIS OUT OF MY SYSTEM, HUH? THEN WE'LL TALK.
WHAM!

BETTER, HUH?
RIGHT— GET THE IMPRESSION YOU THINK THE TWO YOU'RE PROTECTING HAVE PEACEFUL INTENTIONS. I WAS TOLD THEY WERE INTERNATIONAL TERRORISTS. SOMEONE'S BEEN LIED TO, HUH?

NORMALLY IT WOULDN'T BOTHER ME, BUT IN THIS CASE IT DOES. IF THE HIT ISN'T BONA FIDE, MIGHT NOT GET THE BALANCE OF MY FEE, YES?
IN THAT CASE, THE HIRER BECOMES MY NEXT TARGET. BAD FOR FUTURE BUSINESS TO LET PEOPLE DEFAULT, RIGHT?

I HAVE A NASTY SUSPICION WE'VE BOTH BEEN LIED TO, USED... AND THAT HURTS!

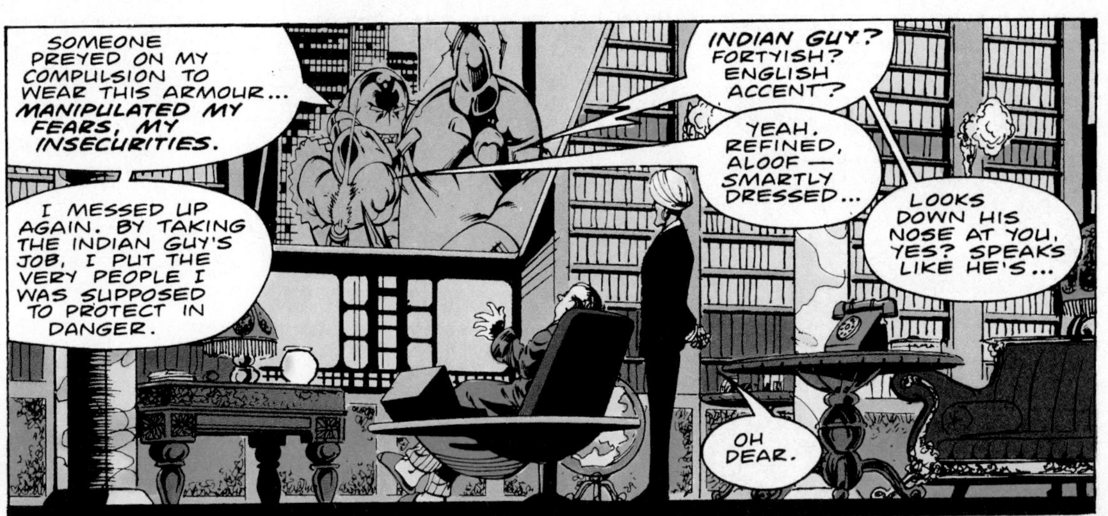
SOMEONE PREYED ON MY COMPULSION TO WEAR THIS ARMOUR... MANIPULATED MY FEARS, MY INSECURITIES.
I MESSED UP AGAIN. BY TAKING THE INDIAN GUY'S JOB, I PUT THE VERY PEOPLE I WAS SUPPOSED TO PROTECT IN DANGER.
INDIAN GUY? FORTYISH? ENGLISH ACCENT?
YEAH. REFINED, ALOOF — SMARTLY DRESSED...
LOOKS DOWN HIS NOSE AT YOU, YES? SPEAKS LIKE HE'S...
OH DEAR.

IT'S THE SAME GUY. BUT WHY?
ATHEY — DO SOMETHING?
I — I...

IT'S LIKE... WE WERE SET UP TO FIGHT EACH OTHER. LIKE COMPETITORS...

...ON TV, YES? A CAMERA... SOMEWHERE. MUST BE CLOAKED. SCANNING...

ATHEY--
TOO LATE, I FEAR. THE MONITOR WASN'T BUILT FOR SPEED— JUST STEALTH.
C-CAN THEY USE IT... TO FIND US?
JUDGING BY HOW EASILY THEY LOCATED IT, I IMAGINE ITS RECEIVING SIGNAL...

"...WILL LEAD THEM RIGHT HERE!"
BRUDDA
BRUDDA

SHRAK!

OH GOD... THEY WENT THROUGH THE PERIMETER DEFENCES LIKE THEY WEREN'T THERE!
THEY'RE INSIDE! ATHEY — DO SOMETHING!
CERTAINLY.

WHA—? ATHEY— HAVE YOU LOST YOUR MIND?
NO, SIR. I AND OTHERS LIKE ME ARE PLACED BY THE DICEMEN COUNCIL BOTH TO SERVE... AND PROTECT!
YOU HAVE TRANSGRESSED THE UNWRITTEN RULE— COMPROMISED THE DICEMEN'S SECURITY. YOU HAVE BECOME A LOOSE END...

...TO BE TIED UP.
BLAM

AND, FOLLOWING A FEW FINAL ARRANGEMENTS...
THERE—I BELIEVE THAT'S EVERY-THING.
GOODBYE, SIR. I'D SAY IT'S BEEN A PLEASURE SERVING YOU... BUT MY MOTHER TAUGHT ME NEVER TO LIE.
EEEEEEE

THIS IS THE PLACE! WE SHOULD FIND--
SKRASH!

GEEZ.
FORGET HIM, HUH? LOOK AT THIS.

THE BALANCE OF OUR FEES, YES?
YES. AND WHAT'S MORE IT'S ALL HERE!
BUT WHY THE DICE? WHY THE DEAD MAN? PERHAPS IF WE SEARCH THE HOUSE WE'LL FIND--

WAIT! INTERNAL SYSTEMS ARE REGISTERING A MASSIVE ENERGY BUILD-UP. UNDERNEATH THE HOUSE!

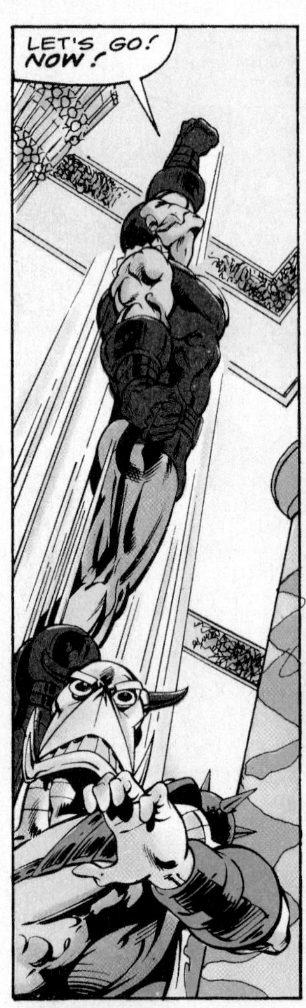
LET'S GO! NOW!

CROSH!

BRADA
DOOM

GUESS SOMEONE WANTED TO LEAVE NO TRACES.
WHO CARES, EH? GOT PAID, DIDN'T WE? THAT'S ALL THAT MATTERS. ACTUALLY BEEN MEANING TO TALK TO YOU ABOUT YOUR ATTITUDE.

BE SURE OF YOURSELF, HUH? EVERYTHING'S STRAIGHTFORWARD WHEN YOU BELIEVE IN WHAT YOU'RE DOING. STRIKE FAST, TAKE THE MONEY...
AND DON'T LOSE YOUR HEAD, YES?

ON HIS WAY, DEATH'S HEAD WAS ***MODERATELY*** SURPRISED TO SEE HIS SPACECRAFT FLY OUT OF A DIMENSIONAL PORTAL.

HE WAS RELIEVED TO SEE THAT THE PILOT BROUGHT THE CRAFT IN FOR A GRACEFUL, CONTROLLED LANDING.

IT WAS HIS FAITHFUL PARTNER AND CHUM, ***SPRATT.*** OF COURSE, DEATH'S HEAD WAS ***DELIGHTED*** TO SEE HIM!

THERE WAS JUST SO MUCH FOR THE CHUMS TO TALK ABOUT, THAT IN THEIR HASTE TO BE AWAY, THEY FORGOT THEIR ***OTHER*** FRIEND...

... BIG SHOT!
YOU CAN'T ESCAPE ME, DEATH'S HEAD! YOU'RE DEAD! YOU HEAR ME — DEAD!
SHE SENT ME HERE TO FIND YOU, DESTROY YOU! AND THAT SUITS ME JUST FINE!
BUT THEY WERE SURE TO MEET UP SOON. AND WHEN THEY DID THEY'D LIVE HAPPILY EVER AFTER!

WALT SIMONSON

BOB WIACEK

WILLIAM ROSADO

# IRON MAN 2020™

WALT SIMONSON
co-plot, script
BOB WIACEK
co-plot, layouts,
pencils pgs. 1-23, inks
WILLIAM ROSADO
pencils pgs. 24-64
JOHN COSTANZA
letters
CHRISTIE SCHEELE
colors
JOE KAUFMAN
design
MICHAEL MARTS
assistant editor
NELSON YOMTOV
group editor
TOM DeFALCO
editor in chief

PROLOGUE:
IT IS THE YEAR 2020
A TIME WHEN THE PEOPLES OF EARTH HOPE THAT THE STRIFE AND DESTRUCTION OF THE 20TH CENTURY WILL HAVE BEEN PUT BEHIND THEM.
WHEN ALL MANKIND WILL LIVE IN ALABASTER CITIES...
...AND TEARS WILL BE FOREVER REPLACED BY THE SOUND OF CHILDREN'S LAUGHTER.
WHEN THE MYTHIC UTOPIA OF SO MANY BROKEN DREAMS WILL AT LAST BE REALIZED...
...AS MAN ASCENDS TO HIS TRUE DESTINY AMONG THE STARS.

AND FROM A DISTANCE, A DISINTERESTED SPECTATOR MIGHT THINK IT SO.
THE REALITY IS MORE PROSAIC.
DEATH AND TAXES ARE STILL THE PRINCIPAL SUBJECTS OF DEBATE AMONG THE INHABITANTS OF EARTH...
...WARS STILL RAGE IN FAR-OFF CORNERS...
...FAMINE STILL FINDS FAR TOO MANY VICTIMS...
...AND PESTILENCE SEEMS AS ENDEMIC AS EVER TO THE HUMAN CONDITION.
BUT THE BUILDINGS ARE TALLER AND SHINIER...
...THE MACHINES ARE BIGGER, FASTER, AND NIFTIER...
...AND IF YOU HAVE THE MONEY, YOU CAN AVOID THE FOUR HORSEMEN FOR A LONG TIME. NOBODY AVOIDS TAXES.
BUT LIFE ISN'T WITHOUT ITS BRIGHT SIDE.
THERE IS STILL... ROMANCE.
ZZZZZZZZZZZZZZZZZZ

LOOK, BRAUN! AN ISLAND! AND DESERTED BY THE LOOK OF IT.
THAT'S GREAT! MAYBE WE CAN BE SHIPWRECKED THERE OR SOMETHING.

YOU KNOW, MAROONED TOGETHER, JUST YOU AND ME, ON A TROPICAL PARADISE? PRETTY ROMANTIC, HUH?

MORE LIKELY WE'D BE EATEN ALIVE BY INSECTS AND COME DOWN WITH SOME EXOTIC TROPICAL DISEASE!
MICKY! MICKY! MICKY! YOU'VE GOT TO GET INTO THE SPIRIT OF THE ADVENTURE.

THAT DOESN'T SOUND HALF BAD. WHEN DOES THE ADVENTURE BEGIN?
ANY TIME YOU WANT. WE'VE GOT AUTO-PILOT.

SPWHRAAAHMM
WHAT THE--?
GEEZ! WHAT THE HELL WAS THAT?
WE'RE LOSING ALTITUDE! FAST!
WE'VE BEEN HIT! THAT WAS A MISSILE!
WE'LL WORRY ABOUT IT LATER! WE'VE HAD IT!
STARBOARD STABILIZER'S GONE DOWN!
GRNNKGRNNKGRNNKGRN
OIL PRESSURE DROPPING!
FIRE IN THE NUMBER THREE THRUSTER! I'M SHUTTING 'ER OFF!
LIFT CONFIGURATION DECREASING, BRAUN! 93%! 85%! 80! 76! 68!
WE'RE GOING IN WHILE WE'VE STILL GOT SOME ABILITY TO MANEUVER! BRACE YOURSELF!

SKREEEAAAMMMMMM
BRAUN!
GET BACK, MICKY! AWAY FROM THE SHIP! FUEL TANKS RUPTURED ON IMPACT!
ANY SECOND NOW SHE'S GOING TO--!

BRAKKAKRHOOOM

GONE! EVERYTHING'S GONE!
BUT WHO COULD HAVE DONE THIS TO US? AND WHY?
I DON'T KNOW, HONEY, BUT I DO KNOW THAT WHOEVER DID IT IS ON THE ISLAND SOMEWHERE!
AND IF YOU CAN STAND, WE'D BETTER GET MOVING.
THEY'LL BE LOOKING FOR US WHERE THE SKIMMER WENT DOWN!
AND THEY'VE FOUND YOU ALREADY!
NO NEED TO RUSH OFF IN SUCH A HURRY, FRIENDS.
AS THE WICKED WITCH ONCE SAID, MY LITTLE PARTY'S JUST BEGINNING!
WHO--?
WE'RE A FEW GOOD-TIME FOLKS LOOKING FOR FUN, MISS.
WELCOME TO *PARADISE ISLAND*, WHERE EVERY MOMENT OF *PLEASURE* IS WORTH A THOUSAND MOMENTS OF PAIN!
*BIND* THEM! AND MAKE SURE IT *HURTS*!

DAWN. ANOTHER DAY. FAR ABOVE THE BUSY STREETS.
NEW YORK CITY. STARK INTERNATIONAL HEAD-QUARTERS.
THE NEXUS OF A HUNDRED INDUSTRIES, A THOUSAND SUBSIDIARIES, AND TEN THOUSAND JOBS.
STARK
IN SHORT, THE SOARING CAPITAL BUILDING OF AN INDUSTRIAL MEGAPLEX...
...AND ALL OF IT RESTING ON THE SHOULDERS OF ONE MAN.

THIS MAN.
ARNO STARK.
SELF-MADE HEIR OF THE LEGENDARY ANTHONY STARK...
...IN WHOSE GIANT SHADOW ARNO HAS BEEN STANDING FOR A LONG TIME.
IN MORE WAYS THAN ONE.
ANTHONY STARK... INDUSTRIALIST, INVENTOR, PHILAN-THROPIST, FOUNDER OF STARK INTER-NATIONAL...
...AND SOMETHING ELSE...
...CREATOR AND CONSTRUCTER OF THE GLEAMING IRONMONGERY...
...THAT EVEN NOW CALLS TO HIS SUCCESSOR...

...IN A VOICELESS ECHO DOWN THE LONG CORRIDOR OF TIME...
...AN ECHO OF A THOUSAND MIGHTY DEEDS, A THOUSAND HEROISMS.

IT IS THE ECHO OF THE ARMORED TREAD... OF THE INVINCIBLE IRON MAN!

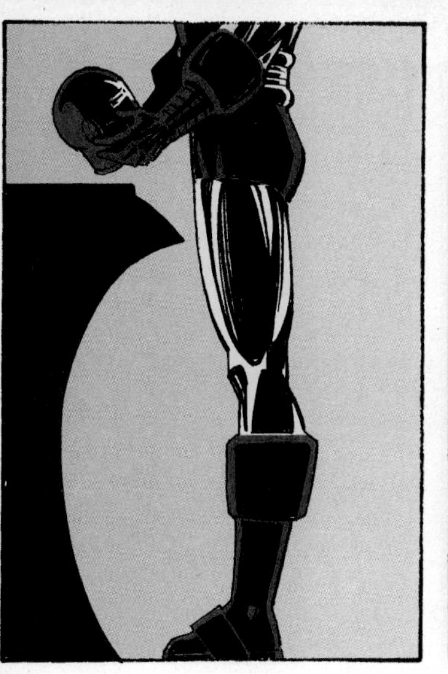

DAMN!

SHATTT TTERRR

AND IT IS AN ALMOST UNBEARABLE BURDEN.

THE RIDE TO THE TOP OF THE SKYSCRAPER TAKES ONLY A FEW MOMENTS...
...BUT MORE THAN ENOUGH TIME FOR A MAN TO COLLECT HIS THOUGHTS.
I GUESS I'VE NO CHOICE. NO CHOICE AT ALL.
I ALREADY HAVE DOUBTS THAT I'M FIT TO WEAR THE ARMOR OF MY PREDECESSOR.
LATELY, I'VE BEGUN TO WONDER IF I'M GOING TO DESTROY THE EMPIRE HE CREATED AS WELL.
THANKS TO THE FAILURE OF THE PEACE INITIATIVE IN RIYADH, OIL PRICES ARE ABOUT TO SKYROCKET. AGAIN.
AND THE LOSS OF THE WESTERN SIBERIAN OILFIELDS TO THE INSURGENTS MEANS THERE'LL BE NO PRICE RELIEF FROM RUSSIAN RESERVES.
STARK INTERNATIONAL IS TEETERING ON THE EDGE OF FINANCIAL RUIN.
WE MUST HAVE AN INFUSION OF CAPITAL AND QUICKLY.
AFTER MY HUMILIATION AT THE HANDS OF THE MACHINE MAN,* I THOUGHT I WOULD NEVER WEAR THE ARMOR AGAIN BUT NOW...
...IT'S THE ONLY THING THAT MIGHT SAVE THE SITUATION...
...AND WELLINGTON MARCUS' OFFER IS TOO TEMPTING TO REFUSE.
*From the legendary MACHINE MAN limited series.
IF I CAN SELL HIM ON THE IDEA.
SKLIKK
BEEP BEEPBEEP BEEP

AND IN THE SPACE OF A SINGLE HEARTBEAT, THE VISIONS OF A NIGHTMARE DANCE BEFORE HIS EYES...
...STILL AS REAL AS EVER. AND AS PAINFUL.
THE INVINCIBLE IRON MAN OF 2020... A MERCENARY...
...HIRED BY SUNSET BAIN OF BAINTRONICS, INC....
...TO DESTROY MACHINE MAN, A ROBOTIC WONDER FROM THE LATE TWENTIETH CENTURY...
...AN ANACHRONISM REBUILT BY A PACK OF MIDNIGHT WRECKERS.
UNTIL THAT MEETING, THE INVINCIBLE IRON MAN WAS JUST THAT... INVINCIBLE.
THE MEMORIES COME UNBIDDEN...
...AND PLAY OUT LIKE AN ENDLESS LOOP OF FILM...
...OVER AND OVER...
...AS THEY HAVE DONE SO MANY TIMES BEFORE.

COME ON, STARK! STAND UP! FACE ME LIKE A MAN!
KRAAANNG
SHOW ME HOW TOUGH YOU ARE!
THE FACT THAT YOU WERE BORN HUMAN DOESN'T MAKE YOU SUPERIOR TO ME!
I COULD EASILY KILL YOU NOW, BUT I WON'T...
...BECAUSE I'M A BETTER MAN THAN YOU!
SPLANNNG
AND JUST LIKE IN THE MOVIES, THE ENDING IS ALWAYS THE SAME.

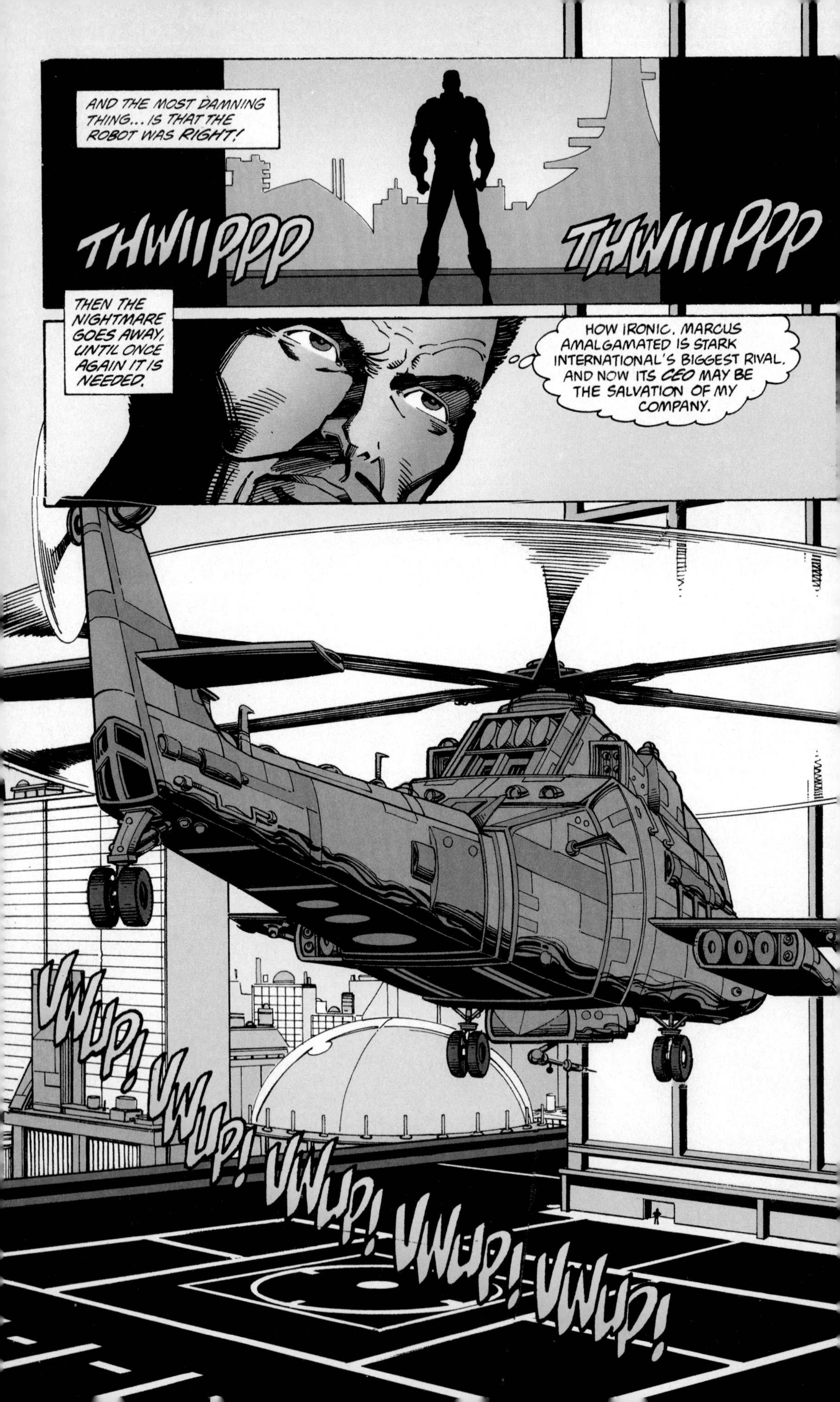
AND THE MOST DAMNING THING... IS THAT THE ROBOT WAS RIGHT!
THWIIPPP
THWIIIPPP
THEN THE NIGHTMARE GOES AWAY, UNTIL ONCE AGAIN IT IS NEEDED.
HOW IRONIC. MARCUS AMALGAMATED IS STARK INTERNATIONAL'S BIGGEST RIVAL. AND NOW ITS CEO MAY BE THE SALVATION OF MY COMPANY.
UWUP! UWUP! UWUP! UWUP! UWUP! UWUP!

FDUB!
FDUB!
FDUB!
FDUB!

HOWARD?
STARK IS POWERED UP, BUT ALL WEAPONS SYSTEMS ARE IN NEUTRAL.
SENSORS INDICATE NO OTHER LIFE-FORMS ON THE TOP THREE FLOORS, AS REQUESTED.
GOOD.

HELLO, WELLINGTON. WELCOME TO--
WE'LL SKIP THE USUAL AMENITIES, STARK.

YOU WOULDN'T BELIEVE ME AND I DON'T WANT TO WASTE ANY MORE TIME.

LET'S GET STRAIGHT TO THE POINT. YOU LOOK VERY NOBLE STANDING THERE IN THE ARMOR, STARK...
...BUT ARE YOU WEARING IT OR IS IT WEARING YOU?
WHAT DO YOU--?
SIMPLE. I'VE DONE MY HOME-WORK.

I KNOW HOW MACHINE MAN TOSSED YOU AROUND LIKE A BEAN BAG.
AND I'VE NO TIME TO WASTE WITH EITHER AMATEURS OR PRIMA DONNAS.
I'VE GOT A JOB THAT NEEDS DOING... AND IT NEEDS DOING FAST.

BUT ONLY THE BEST WILL DO, STARK. IS THAT YOU?
THERE'S ONLY ONE WAY TO FIND OUT, MARCUS.
DRINK, SIR?
NO, THANKS.

I UNDERSTAND YOUR CONCERN BUT YOU NEEDN'T WORRY. MACHINE MAN WAS A ONE-OF-A-KIND, A FREAK. AND I'VE MADE A NUMBER OF MODIFICATIONS IN THE ARMOR SINCE THEN.

EVEN HE WOULDN'T STAND A CHANCE AGAINST ME NOW.
THERE'S NOTHING... AND NOBODY... I CAN'T--?

!

KKREEASSSH
WE'RE IN! KILL HIM!
BEEYOW!
BEEYOW!

AIM FOR HIS HEAD!
BEEYOW!

YOU MISSED, PUNK! AND YOU HAD YOUR SHOT!
SCHREEEEEEEEE!

SCHWOOOOOOOSHHH
AIIEEEEEEEEE
HUMMMMPH.
GEEZ! HE NAILED CALEB! GET HIM, ETHAN! GET HIM!
BEEYOWW
MMMMMMM.
BLLAAARRMM!
KISS ETHAN GOODBYE, BUSTER! HE WON'T BE NEEDING HIS PENSION EITHER!
EEEEEEEEEE!

MMM.
OOOO

OH NO!
BEEYOOW!
IT'S CALLED A NEUTRALIZER SCREEN, PUNK!

BUT DON'T BOTHER TO REMEMBER IT.
SKREEAACK

SPTHANNG

SPTHINNG
UGGGH!
PTHUMP!

JUST COUNT YOURSELF LUCKY THAT I'VE DECIDED TO TAKE ONE PRISONER!

BUT I'M ALREADY OUT OF PATIENCE. YOU'VE GOT JUST THREE SECONDS TO TELL ME WHO SENT YOU...
...OR I'LL TOSS YOU OUT AFTER YOUR BUDDY!

I... CAN'T...
RELEASE HIM, STARK. I SENT HIM.
OH, PLEASE. ISN'T THE "LET'S TEST HIM" PLOY A LITTLE OLD BY NOW?

PERHAPS. BUT AS I SAID, I'VE DONE MY HOMEWORK...
...AND I NEEDED TO SEE FOR MYSELF. HOWARD?

5.294 SECONDS, SIR. THAT'S BETTER THAN TWO SECONDS OFF THE RECORD OF YOUR OWN SECURITY FORCES.
HMMMM. IT'LL DO. IT'LL HAVE TO.
AND WHO IS THIS ANYWAY? I THOUGHT OUR MEETING WAS PRIVATE.
HOWARD IS MY PERSONAL ASSISTANT... AND BODYGUARD. PRACTICALLY SPEAKING, HE IS MERELY AN EXTENSION OF MYSELF.
AND JOSH HERE IS AS NOTHING.
SECURITY STASIS FIELD, JOSH. IMMEDIATELY.
YESSIR!

THIS WILL PREVENT ANY EAVES-DROPPING.
AND MY WINDOW?

PFAUGH! I SEE IT'S SELF-REPLACING.

YOU WILL BE MORE THAN ADEQUATELY COMPENSATED IF YOU SUCCEED IN THE TASK I AM ABOUT TO SET YOU.

FIELD ON, SIR. ANYTHING ELSE?
YES.

YOU'RE FIRED.
BUT--?

COLLECT YOUR GEAR AND GET OUT!

WAS THAT NECESSARY, MARCUS? HE DIDN'T HAVE A CHANCE AGAINST ME AND YOU KNOW IT.
I DON'T TOLERATE FAILURE, STARK.
THE VERY FACT THAT HE'S ALIVE PROVES HE DIDN'T DO HIS JOB.

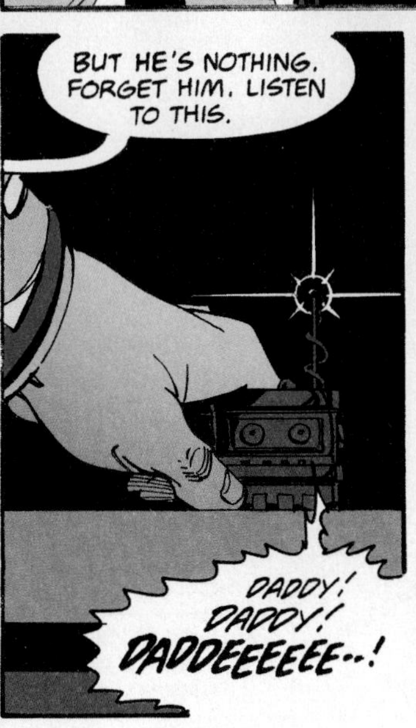
BUT HE'S NOTHING. FORGET HIM. LISTEN TO THIS.
DADDY! DADDY! DADDEEEEEEE--!

THEY'VE GOT MY DAUGHTER, STARK. MY DAUGHTER.
AND I WANT HER BACK.

I'D GIVE THE WORLD IF I COULD. I DON'T OWN IT.

"BUT I OWN ENOUGH."
THE COLD WAR MAY BE A FADING MEMORY...
...BUT GIVEN MAN'S AGGRESSIVE INSTINCTS...
...CONFLICT IS STILL AN IMPORTANT WAY TO SETTLE DIFFERENCES OF OPINION IN MANY PARTS OF THE GLOBE.
SKREEEE
AN ENTERPRISING MERCENARY NEEDS TO BE ABLE TO DELIVER HIS SERVICES TO HIS CUSTOMERS AS QUICKLY AND EXPEDITIOUSLY AS POSSIBLE.
THANKS TO STARK INTERNATIONAL'S MILITARY DEVELOPMENT DIVISION...
...SUPERSONIC STEALTH TECHNOLOGY CAN PUT IRON MAN 2020 IN ANY PART OF THE GLOBE IN A HURRY.
AND BEST OF ALL, THE TRIP'S A WRITE-OFF.

MR. STARK? WE HAVE TO MAKE A SLIGHT DETOUR AROUND TROPICAL STORM HARRIS.
REVISED ETA IS 22:00 HOURS.
THANK YOU, WATERS.
AND IN THE PLANE'S MODIFIED CARGO BAY...
STATUS REPORT UPDATE, PLEASE, COMPUTER.
WEAPONS' SYSTEMS FULLY CHARGED.
PROPULSION AND GUIDANCE SYSTEMS ENERGIZED.
ALL INTERNAL COMPUTERS ON LINE.
SLIGHT ENERGY DRAIN IN STARBOARD GYRO...
REPLACEMENT UP-GRADE TO VERSION 4.5 LOADED. LOCKED.
REFUELING 84% COMPLETE.
SUIT FULLY OPERATIONAL IN 24 SECONDS.
GOOD.
BRING UP THE MARCUS TAPE, PLEASE.
CLLICK!
SUBJECT FILE 629. UPLOADING.
ACCESSING...

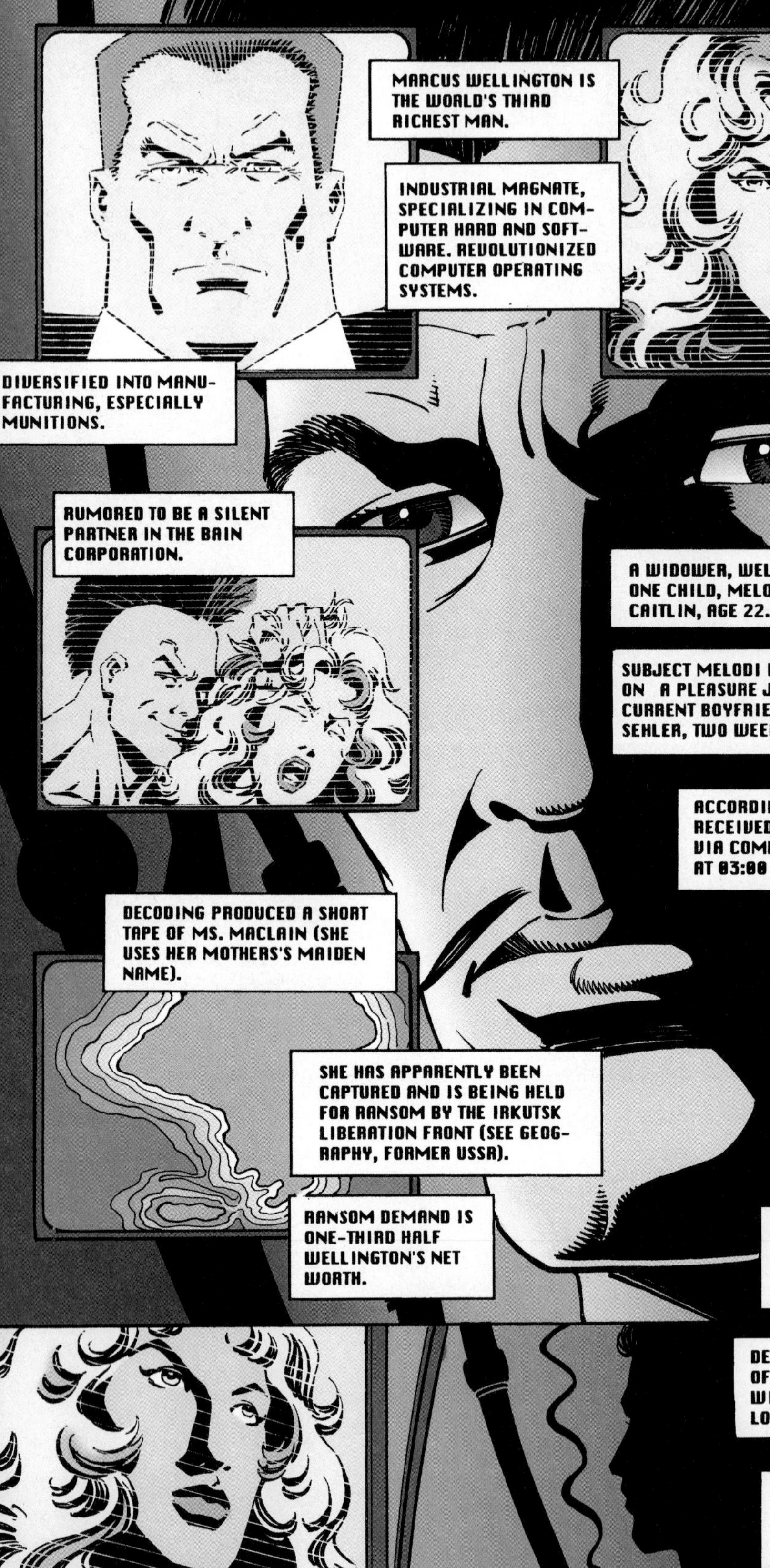
MARCUS WELLINGTON IS THE WORLD'S THIRD RICHEST MAN.
INDUSTRIAL MAGNATE, SPECIALIZING IN COMPUTER HARD AND SOFTWARE. REVOLUTIONIZED COMPUTER OPERATING SYSTEMS.
DIVERSIFIED INTO MANUFACTURING, ESPECIALLY MUNITIONS.
RUMORED TO BE A SILENT PARTNER IN THE BAIN CORPORATION.
A WIDOWER, WELLINGTON HAS ONE CHILD, MELODI (MICKY) CAITLIN, AGE 22.
SUBJECT MELODI DISAPPEARED ON A PLEASURE JAUNT WITH CURRENT BOYFRIEND, BRAUN SEHLER, TWO WEEKS AGO.
ACCORDING TO WELLINGTON, HE RECEIVED A PRIVATE MESSAGE VIA COMPUTER INTERNET TODAY AT 03:00 HOURS.
DECODING PRODUCED A SHORT TAPE OF MS. MACLAIN (SHE USES HER MOTHERS'S MAIDEN NAME).
SHE HAS APPARENTLY BEEN CAPTURED AND IS BEING HELD FOR RANSOM BY THE IRKUTSK LIBERATION FRONT (SEE GEOGRAPHY, FORMER USSR).
RANSOM DEMAND IS ONE-THIRD HALF WELLINGTON'S NET WORTH.
RANSOM DROP TO BE MADE IN A REMOTE LOCATION IN THE MARSHAL ISLANDS IN THE PACIFIC.
DEPFORD IMAGING ANALYSIS OF KIDNAPPERS COMBINED WITH WEINTRAUB PSYCHOLOGICAL PROFILE WORKUP...
... INDICATES A 73% PROBABILITY SUBJECT WILL BE KILLED UPON DELIVERY OF RANSOM.
AND AS HE LOOKS AT THE BRIGHT YOUNG FACE ON THE SCREEN BEFORE HIM...

...ARNO STARK AGAIN HEARS WELLINGTON MARCUS' FINAL WORDS.
"HER MOTHER'S BEEN DEAD FOR TEN YEARS, ARNO. SHE'S ALL I'VE GOT LEFT."
AND UP AHEAD, SOMEWHERE IN THE MARSHALL ISLANDS...
I'M SORRY WE CAN'T OFFER YOU FANCIER ACCOMMODATIONS, MS. MACLAIN...
...BUT THESE OLD BUILDINGS LEFT OVER FROM THE JAPANESE OCCUPATION ARE ABOUT ALL WE COULD AFFORD.
A SAD STATE OF AFFAIRS THAT SHOULD BE CHANGING SHORTLY.
THANKS TO YOUR FATHER.
IF YOU THINK MY FATHER WILL GIVE UP ONE RED CENT TO SAVE ME, YOU'RE SADLY MISTAKEN.
HE HATES MY GUTS!

JUST LIKE HE HATES EVERYBODY!
NOW, MS. MACLAIN, YOU'RE UNDERVALUING YOURSELF.
I SUSPECT YOU'RE WORTH MORE TO HIM THAN YOU KNOW.
I MYSELF HAVE LONG BEEN AN ADMIRER OF MARCUS WELLINGTON'S.
RICH, RUTHLESS... A MAN WHO DOES BUSINESS THE WAY BUSINESS SHOULD BE DONE.
WITHOUT APOLOGY.
AND OF COURSE, HIS SOFTWARE INNOVATIONS ARE NOTHING SHORT OF GENIUS.
THE LAUGH'S ON YOU, BUSTER. MY FATHER'S HIRED GUNS DO THE THINK-TANK WORK.
WITH HIS MONEY, HE HIRES THE BEST.
MAYBE, BUT IN YOUR CASE, HE USED LOW-GRADE HELP.
DID HE THINK PRETTY BOY HERE WOULD PROTECT YOU?
I DON'T NEED PROTECTION!
HAHAHA HAHAHAHA

I'M GLAD YOU THOUGHT SO. MADE IT THAT MUCH EASIER FOR US!
AFTER THIS, THE IRKUTSK LIBERATION FRONT WILL AT LAST BECOME A SERIOUS PLAYER ON THE WORLD STAGE!
OH, PLEASE! YOU CAN'T FOOL ME.
YOU DON'T HAVE THE COURAGE OF ANY POLITICAL CONVICTIONS!
YOU'RE JUST IN IT FOR THE MONEY! EVERYBODY ALWAYS IS.

SHUT YOUR MOUTH, YOU RICH--!
SLAPPP!
OHHH!

GENTLY. GENTLY, DORA.
WE WOULDN'T WANT TO DAMAGE THE MERCHANDISE NOW, WOULD WE?
WHO CARES, CAESAR! IT ISN'T LIKE--
BE QUIET. IT'S NEARLY TIME FOR THE DROP.
TAKE ANTÓN AND THE PORTABLE SIDEWINDER LAUNCHERS...

MAKE SURE THE MONEY SHOWS UP.
AND OF COURSE, KILL WHO-EVER BROUGHT IT.
LIKE YOU'RE GOING TO KILL ME?
NOT QUITE, DOLL.
YOU AND I ARE GOING TO HAVE A LITTLE FUN FIRST.

IT'S ALL PART OF THE FRIENDLY SERVICE.
LIKE HELL!

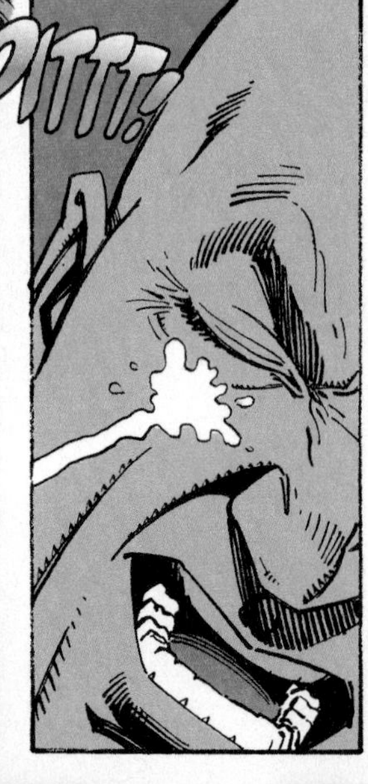
SPITTT!

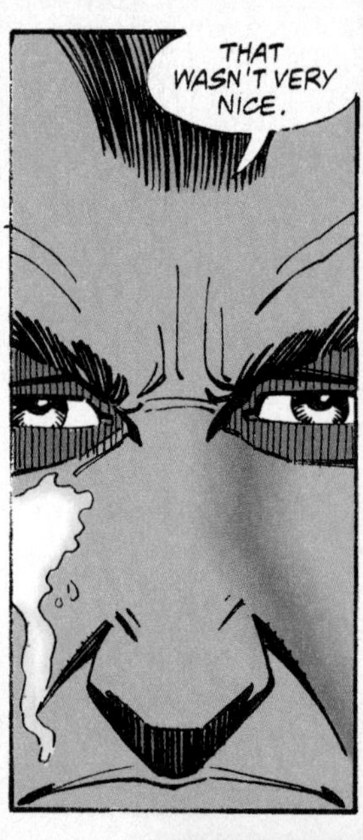
THAT WASN'T VERY NICE.

NO? THEN TRY THIS ON FOR SIZE!
UHHHHHH!!
THAT... HURT!
KICCCKK!
MICKY!

WELL, DOLL, I LIKE IT ROUGH, TOO!
THWRAKK!

I SAID I DIDN'T WANT DAMAGED MERCHANDISE...
... BUT REALLY, I JUST LIKE TO DAMAGE THE MERCHANDISE MYSELF!
NO!

BACK OFF, PAL. THE LADY SAID "NO"!
HUH?
AND PERSONALLY, I REALLY OBJECTED TO THAT "PRETTY BOY" CRACK!
BRAUN!

COME ON, MICKY! WE'VE GOT TO GET OUT OF HERE!
HOW--?
THESE GUYS OBVIOUSLY FLUNKED KNOT TYING!
YOU'D THINK TERROR-ISTS WOULD KNOW A LEAST AS MUCH AS ANY REGULATION BOY SCOUT!
--AND I NAILED JERKWATER OVER THERE WHILE HE WAS WATCHING CAESAR ROUGH YOU UP!
C'MON! MOVE IT BEFORE ANY MORE OF THEM--!

HEY! HEY YOU!
BLAST IT!

THERE THEY GO!
BRUNO! CUT OVER ALONG THE BEACH!
WE'LL DRIVE THEM TOWARD YOU!
I DON'T CARE IF YOU KILL THE GUY...
...BUT I WANT THAT GIRL ALIVE!

BRAUN--!
I HEARD.
BEAR TO THE LEFT. WE'LL TRY TO STAY AS FAR AWAY FROM BRUNO AS WE CAN!

MICKY! LOOK!
A CAVE?
EVEN BETTER! CAESAR SAID THIS WAS AN OLD JAPANESE BASE FROM WORLD WAR II.

THE JAPS RAN TUNNELS EVERYWHERE!
SUPPLY STORAGE, BOMB SHELTERS, YOU NAME IT!
WE CAN LOSE THOSE GUYS IN HERE!
KLING KLING KLING KLING KLING KLING KLING
AND MAYBE OUR-SELVES!

SWEETHEART, WE'RE *ALREADY* LOST!
AT LEAST WE WILL BE UNTIL WE CAN FIGURE OUT HOW TO LET SOMEBODY IN THE OUTSIDE WORLD KNOW WHERE WE ARE.
I DON'T SUPPOSE THE RADIO FROM OUR SKIMMER STILL WORKS.
ONLY IF IT SURVIVED BEING BLOWN UP.
WHICH I DOUBT.
SOONER OR LATER, WE'RE GOING TO HAVE TO CIRCLE BACK TO THE PLACE THEY HELD US CAPTIVE AND SEE WHAT WE CAN FIND.
BRAUN, *SHHHHHH!* LISTEN.
...AIN'T NOBODY DOWN HERE!
...DON'T KNOW WHY CAESAR INSISTED ON KEEPING THE TWO OF THEM ALIVE IN THE FIRST PLACE...
...KNEW WE WEREN'T GOING TO LET 'EM GO AFTER THE MONEY DROP...
...WE SHOULDA JUST WASTED 'EM AFTER THEY CRASHED.

BUT YOU DIDN'T!
AND NOW IT'S TOO LATE!
HEY!!
SPLASSSSH
THE SCUFFLE IS SHORT AND SHARP!
SUDDENLY...
BRAUN!
YOU... KILLED HIM!
I'M REAL SORRY, MICKY, BUT HE WAS TRYING TO KILL ME.
AND YOU HEARD THE GUY.
IT'S US OR THEM NOW.

BRAUN! WAIT!
I'VE GOT SOMETHING TO TELL YOU. YOU'RE RIGHT. IT IS LIFE OR DEATH NOW...
...AND IF I DON'T GET OUT OF HERE ALIVE, YOU MIGHT.
WHAT ARE YOU TALKING ABOUT? WE'RE BOTH GONNA MAKE IT!
I LIKE YOU, BRAUN, BUT THE REAL REASON I CAME SKIMMING WITH YOU IS THAT I NEEDED TO GET AWAY!
FROM MY FATHER!
HE WANTS TO CATCH ME... ALIVE OR DEAD!
WHAT?
I'M NOT VERY FLATTERED BUT WHY SHOULD HE WANT TO DO SUCH A THING?
BECAUSE I KNOW HIS SECRET.
I'M ACTIVE IN SEVERAL GREEN WORLD ORGANIZATIONS.
MY FATHER'S INDUSTRIES DESTROY A LOT OF THIS PLANET EVERY YEAR! I PREVENT WHAT I CAN.
I SEE. YOU SPY ON HIM.
LET'S JUST SAY I KEEP TABS ON HIM. AND HIS ACTIVITIES.
TWO DAYS AGO, I WAS... INVESTIGATING... HIS PERSONAL FILES.
HE THINKS THEY'RE PROTECTED. THEY'RE NOT.
AND I FOUND SOMETHING SO SCARY THAT EVEN I DON'T REALLY BELIEVE IT.
HE'S DEVELOPED A COMPUTER VIRUS OF SUCH MAGNITUDE, POWER, AND SPEED...
...THAT IT WOULD VIRTUALLY DESTROY COMPUTER NETWORKS WORLD-WIDE, IN SECONDS!
"AND THAT'S EXACTLY WHAT HE PLANS TO DO!"

THE MEGAVIRUS WILL BE INTRODUCED INTO THE NET THROUGH A COMPUTER RESEARCH FACILITY IN OLD RUSSIA.
NOBODY'LL CONNECT IT WITH MARCUS AMALGAMATED AND BY THE TIME PEOPLE REALIZE HOW SERIOUS IT IS, IT'LL BE ALL OVER THE WORLD!
IT'LL BE TOO LATE!
BUT... HOW DOES THIS HELP HIM? HIS WHOLE BUSINESS IS COMPUTERS!
BECAUSE HE'S ALREADY DEVELOPED THE ANTIDOTE.
IN THE ENSUING PANIC, HE'LL MAKE A KILLING!

AND ENSURE THAT HIS OPERATING SYSTEMS BECOME THE NEW WORLDWIDE STANDARD AFTERWARDS.
WE'RE TALKING ABOUT BILLIONS, MAYBE EVEN TRILLIONS!

THERE'S A COPY OF THE VIRUS AND THE ANTIDOTE ON THIS ANALOG CORTEX DISK.

ONE OF US HAS TO GET OUT SO THAT THIS KNOWLEDGE CAN SAVE THE WORLD!

DON'T YOU WORRY, MICKY. BELIEVE ME, ONE OF US WILL GET OUT.
RIGHT, BOYS?

YOU BET.
BRAUN! NO!
UNFORTUNATELY, IT'LL BE ME.
WHERE'S FRANZ?
SACRIFICED FOR THE GREATER GOOD.

NOW WE ONLY HAVE TO SPLIT THE MONEY FIVE WAYS.
YOU WERE RIGHT, SWEETHEART, IT WAS ABOUT MONEY!
BUT THIS IS EVEN BETTER!

AND SOMEWHERE ABOVE IN THE DARK...
T MINUS ONE MINUTE TO DROP ZONE.
ARNO, LISTEN TO ME! DON'T DO THIS!
WE DON'T NEED MARCUS'S MONEY THIS BADLY!
YES, WE DO.
KLICKT!
I KNOW YOU'RE WORRIED ABOUT OUR DEBT, ABOUT THE CORPORATION!
BUT THIS ISN'T ABOUT THAT!
THIS IS ABOUT THAT LOUSY ARMOR, ISN'T IT!
NOBODY EXPECTS YOU TO BE TONY STARK!
IT WON'T DO ANYBODY ANY GOOD IF YOU GET KILLED!
SLISSSH!
T MINUS THIRTY SECONDS TO DROP ZONE.
I WON'T GET KILLED.
BILL, YOU'RE MY BROTHER-IN-LAW AND THE CHIEF OPERATING OFFICER OF STARK INTERNATIONAL.
YOU'RE NOT MY CONSCIENCE.
WELL DAMMIT, SOMEBODY SHOULD BE!
IF I SUCCEED, WE GET COMPLETE SPECS ON MARCUS'S CORPORATION'S ADVANCED OPTICAL LASER TECHNOLOGY! CUTTING EDGE COMPUTERS!
PLUS A FORTUNE! WE'LL BE ABLE TO MAKE STARK INTERNATIONAL MORE POWERFUL THAN ANYTHING TONY STARK EVER DREAMED OF!

ARNO!
T MINUS FIVE, FOUR, THREE, TWO, ONE...
IGNITION.
THAT'S WHAT THIS IS ABOUT!
THAT... PLUS THE ARMOR!
I'LL BE HOME FOR DINNER.

AND INTO THE NIGHT, RIGGED FOR SILENT RUNNING, SOARS THE GOLDEN AVENGER...
...FLYING ON A HISTORY OF PAST GLORIES...
...AND A REMEMBRANCE OF FAILURE...
...INTO THE UNCERTAIN HOPE OF THE FUTURE.

THE ISLAND THE KIDNAPPERS SELECTED FOR THE MONEY DROP WAS WELL CHOSEN.
IT'S ON THE EASTERN PERIMETER OF THE MARSHALLS, FAR FROM ANY REAL HABITATION.
THEY'LL BE ABLE TO MONITOR EVERY AIRCRAFT OR SHIP APPROACH FOR MILES...
...AND KILL MS. MACLAIN IF SOMETHING GOES WRONG BEFORE THE MONEY'S DELIVERED.
REMOTE SENSOR SCAN FROM THE PLANE INDICATED SIX PEOPLE PRESENT ON THE ISLAND.
THE DROP SHIP ARRIVES IN THREE MINUTES.
TIME TO HIT THEM IS WHILE THEY'RE SPLIT UP...
...AND I SEE THAT TWO OF THEM ARE AT THE RENDEZVOUS SITE NOW.
ALL PORTS CLOSED...
...DEFLECTORS TO FULL POWER.
BEEP BEEP!
ORDINARY RESCUERS MIGHT BE DETECTED BUT IRON MAN IS ANOTHER STORY.
SHIFT TO SUBMERSION MODE.

LET'S DO IT!
SPLASSH

HEAR THAT, DORA? THAT'S NO WHALE!
THAT'S THE BOOGIEMAN COMING TO GET YOU!
OH, SHUT UP, ANTON.
THERE ARE TIMES WHEN YOU ARE SUCH A--
THUP THUPTHUPTHUPTHUPTHUPT
LISTEN! NOW THERE'S SOMETHING WORTH HEARING!

IT'S THE MONEY!
THUPTHUPTHUPT
GET YOUR SIDEWINDERS READY TO NAIL HIM AS HE FLIES AWAY!

HIS LOUSY LANDING LIGHTS ARE BLINDING ME!
SHUT 'EM OFF! SHUT 'EM OFF!
HE CAN'T HEAR YOU, IDIOT! I CAN'T SEE A BLOODY THING!
YOU DON'T THINK--?

IT DOESN'T MUCH MATTER *WHAT* HE THINKS NOW, DOES IT?!
BLHOO
OH GEEZ!
IRON MAN!

WASTE HIM!
THWOOSH
THWOOSH
OH GEEZ! OH GEEZ! OH GEEZ!
I COULD SHRUG OFF THIS MINOR LEAGUE STUFF ALL DAY...
...BUT I'M SHORT ON TIME...
BWAMM
BWHAMM
I WANT TO KNOW EXACTLY WHERE THE GIRL IS!
SSHRAKKLE
THE OTHER GIRL!
SPOW
ARRRGH!
OH GOD! YOU KILLED DORA!
SPOW
WRONG ANSWER!
OWWWW!

WHEN THEY FIND OUT WHAT'S HAPPENED, THEY'LL KILL HER!
TOO BAD, SONNY. IF SHE LIVES, I GET THE TECHNOLOGY I NEED... AND I'LL NAIL MARCUS'S HIDE TO THE WALL WITH IT!
IF SHE DIES, HE'LL LOSE EVERYTHING HE LIVES FOR... AND THAT'LL GIVE ME THE EDGE ANYWAY!
KKRA-CCKL

I'M IN A NO LOSE SITUATION. WHICH IS MORE THAN I CAN SAY FOR YOU.
UGGGH!
EXPERIMENTAL MAGNETIC TRACTOR CLAMPS.
YOUR BANDOLEER IS ALL THAT'S HOLDING YOU UP... AND THE CLAMPS AREN'T PERFECTED YET.
THAT MEANS THAT SHORTLY...
...YOU'LL BE FALLING AT THIRTY-TWO FEET PER SECOND PER SECOND.

ALTIMETER SHOWS WE'RE A QUARTER OF A MILE UP. THAT'S 1,320 FEET.
SO HOW LONG HAVE YOU GOT BEFORE YOU HIT?

OH GEEZ! OH GEEZ! OH GEEZ!
WHAT WAS THAT? I DIDN'T HEAR YOU!

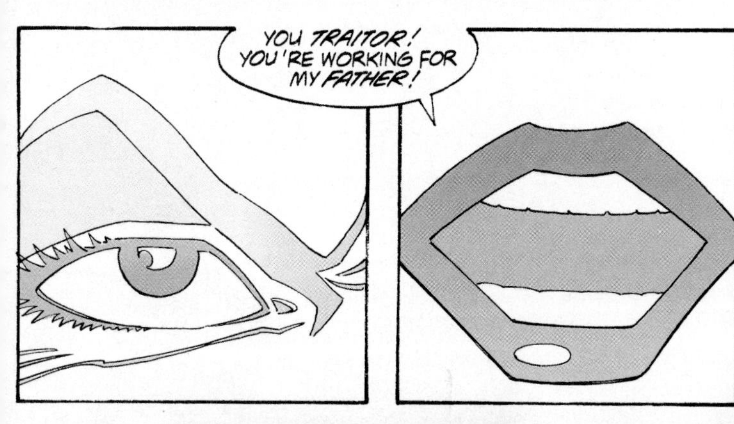
YOU TRAITOR! YOU'RE WORKING FOR MY FATHER!
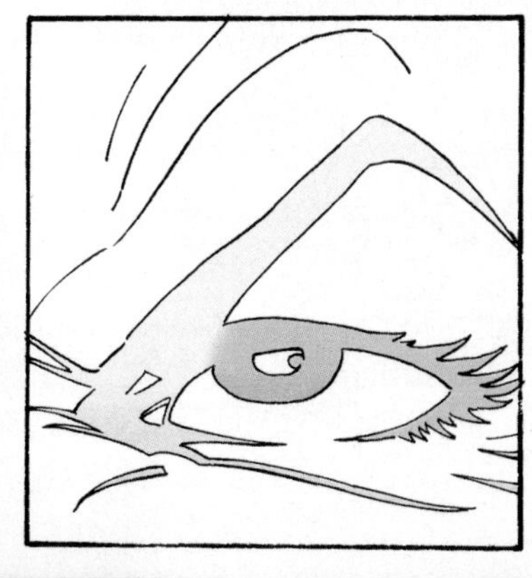

SWEETHEART, GIVE ME SOME CREDIT!
EVEN I'M PARTICULAR ABOUT THE COMPANY I KEEP.
I WAS JUST RUNNING YOU AROUND FOR FUN.
WE HAD SOME TIME TO KILL AND I ENJOY A GOOD GAME OF HIDE AND SEEK.

I NEVER EXPECTED TO TURN UP SUCH A LOVELY BONUS.
BESIDES, I REALLY WANTED TO SKIN YOUR OLD MAN. WHAT A CREEP!
BUT THIS VIRUS AND ITS ANTIDOTE ARE WORTH MORE THAN ANY LOUSY RANSOM!
WHAT'S THE GOOD WORD, CAESAR?

DORA AND ANTON HAVEN'T CHECKED IN, BRAUN.
THAT'S BAD. I DON'T LIKE THAT.

BETTER KILL LITTLE MISS "LET'S SAVE THE WORLD" AND GET OUT OF HERE.

WHAT ABOUT DORA AND ANTON?
GONE BUT NOT FORGOTTEN.
THINK OF THEM AS TWO FEWER SHARES AND A LOT MORE MONEY!
SO LONG, SWEETHEART. I REALLY LIKED YOUR STYLE, BUT FOR TRILLIONS...
...I CAN ALWAYS GET ANOTHER GIRLFRIEND.
BRAUN! NO!! DON'T DO IT!
TIINK!
KATHINK
KRUNKK
IT CAN'T BE!
I THOUGHT YOU GUYS WERE NEVER GOING TO SHOW UP!
WHAT THE--?

VERY GOOD. LET'S HEAR IT FOR THOSE FRESH NEW CLICHÉS!
PAUM!! PAUM!!
AIEEEE!
GAAAAHHH!
PTHEEEEOOWWW

BAKKOWWW!
THAT'S GOT A MUCH MORE IMPRESSIVE PUNCH THAN THOSE PEA-SHOOTERS YOUR FRIENDS WERE CARRYING.
BUT IF YOU REALLY WANT TO DAMAGE ME, YOU'D BETTER BE PACKING TACTICAL NUKES!
OR MAYBE CUT DOWN ON YOUR RELOADING TIME.
NO!
SCHLICCT
I'M AFRAID SO.
IT'S THE PROVERBIAL END OF THE LINE, PARTNER!
I LIKE CLICHÉS MYSELF!
PAUMMMM
WHAT, BRAUN? GOING SO SOON? I WOULDN'T HEAR OF IT!
WHY, MY LITTLE PARTY'S JUST--OH FORGET IT!
FLIKK!
I JUST HIT CLICHÉ OVERLOAD!
THUUPP
OHHHH!

DON'T KILL ME!
MARCUS DIDN'T GIVE ME ANY SPECIAL ORDERS REGARDING YOU GUYS.
AND I ADMIRE ENTREPRENEURIAL INITIATIVE. BUT--
PLEASE DON'T KILL ME!
I'VE GOT SOMETHING HERE WORTH TRILLIONS! IT'S ALL YOURS!
JUST LET ME GO! IT'S--
BLAM!
ARRRGH!
WELL. THAT SHOWED A CERTAIN AMOUNT OF SPUNK!
DON'T PATRONIZE ME, IRON MAN. HE DESERVED IT.
I DON'T DOUBT IT, I'M MERELY SURPRISED YOU HAD IT IN YOU!
IT'S 2020, IRON MAN. I'M AN ACTIVIST, NOT A PACIFIST.
"THEN ACTIVATE YOURSELF INTO THE PLANE. YOU'RE GOING HOME."
I DON'T WANT TO GO HOME.
WHAT KID DOES? WHAT WAS THAT ABOUT TRILLIONS?
I... UH... I...
LOOK, MS. MACLAIN. I'M BEING PAID A FORTUNE TO TAKE YOU HOME. AND I AM, SO SIT DOWN.
FOR A BIGGER FORTUNE, WOULD YOU LET ME OFF SOME-WHERE?
NOPE. BAD FOR BUSINESS.
I DIDN'T WANT TO TELL YOU THIS BUT YOU LEAVE ME NO CHOICE. YOU HAVE TO LET ME OFF.
MY FATHER IS GOING TO KILL ME. AND HERE'S WHY.

A FEW HOURS LATER...
"BUT WHY WON'T YOU LET ME ESCAPE? YOU KNOW WHAT HE'LL DO TO ME!"
"I'M SORRY, MS. MACLAIN, BUT THIS IS TOO GOOD AN OPPORTUNITY TO PASS UP.
"I'LL SEVER STARK INTERNATIONAL COMPUTER NETS FROM ALL EXTERNAL INPUT...
"...LET THE VIRUS RUN WILD...
"...AND BE READY TO PICK UP THE PIECES.
"MARCUS'LL BE FINISHED WHEN THE WORLD LEARNS THAT HE WAS RESPONSIBLE FOR THE MESS. AS THEY WILL.
"AND I'LL BE LEFT WITH THE ONLY OPERATING COMPUTER NETWORK IN THE WORLD! I'LL STILL WIN!"
"I DON'T BELIEVE THIS! YOU'RE JUST AS BAD AS HE IS!"
"THANK YOU. I WAS BEGINNING TO WONDER."
"STARK'S PLANE IS ENTERING AMALGAMATED AIRSPACE, SIR."

HE'S GOT MELODI, MR. WELLINGTON... AND HE'S CIRCLING.
HE SAYS THE TWO OF YOU NEED TO TALK.
AS IF THERE WERE ANYTHING TO SAY.
I WISH, HOWARD, THAT HE HAD COME SUITED UP. IT WOULD HAVE BEEN FUN, TAKING HIM APART PIECE BY PIECE.

YOU'RE A GOOD DESIGNER. THE BEST.
ENGAGE AUTO-TRACKING OF UNIDENTIFIED AIRCRAFT.
SIGNAL THE GUNNERS TO ACTION STATIONS.
AND OPEN A COMLINK TO THE PLANE.

HELLO, STARK.

I'VE GOT YOUR DAUGHTER, MARCUS. I'VE GOT YOUR VIRUS.
IT'S TIME WE CUT A NEW DEAL.
STARTING WITH YOUR DAUGHTER'S SAFETY.
WHAT? BUT I THOUGHT--
YOU THOUGHT I WAS JUST AS NASTY AS YOUR OLD MAN. MAYBE I AM.
MAYBE I'M JUST HAVING SECOND THOUGHTS.
BUT WITH HIS MONEY HUNTING YOU, YOU'D NEVER HAVE GOTTEN AWAY.
BETTER TO SOLVE YOUR TROUBLES NOW AND LIVE PEACEFULLY LATER.
THAT WAS ALWAYS YOUR PROBLEM IN BUSINESS, ARNO. YOU NEVER WERE RUTHLESS ENOUGH.
BLHWHAMM!
FORTUNE FAVORS THE BOLD!
OH!
THAT SON OF A--!
STRAP YOURSELF IN! FAST!
DON'T FLATTER HIM!
I PRESUME MY DAUGHTER HAS BEEN EXPLAINING THINGS TO YOU, STARK.
I RATHER HOPED SHE WOULDN'T.

IT WOULD HAVE BEEN AMUSING TO GIVE YOU INFECTED COMPUTER TECHNOLOGY AND TOTALLY DESTROY STARK ENTERPRISES.
OH WELL. ONE MUST BEAR LIFE'S LITTLE DISAPPOINTMENTS.
FIRE!
SKREEEEACK!!
GOOD REFLEXES. LOOK AT THAT!
HE'S JETTISONED THE ESCAPE POD!
EXCELLENT!
WE'LL HAVE THE CHANCE TO TRY OUT OUR PROTOTYPE AFTER ALL!
LAUNCH!
THE SUIT'S COMPLETELY POWERED UP, SIR. ALL SYSTEMS OPERATIONAL.
"GOOD. STAND BY THE MONITORS, HOWARD. I'LL BE READY IN A MOMENT."
KABOOOM

THIRTY SECONDS TO TOUCHDOWN.
YOU KNOW, I'M BEGINNING TO THINK THAT CUTTING A DEAL WITH MARCUS WASN'T SUCH A GOOD IDEA!
I TRIED TO TELL YOU!
DON'T RUB IT IN!
WHAT ARE YOU DOING?
USING YOUR ORIGINAL IDEA.
I'LL HAVE TO DEAL WITH WHATEVER YOUR FATHER'S LINED UP.
I'VE GOT FAITH IN MY ARMOR BUT I WANT YOU TO GET THE HELL OUT OF HERE WITH THE DISK!
AND IF YOU DON'T MAKE IT, WE'RE GOING TO NEED A COPY OF THE ANTIDOTE.
I'VE COPIED THE ENTIRE DISK INTO MY SUIT IN A MOBIUS LOOP.
IT WON'T AFFECT MY ARMOR BUT IF I LIVE... WELL, IT'S ONE MORE CHANCE FOR THE WORLD!
AND WHO KNOWS? MAYBE I CAN STILL TALK SOME SENSE INTO HIM.
TALK TO HIM? MY FATHER IS A MADMAN!
I JUST CAN'T MAKE UP MY MIND ABOUT YOU!
SPHWRAAHM!!

I THINK THE WORD YOU'RE LOOKING FOR IS "IDIOT!"

HELLO, MELODI, MY DEAR. STARK. THANKS FOR DROPPING IN.
AND NOW... I WANT MY VIRUS BACK!

IT'S HIDDEN WHERE YOU'LL NEVER FIND IT!
BREAAPPPPP
I'D LIKE TO BELIEVE YOU, ARNO.
REALLY I WOULD.
BUT I'M AFRAID I'LL HAVE TO LOOK FOR MYSELF.
THWRSHINNNG
NICE TRY, ARNO! BUT HOWARD AND I KNEW THAT THIS DAY WOULD COME!
AND THIS TIME, I'VE BUILT THE BETTER MOUSE-TRAP!

THIS IS SOMETHING SPECIAL WE DESIGNED JUST FOR YOU!
IT'S A SORT OF CONCENTRATED EMP BURST!
GUARANTEED TO TOTALLY DISRUPT YOUR COMPUTER AND INTERNAL GUIDANCE SYSTEMS!
KREEEEEEEEEEEEEEE
NICE, EH?
WHAT--?
I'D REREAD THE GUARANTEE IF I WERE YOU!
IT WOULD BE...
...IF IT WORKED!
BUT I DO UPGRADE MY SUIT'S REFRACTIVE COATING AND SHIELDING FROM TIME TO TIME!

THLABLAM!
THLABLAM!
THAT WON'T BE NECESSARY.
THE SIZE OF MY ARMOR PUTS ANY NUMBER OF OFFENSIVE WEAPONS AT MY DISPOSAL.
THAKKH
GUHHHHH!
SUCH AS THESE MAGNIFIED POSITRON BURSTS!
AN
NGGG
I DON'T BELIEVE IT! THAT BLAST SHUT DOWN MY MAIN BOARDS! I'M RUNNING ON AUXILIARIES!
I KNEW MARCUS WAS BIG IN COMPUTERS BUT HOW IN BLAZES DID HE COME UP WITH THIS KIND OF STUFF?
IF I DON'T GET A COUPLE OF SECONDS TO RECONFIGURE MY SYSTEMS, I'M TOAST!
DAD! NO!
MELODI! HOW KIND OF YOU TO WAIT FOR ME TO FINISH WITH ARNO.
UH OH!

I AM TRULY SORRY, MY DARLING...
...BUT REALLY, YOU'RE FAR TOO MUCH LIKE YOUR LATE MOTHER.

OHHH!
WHOPT!
IF ONLY YOU'D BEEN MORE LIKE ME!

THRWEEEEEEEE!
I WAS HOPING THAT STARK WOULD FOUL UP...

...THEREBY GETTING YOU KILLED AND FINALLY AND COMPLETELY DISCREDITING HIMSELF!
IMAGINE MY SURPRISE WHEN HE TURNED OUT TO BE AS GOOD AS HE SAID HE WAS.
NOW I'LL HAVE TO DO THE JOB MYSELF!
THIS BEAM DISRUPTS YOUR NEURAL SYNAPSE PATTERNS.
IT DOESN'T LAST VERY LONG BUT IT DOES TURN YOUR ENTIRE BODY INTO JELLO...
UH UH UH!
...AS YOU'VE NOTICED...

...AND IT ACTS AS A TEMPORARY ANESTHETIC.
COME, MY DEAR. LET ME HAVE THE DISK AND WE'LL PUT THIS UNPLEASANT BUSINESS BEHIND US.
IT WON'T HURT A BIT.

HUH?
GRABB
YOUR PROBLEM, WELLINGTON, IS THAT YOU NEVER FINISH WHAT YOU START!

YOU DIDN'T GUARD YOUR VIRUS EFFECTIVELY, YOU DIDN'T KEEP MICKY FROM ESCAPING...
...AND YOU DIDN'T KILL ME WHEN YOU HAD THE CHANCE!
SKRAAKKKT
ARRRRGH!
GOT TO GO TO EMERGENCY POWER EVEN THOUGH IT MIGHT BURN OUT MY ARMOR!
THIS COULD BE THE ONLY CHANCE I'LL GET!

KLANNK!
YOU'RE RIGHT! I SHOULD HAVE KILLED YOU WHEN I HAD THE CHANCE!

I'LL RECTIFY THAT MISTAKE RIGHT NOW! ONE-HANDED OR NOT!

UGGGGH! MY ARMOR'S SYSTEMS ARE STARTING TO DECAY!
POWER RESERVES DEPLETED.
HE'S CRACKING MY OUTER SHELL!
I'VE HAD IT!
MICKY! GET OUT OF HERE!

WAIT A SECOND! ONE LAST CHANCE!
IF I CAN...
SQUICKK
...JUST BREAK THE...

...MOBIUS LOOP...
...INFECT MY OWN ARMOR WITH THE VIRUS...
THIKTHIKTHIKTHIK

...AND INJECT IT INTO MARCUS'S SUIT...
KKKRTKKKKKKN

UHHH! DON'T... THINK I--
LOOK WHAT YOU'VE DONE TO MY ARMOR!
DO YOU HAVE ANY IDEA HOW MUCH IT COST?

YOU...COULD ALWAYS... BILL ME.
I'LL DO BETTER THAN THAT, YOU PATHETIC FAILURE!

I'LL KILL YOU!
SKLATHAAM!!!

I CAN MOVE AGAIN!
ARNO WAS RIGHT! I SHOULDN'T HAVE STAYED HERE!
GOT TO SPLIT WHILE THEY'RE STILL FIGHTING!

MAYBE I CAN FIND SOME HELP!
THE POLICE! THE ARMY! THE NATIONAL GUARD!
C'MON, BABY! C'MON!
BBRRAAOOOOM

LET'S GET THE HECK OUT OF HERE!
MELODI!!
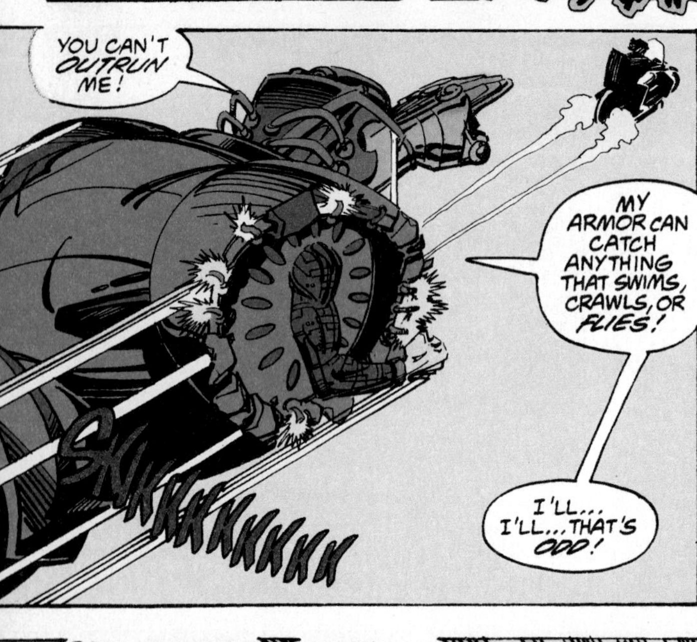
YOU CAN'T OUTRUN ME!
MY ARMOR CAN CATCH ANYTHING THAT SWIMS, CRAWLS, OR FLIES!
I'LL... I'LL... THAT'S ODD!
SKKKKKKKKKK

I'M GETTING RED FLAG INDICATORS!
MY SENSOR DISPLAYS ARE GOING WILD!
POWER'S CUTTING OUT!

BACK-UP SYSTEMS ARE FAILING!
WHAT'S HAPPENING?
SPAATHWRING!
MY HAND!

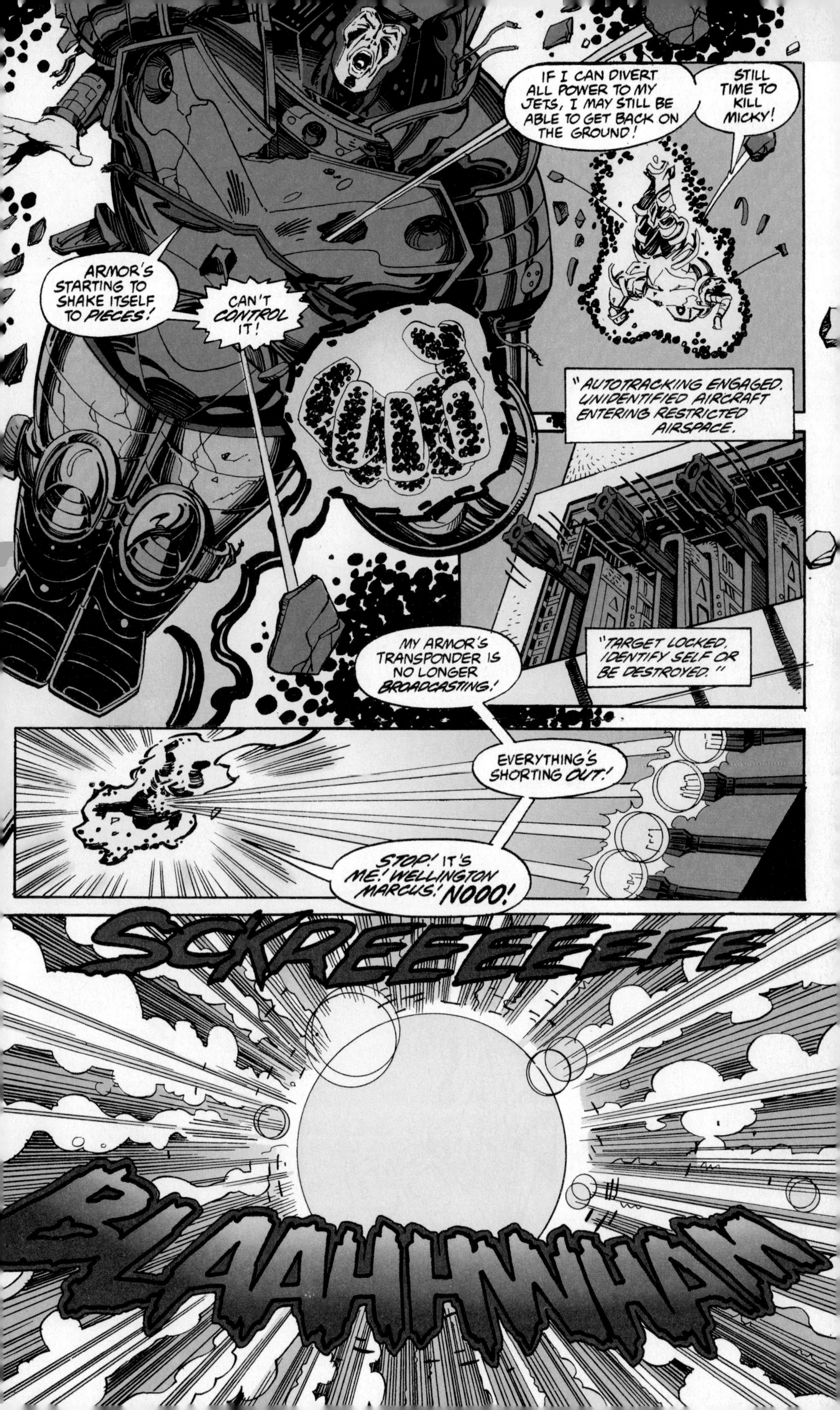
IF I CAN DIVERT ALL POWER TO MY JETS, I MAY STILL BE ABLE TO GET BACK ON THE GROUND!
STILL TIME TO KILL MICKY!
ARMOR'S STARTING TO SHAKE ITSELF TO PIECES!
CAN'T CONTROL IT!
"AUTOTRACKING ENGAGED. UNIDENTIFIED AIRCRAFT ENTERING RESTRICTED AIRSPACE.
"TARGET LOCKED. IDENTIFY SELF OR BE DESTROYED."
MY ARMOR'S TRANSPONDER IS NO LONGER BROADCASTING!
EVERYTHING'S SHORTING OUT!
STOP! IT'S ME! WELLINGTON MARCUS! NOOO!
SCKREEEEEEEE
BLAAHHWHAM

AND SO...
I...I'M TRULY SORRY ABOUT YOUR FATHER, MS. MACLAIN.
I'M NOT.
OR MAYBE I AM. I DON'T EVEN KNOW AT THIS POINT.
I JUST FEEL DUMB.
I'M GLAD YOU WON.
THANK YOU. YOU'LL BE ALL RIGHT. I'D DESTROY THAT DISK IF I WERE YOU.
CAN'T EVEN RISK THE INFECTED ARMOR.
THIS WILL ALL HAVE TO BE MELTED DOWN.
YOU'RE NOT AS HARD AS YOU PRETEND TO BE, ARE YOU, ARNO?
YOU TRIED TO FULFILL YOUR CONTRACT AND STILL KEEP ME SAFE.
THAT'S JUST GOOD BUSINESS, NO MATTER WHAT YOUR FATHER SAID.
I... FUL-FILLED A CONTRACT WITH MARCUS AMALGAMATED.
YOU DIDN'T HAVE TO COME HERE. YOU COULD HAVE HAD ME DELIVERED.
I EXPECT THE COMPANY TO HONOR IT.

YOU DON'T OWE ME ANYTHING.
...

REALLY?

YES, MA'AM.
ARNO! WAIT! THIS MIGHT INTEREST YOU.
I NOW OWN THE CONTROLLING SHARES OF STOCK IN MARCUS.

YOU DO?
AT LEAST UNBEND ENOUGH TO LET ME THANK YOU PROPERLY. WE MIGHT... DISCUSS A BONUS?
AND SINCE I'M GOING TO BE YOUR COMPETITION, MAYBE YOU SHOULD GET TO KNOW ME BETTER.
I HAVEN'T PRACTICED THE SOCIAL GRACES MUCH. TOO BUSY, I GUESS.
UMMM... MAYBE I WAS A LITTLE HASTY.

I... I'M NOT SURE... WHAT TO DO.
ASK ME TO DINNER.
WELL, I'M VISITING FAMILY, BUT MY BROTHER-IN-LAW IS A GREAT CHEF. IT'S NOT MUCH BUT...
WHAT I MEAN IS... WOULD YOU HONOR ME BY HAVING DINNER WITH ME... MELODI?
I'D BE DELIGHTED... ARNO.

AND TWO MERGING EXECUTIVES WALK OFF INTO THE MORNING.
MIDTOWN. A FEW HOURS LATER, IN A PRIVATE SUITE...
THAT WAS A GOOD DAY'S WORK.

MARCUS HAS AT LONG LAST RECEIVED HIS JUST DESERTS.
I EXPECT THAT STARK ENTERPRISES WILL EVENTUALLY MERGE WITH MARCUS AMALGAMATED AND BECOME STRONGER THAN EVER...
...AND WITH MICKY'S HELP, ARNO STARK WILL AT LAST BECOME THE MAN HE WAS DESTINED TO BE...
...A MAN WHO NO LONGER MEASURES LIFE BY THE LENGTH OF A DOLLAR...

...BUT WHO KNOWS WHAT IT IS TO HELP PEOPLE FOR THEIR OWN SAKE.
AND THEN, PERHAPS HE WILL FINALLY FEEL THE THRILL I ONCE FELT WHEN I WAS A GOLDEN AVENGER...
...A MAN WHO WILL BE PROUD TO BE... THE IRON MAN OF 2020!
YES. IT'S BEEN A GOOD DAY...
MAYBE I'LL BE ABLE TO MAKE A FEW SUGGESTIONS ABOUT IMPROVING HIS ARMOR WHEN HE REBUILDS IT.
End

Arno Stark. Wealthy industrialist and prominent corporate figure. Heir to the vast technological and financial empire that is Stark International.

Arno Stark. Armored avenger and prominent American hero. Heir to the legendary and demanding task of being Iron Man.

The year is 2020. The times are desperate. When a cutthroat business rival approaches Stark with a lucrative offer to perform a rescue operation as Iron Man . . .is the price to pay too high? To save the weakened remains of Stark International, will Stark essentially sell out his services as Iron Man?

Walter Simonson, Bob Wiacek and Will Rosado deliver an intriguing and pulse-pounding tale about a man attempting to escape the overwhelming shadow of his ancestor, Tony Stark.

Meet a man placing his life in jeopardy in an effort to save his company.

Meet Arno Stark – Iron Man 2020!

WOLVERINE & PUNISHER • IRON MAN 2020 • SPIDER-WOMAN • MOJOWORLD
ASTONISHING TALES
MARVEL
ISSUE 3

NEW YORK.
Buddy List
9:46 PM
I'M JAMMING YOUR PHONE, IDIOT.
Clear
OH GOD.
2023 A.D.
PLEASE LET THE COPTER STILL BE THERE...
A FASTER FUTURE.
YES! I'M GOING TO MAKE IT!
I'M ACTUALLY GOING TO--
NO!
NO.
YOU'RE NOT GOING TO MAKE IT.
DON'T HURT ME!
I'LL GIVE THEM BACK! I'LL GIVE THE SCHEMATICS BACK!

ARNO STARK.
CURRENT OWNER AND SOLE OPERATOR OF THE IRON MAN PERSONAL COMBAT SYSTEM.
OH PLEASE.
I'VE ALREADY WIPED EVERY HARD DRIVE, DATA-CRYSTAL AND MEM-DUMP IN A ONE BLOCK RADIUS.
THEN... THEN WHAT IS IT YOU--
HOW MUCH DID YOU SEE WHEN YOU WERE DOWNLOADING THOSE SCHEMATICS?
HOW MUCH COULD AIM'S PSYCHICS PULL FROM YOUR HEAD?
I...I DIDN'T...OH GOD, PLEASE, I'LL DO ANYTHING.
JUST DON'T HURT ME AND I'LL DO WHATEVER YOU WANT.
WELL NOW...
...THAT'S A BIT MORE COOPERATIVE, ISN'T IT?
LET'S SEE IF WE CAN COME TO SOME AGREEABLE TERMS.

ARNO STARK.
BILLIONAIRE CEO OF STARK INTERNATIONAL.
FIRST COUSIN ONCE REMOVED OF DECEASED PHILANTHROPIST, TONY STARK.

YOU BAAAAAA-ASTARD!

ARNO STARK.
ABSOLUTELY.
ABSOLUTE BASTARD.

IRON MAN 2020
ENDLESS STOLEN SKY PART 1
WRITER: DANIEL MERLIN GOODBREY
PENCILER: LOU KANG
INKER: CRAIG YEUNG
COLORIST: CHRIS SOTOMAYOR
LETTERER: DAVE SHARPE
ASST. EDITOR: MICHAEL HORWITZ
EDITOR: JOHN BARBER
EDITOR IN CHIEF: JOE QUESADA
PUBLISHER: DAN BUCKLEY
WED
7
STARK
SNN
PAN
BY
MIN

CYNTHIA, CONTACT COMMANDER DREW. TELL HER OUR DATA-LEAK IS PLUGGED AND SHE'S CLEAR TO PROCEED WITH THE LIVE TRIAL.
YES, ARNO.
HOW LONG TO THE HELIDOCK FROM HERE AT TOP SPEED?
13 MINUTES, 32 SECONDS.
TIME TO KILL THEN. SET FLIGHT SYSTEMS TO AUTOMATIC AND ACTIVATE EXTREMIS™ A.R..

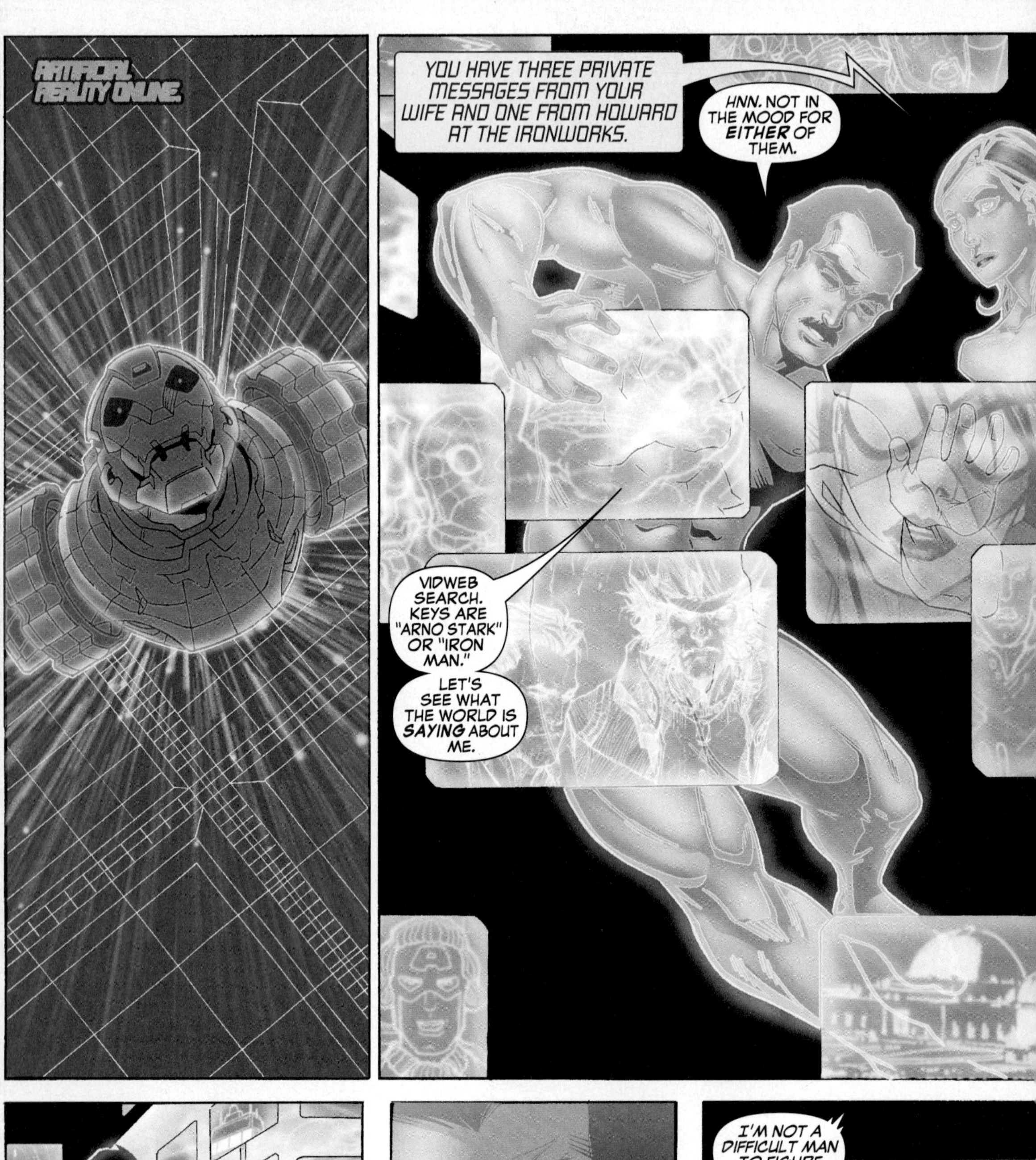
ARTIFICIAL REALITY ONLINE.
YOU HAVE THREE PRIVATE MESSAGES FROM YOUR WIFE AND ONE FROM HOWARD AT THE IRONWORKS.
HNN. NOT IN THE MOOD FOR EITHER OF THEM.
VIDWEB SEARCH. KEYS ARE "ARNO STARK" OR "IRON MAN."
LET'S SEE WHAT THE WORLD IS SAYING ABOUT ME.

HMM... MOSTLY CHATTER ABOUT THE SPIRIT...

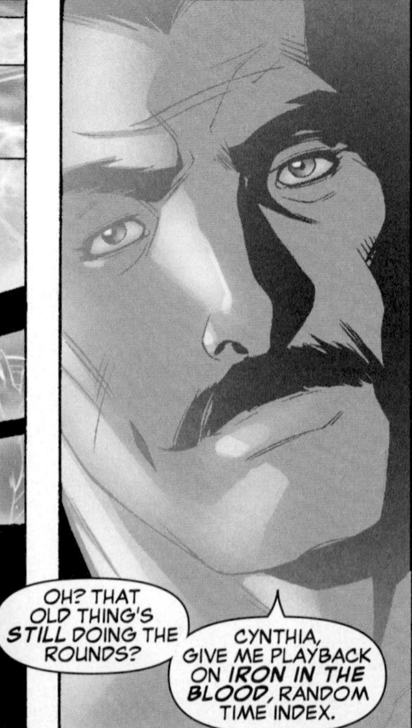
OH? THAT OLD THING'S STILL DOING THE ROUNDS?
CYNTHIA, GIVE ME PLAYBACK ON IRON IN THE BLOOD, RANDOM TIME INDEX.

I'M NOT A DIFFICULT MAN TO FIGURE OUT.
THERE'S ONLY REALLY TWO THINGS YOU NEED TO KNOW ABOUT ME.
WITH

ONE, I'M VERY RICH. AND LIKE ALL THE VERY RICH, I WANT TO BE RICHER.
TWO, I BORE EASILY. AND BEING VERY RICH AND VERY BORED MAKES ME SOMETHING ELSE.
INDEPTH WITH ARNO

INCREDIBLY DANGEROUS.

HEH. WHAT A HAM.
TIME TO UPDATE THE OLD P.R. A BIT, CYNTHIA.
THERE ARE CURRENTLY SIX DIRECTORS WITH DECLARED INTEREST IN FILMING YOUR BIOPIC.
SHOW ME THE LIST.

OKAY. GET IN TOUCH WITH HERZOG'S PEOPLE. TELL THEM I'LL DO IT, BUT I WANT TO FIGHT KLAUS KINSKI IN THE FINAL REEL.
BRAFF, ZACH
DIRECTOMATIC 45
DIRECTOMATIC 87
HERZOG, WERNER
ACTOR KLAUS KINSKI HAS BEEN DECEASED FOR 32.6 YEARS.

THAT'S WHY GOD INVENTED TIME TRAVEL.

NOW IN VISUAL RANGE OF HELIDOCK.
DEACTIVATE A.R.. FLIGHT CONTROLS TO MANUAL.
SHE'S QUITE A SHIP, ISN'T SHE?
INSUFFICIENT PARAMETERS. PLEASE RESTATE QUERY.
NEVER MIND.
STARK INTERNATIONAL PROTOTYPE CIVILIAN HELILINER, THE SPIRIT OF FREE ENTERPRISE.
ALL EYES ARE ON STARK INTERNATIONAL THIS WEEK AS THEY PREPARE THE SPIRIT OF FREE ENTERPRISE FOR ITS STAR-STUDDED INAUGURAL CRUISE.
IVE AT THE HELIDOCK with EDNA TRILBY
VID WEB NEWS
SNN
MANY PUNDITS HAVE HAILED THE PROTOTYPE HELILINER AS THE BEST SOLUTION TO THE CRISIS THAT'S FACED THE AVIATION INDUSTRY SINCE U.N. ENVIRONMENTAL RESTRICTIONS ON JET ENGINE TRAVEL CAME INTO FULL EFFECT IN 2021.

EXCLUSIVE
LIVE
ARNO STARK JOINS US NOW LIVE OUTSIDE HIS HELIDOCK FACILITY IN A VIDWEB NEWS EXCLUSIVE INTERVIEW.
ALWAYS A PLEASURE, EDNA.
VID WEB NEWS
SNN

THE SPIRIT OFFERS A TRUE REVOLUTION IN AIR TRAVEL. SPEED, SAFETY AND LUXURY DELIVERED WITH ZERO ATMOSPHERIC POLLUTION.
SHE'LL BE THE GREATEST SHIP TO EVER SAIL THE SKY!
VID WEB NEWS
SNN

GREATEST SHIP?! GREATEST SHIP?!

HAH!
COMMODORE...

...IS THERE SOMETHING WRONG?
OH, JENNY...

...I USED TO THINK THE SKY WAS ENDLESS.
SO MANY POSSIBILITIES. SO MANY FUTURES.
BUT THEY TOOK THEM FROM ME. STARK AND HIS CRONIES.
COMMODORE Q.
ONE BY ONE THEY STOLE ALL MY TOMORROWS.
SPIRITED THEM AWAY LIKE THIEVES IN THE NIGHT.
THEN YOU'LL STEAL THEM BACK, GRANDFATHER.
INDEED I WILL, LASS. INDEED I WILL.
ATOMIC TURBINES TO SPEED, BOYS!
AYE-AYE, CAP'N!
LET'S SHOW THEM THE FUTURE'S STILL GOT TEETH.
TO BE CONTINUED...

IRON MAN 2020
ENDLESS STOLEN SKY PART 2
WRITER: DANIEL MERLIN GOODBREY
PENCILER: LOU KANG
INKER: CRAIG YEUNG
COLORIST: CHRIS SOTOMAYOR
LETTERER: DAVE SHARPE
ASST. EDITOR: MICHAEL HORWITZ
EDITOR: JOHN BARBER
EDITOR IN CHIEF: JOE QUESADA
PUBLISHER: DAN BUCKLEY
THE STARK HELILINER, THE SPIRIT OF FREE ENTERPRISE.
MAKING BEST SPEED ACROSS THE ATLANTIC SKY.
FORWARD OBSERVATION DECK ONE.
GALA RECEPTION FOR MAIDEN VOYAGE DIGNITARIES.
NO, SADLY MY WIFE WAS UNABLE TO ATTEND...
...MELODI IS CURRENTLY TOURING OUR DISASTER RELIEF FACILITIES ON MOON TWO. SHE'S--
ARNO STARK!

A PENNY FOR YOUR THOUGHT PATTERNS?
MADAME MODOC.
CEO OF ADVANCED IDEA RESEARCH
MADAME MODOC...
...YOU LOOK POSITIVELY STUNNING AS EVER.
STARK, YOU SILVER-TONGUED DEVIL. HOW LONG HAS IT BEEN?
TOO LONG MADAM, TOO LONG.
BUT IT SEEMS LIKE ONLY YESTERDAY I WAS THROWING ONE OF YOUR MEN OFF A ROOF.
COME NOW, ARNO.
YOU KNOW ADVANCED IDEA RESEARCH NO LONGER HOLDS ANY ASSOCIATIONS WITH OUR...MISGUIDED PARENT GROUP.
OF COURSE. HOW FOOLISH OF ME.
BE ASSURED THAT I WILL PERSONALLY SEE THE FULL FORCE OF STARK INTERNATIONAL'S HOSPITALITY EXTENDED TO YOUR PARTY DURING OUR VOYAGE.

CYNTHIA, DOUBLE THE SECURITY DETAIL ON THE A.I.R. DELEGATION. FULL SURVEILLANCE, 24-7.
YES, SIR.
AMBASSADOR!
YOU'VE LOST WEIGHT!
OF COURSE, YOUR HOLINESS.
IF THE VATICAN IS INTERESTED, I'M SURE WE CAN--
QUITE A SHIP YOU'VE BUILT HERE, STARK.

IMPRESSIVE WORK. FOR A FLATSCAN.
WARREN WORTHINGTON IV.
CEO OF WORTHINGTON AVIONICS.
HIGH PRAISE FROM A WORTHINGTON.
IF THIS CRATE MEETS UP WITH EVEN HALF ITS HYPE YOU'LL HAVE EARNED IT.
WAY I FIGURE IT, THOUGH, A LOT OF AIRPORTS ARE JUST GOING TO BE TOO SMALL TO DEAL DIRECTLY WITH SHIPS OF THIS SIZE.
YOUR POINT BEING?
MAYBE WE SHOULD TALK IS ALL.
THAT'S AN INTERESTING PROPOSAL. THE SPECS I'VE SEEN ON YOUR THOPTERS ARE CERTAINLY IMPRESSIVE, PROVIDING THEY CAN--
RAND, YOU HAVE AN INCOMING TRANSMISSION ON YOUR SECURE A.A. LINE.
DAMN. SORRY WARREN, THERE'S A CALL COMING IN I'M GOING TO HAVE TO TAKE.
BUT WE'LL TALK?
DEFINITELY. GET YOUR PEOPLE TO SET A DATE WITH MINE.

ARTIFICIAL
REALITY
ONLINE.

COMMANDER
ESSICA DREW.
DIRECTOR
OF S.H.I.E.L.D.
GOOD PARTY IS IT, TARK? HAVING OTS OF FUN ON S.H.I.E.L.D.'S DOLLAR?
OH 'EAR...

...NOT STILL BITTER, ARE WE, COMMANDER?
HELICARRIER TECHNOLOGY SHOULD HAVE BEEN OPENED UP TO THE PUBLIC YEARS AGO AND YOU KNOW IT.
THE VERY HIGH-PAYING PUBLIC, I NOTICE.

FOR ALL HER GRANDEUR, THE SPIRIT IS STILL A PROTOTYPE.
ONCE WE GO INTO FULL PRODUCTION, HELILINER TRAVEL WILL BE OPEN TO ALL.
SAVE IT FOR THE PRESS RELEASE, ARNO.

FINE. BUT S.H.I.E.L.D. HARDLY FARED BADLY FROM OUR LITTLE DEAL, DID THEY?
I ASSUME YOU ARE CALLING TO CONFIRM THE SUCCESS OF THE NEW TOY I'VE BUILT YOU?

OKAY, I ADMIT IT. THE TECHS ALL SAY SHE'S HANDLING LIKE A DREAM.
HAH!
NO PROBLEMS WITH THE DRIVE AT ALL?
NONE. OUR S.W.O.R.D. OBSERVERS ARE STARTING TO LOOK A LITTLE JEALOUS, ACTUALLY...
...THIS THING IS EVEN OUT-PERFORMING SOME OF THEIR OFF-WORLD TECH.
I ASSURE YOU, THE SYSTEM IS 100% EARTH-DERIVED. YOU WON'T BE BREAKING ANY OF S.W.O.R.D.'S PRECIOUS TREATIES WHEN YOU USE IT.
NOW, GLAD AS I AM TO HEAR THAT THE PROVING RUN HAS BEEN A SUCCESS, I DO HAVE A PARTY TO GET BACK TO. SO IF YOU'LL EXCUSE ME--
ALL THOSE WELL-TO-DO RICH FOLK IN ONE NICE REMOTE LOCATION.
I HOPE YOU REALIZE HOW BIG A TARGET YOU'VE PAINTED ON YOURSELF, STARK.
COMMANDER DREW, YOUR CONCERN IS TRULY TOUCHING.
BUT I'VE A FULL SQUADRON OF MY BEST IRON-BOT PILOTS ONBOARD AND MY OWN ARMOR PREPPED AND READY FOR EMERGENCY LAUNCH.
IF ANYONE'S FOOLISH ENOUGH TO THINK THEY POSE THIS SHIP A SERIOUS THREAT, THEN I WELCOME THEM TO TRY.

SPIRIT OF FREE ENTERPRISE BRIDGE.
CAPTAIN?
YES, LIEUTENANT?
CAPTAIN NIGEL MERRIWEATHER COMMANDING.
I'M GETTING SOME FUNNY READINGS ON THE CLOUDBANK UP AHEAD, SIR.
ON SCREEN.
WELL? WHAT'S FUNNY ABOUT IT? LOOKS PERFECTLY NORMAL TO ME.
BUT IT'S TOO HIGH UP, SIR. AND I'M GETTING A WEIRD READING FROM IT ON RADAR.
DEFINE WEIRD, LIEUTENANT...
UM...NON-STANDARD, SIR. IF I DIDN'T KNOW BETTER, I'D SAY IT WAS--
MISSILE LOCK DETECTED!
WHAT?!
WE'VE GOT INCOMING...!
...TWO CONTACTS... SMALL, FAST-MOVING...
ACTION STATIONS!
REPULSOR FIELDS TO MAXIMUM!

TO BE CONTINUED...

IRON MAN 2020
ENDLESS STOLEN SKY PART 3
WRITER: DANIEL MERLIN GOODBREY
PENCILER: LOU KANG
INKER: CRAIG YOUNG
COLORIST: CHRIS SOTOMAYOR
LETTERER: DAVE SHARPE
ASST. EDITOR: MICHAEL HORWITZ
EDITOR: JOHN BARBER
EDITOR IN CHIEF: JOE QUESADA
PUBLISHER: DAN BUCKLEY
ARNO STARK.
OVERSEEING THE MAIDEN VOYAGE OF THE PROTOTYPE HELILINER, THE SPIRIT OF FREE ENTERPRISE.
HOW'S OUR LITTLE SOIRÉE BEEN PROGRESSING WITHOUT ME, CYNTHIA?
FRIVOLITY LEVELS ARE HOLDING WITHIN ACCEPTABLE PARAMETERS, ARNO.

WHAT THE--
AAAAHHH!
WHAT'S HAPP--
TERRORISTS! OH GOD, IT MUST BE--
KEEP FILMING!
--ELP! HELP ME!
DAMAGE REPORT!
REPULSOR FIELDS HOLDING AT 80%!
NO MAJOR DAMAGE BUT REPORTS OF FIRES IN SEVERAL MINOR SYSTEMS THROUGHOUT THE SHIP. REPAIR CREWS RESPONDING.
ALL EXTERNAL COMMS ARE NON-RESPONSIVE!
I THINK... I THINK SOME-ONE'S JAMMING US, CAPTAIN.
ONE GUESS AS TO WHOM. WHAT CAN YOU TELL ME ABOUT HER?
HEAVILY ARMED AND ARMORED, SIR. PROFILE DOESN'T MATCH ANYTHING IN OUR DATABASE.

LOOK AT THE GUNS ON THAT THING.
THOSE MISSILES WERE JUST TO GET OUR ATTENTION; SHE CAN SINK US ANYTIME SHE WANTS, REPULSOR FIELDS OR NO.
CAPTAIN, WE'RE GETTING REPORTS FROM THE SECURITY STATIONED AT FORWARD OBS ONE. SOUNDS LIKE IT'S A BIT OF MESS, SIR.
DAMN IT, THE CIVILIANS.
GET MEDICAL CREWS AND WHATEVER EXTRA SECURITY WE CAN SPARE DOWN THERE AT ONCE.
CAPTAIN. WHAT THE HELL IS GOING ON?
MR. STARK, SIR. I'M AFRAID TO REPORT WE'RE UNDER ATTACK.
WHAT?! FROM WHO?
UNKNOWN HEAVILY ARMED FLYING BATTLE-SHIP, SIR.
FLYING WHAT?!
INCOMING TRANSMISSION, CAPTAIN!
IT'S OVERRIDING THE JAMMING SIGNAL-- I THINK IT MUST BE COMING FROM THE ENEMY VESSEL, SIR.
ON SCREEN!

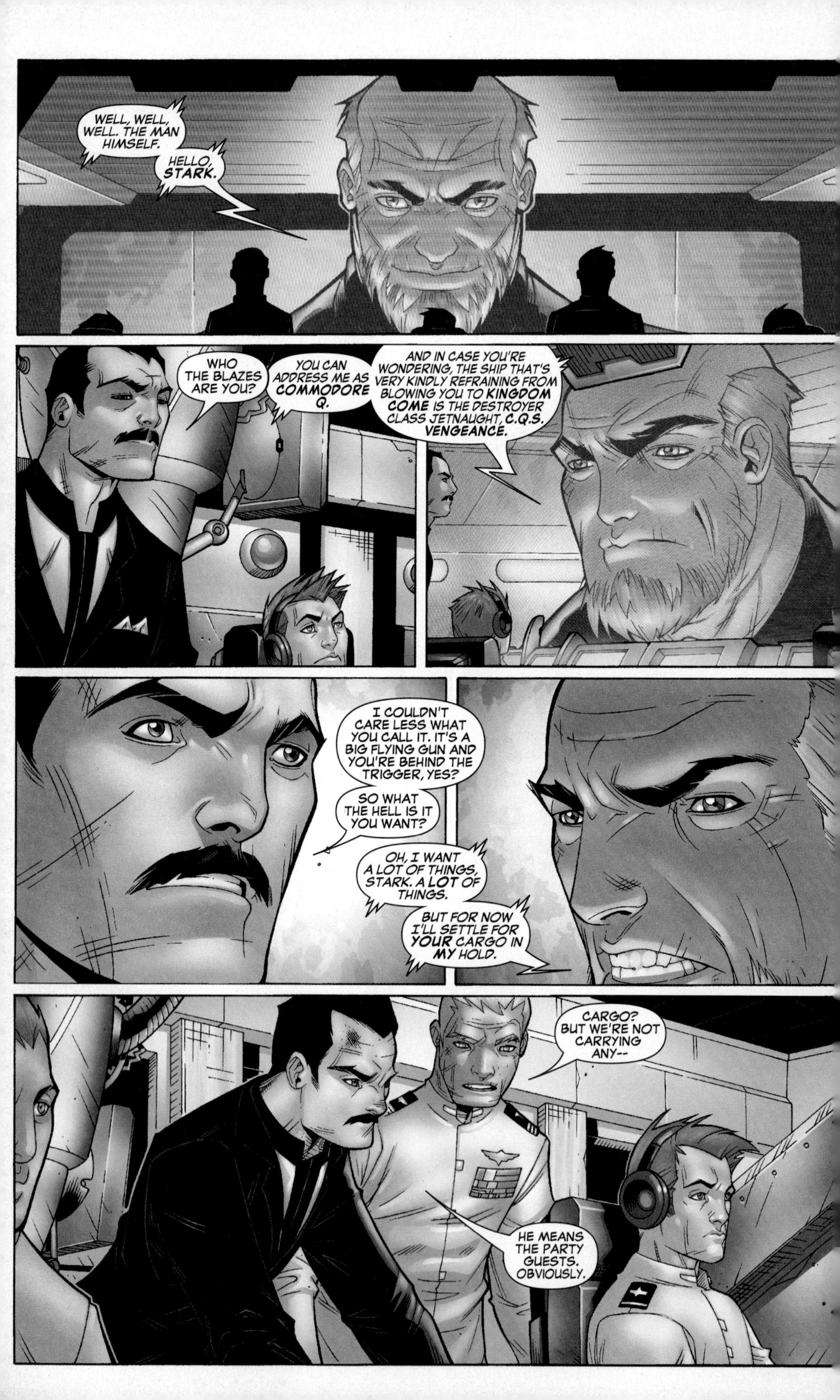

WELL, WELL, WELL. THE MAN HIMSELF.
HELLO, STARK.
WHO THE BLAZES ARE YOU?
YOU CAN ADDRESS ME AS COMMODORE Q.
AND IN CASE YOU'RE WONDERING, THE SHIP THAT'S VERY KINDLY REFRAINING FROM BLOWING YOU TO KINGDOM COME IS THE DESTROYER CLASS JETNAUGHT, C.Q.S. VENGEANCE.
I COULDN'T CARE LESS WHAT YOU CALL IT. IT'S A BIG FLYING GUN AND YOU'RE BEHIND THE TRIGGER, YES?
SO WHAT THE HELL IS IT YOU WANT?
OH, I WANT A LOT OF THINGS, STARK. A LOT OF THINGS.
BUT FOR NOW I'LL SETTLE FOR YOUR CARGO IN MY HOLD.
CARGO? BUT WE'RE NOT CARRYING ANY--
HE MEANS THE PARTY GUESTS. OBVIOUSLY.

AND THAT'S ALL, IS IT?
I HAND OVER MY LITTLE CACHE OF THE RICH AND RICHER AND WE'RE DONE?
YOU AND YOUR BOAT WILL BE FREE TO GO. YOU HAVE MY WORD.
I NEED FIFTEEN MINUTES TO CONSULT WITH MY LEGAL DEPARTMENT.
WHAT?
I HAD ALL MY GUESTS SIGN LIABILITY WAIVERS BEFORE THEY BOARDED.
I NEED TO CHECK THAT STARK INTERNATIONAL IS COVERED AGAINST MASS KIDNAPPING.
HAH! YOU'RE A PIECE OF WORK, STARK.
TEN MINUTES. NOT A SECOND MORE.

I CAN'T BELIEVE YOU'RE SERIOUSLY GOING TO JUST HAND HIM THE PASSENGERS.
DON'T BE AN IDIOT, CAPTAIN.
THE INSTANT THE LAST PASSENGER LEAVES THIS SHIP, Q'S GOING TO BLOW US CLEAN OUT OF THE SKY.
THE MAN HATES ME. FOR REASONS I FIND UNFATHOM-ABLE.
BUT FORTUNATELY FOR ALL OF US I'M A MUCH BETTER LIAR THAN HE IS.
WE SHOULD GET THE GUESTS TO THEIR QUARTERS THEN. THEY'LL BE MORE SECURE THERE.
NO. KEEP THEM ALL EXACTLY WHERE THEY ARE ON THE OBSERVATION DECK.
BUT MR. STARK--
WE NEED THEM VISIBLE! RIGHT NOW THEY'RE THE ONLY THING KEEPING US IN THE AIR.
YOU! YOU SAID OUR COMMUNICA-TIONS ARE BEING JAMMED?
Y-YES SIR! I'M POSITIVE THE SIGNAL'S COMING FROM SOMEWHERE ON THE ENEMY SHIP, SIR.
GOOD! I'LL BE ABLE TO FIND THE PRECISE ORIGIN ONCE I'M IN THE AIR. THEN ALL WE NEED TO DO IS KNOCK OUT THAT JAMMER.
AND THEN WHAT? SIGNAL FOR HELP? THERE'S NO ONE OUT THERE WHO CAN POSSIBLY REACH US IN TIME!
IS THERE?

THIS IS ARNO STARK TO ALL IRON-BOT CREWS.
PREP PILOTS FOR INSERTION AND READY ALL SUITS FOR IMMEDIATE LAUNCH.
DISENGAGING A.R. CRADLE.
CYCLING OUT OF REM SLEEP.
EXTREMIS™ FOETAL ENHANCILE GOLD ONE REPORTING FULL WAKING STATE.
ALL LIFE SIGNS READING GREEN.
PSYCHOSIS LEVELS HOLDING AT AMBER.
1
READY FOR ARMOR INSERTION ON MY MARK.
YOU BOYS READY FOR SOME *FUN*?

COPY THAT, GOLD LEADER.
WHAT DO WE GET TO KILL TODAY, BOSS?
EVERYTHING THAT GETS IN OUR WAY.
TO BE CONTINUED...

THE CQS VENGEANCE.
CQS VENGEANCE
COMMODORE Q. COMMANDING.
SIX--NO, SEVEN CONTACTS. PROFILE SUGGESTS EITHER A MECH OR POWERED ARMOR DEPLOYMENT.
THAT SNAKE STARK WAS JUST BUYING TIME TO GET HIS ARMOR IN THE AIR.
ORDER ALL GUNNERY STATIONS TO TARGET APPROACHING HOSTILES AND FIRE AT WILL!
GOLD LEADER TO GOLD SQUADRON.
INITIATE EVASIVE MANEUVERS!
IRON MAN 2020
ENDLESS STOLEN SKY PART 4
WRITER: DANIEL MERLIN GOODBREY
PENCILER: LOU KANG
INKER: CRAIG YEUNG
COLORIST: CHRIS SOTOMAYOR
LETTERER: DAVE SHARPE
ASSISTANT EDITOR: JODY LEHEUP
EDITORS: JOHN BARBER AND NICOLE BOOSE
EDITOR IN CHIEF: JOE QUESADA
PUBLISHER: DAN BUCKLEY
EXECUTIVE PRODUCER: ALAN FINE

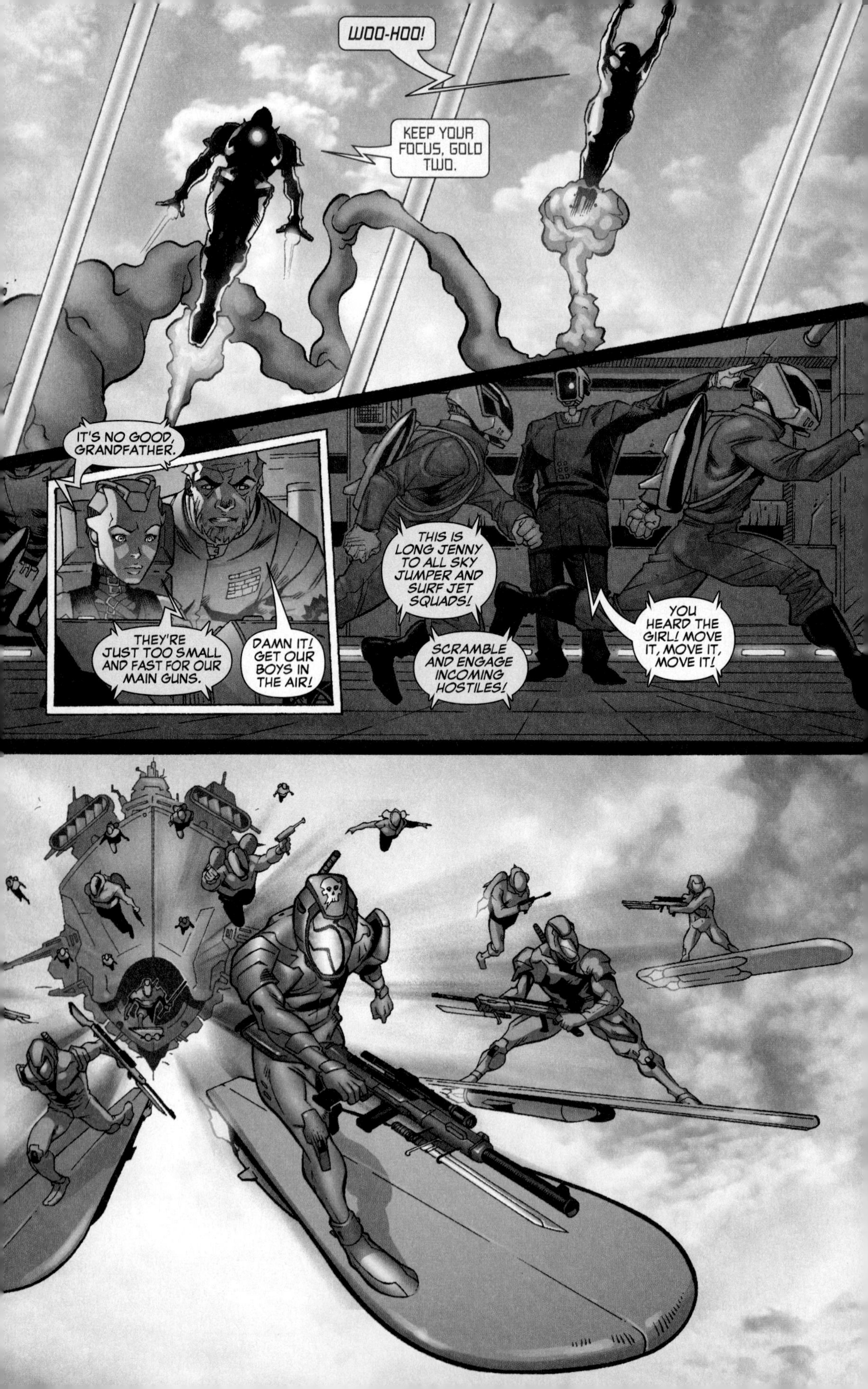
WOO-HOO!
KEEP YOUR FOCUS, GOLD TWO.
IT'S NO GOOD, GRANDFATHER.
THEY'RE JUST TOO SMALL AND FAST FOR OUR MAIN GUNS.
DAMN IT! GET OUR BOYS IN THE AIR!
THIS IS LONG JENNY TO ALL SKY JUMPER AND SURF JET SQUADS!
SCRAMBLE AND ENGAGE INCOMING HOSTILES!
YOU HEARD THE GIRL! MOVE IT, MOVE IT, MOVE IT!

WE'VE GOT INCOMING!
SENSOR SWEEP IS READING LIFE-SIGN NEGATIVE.
ROBOTS.
GO TO TOWN, BOYS.
DAMN ROBOTS!
DAMN!

CYNTHIA?
COMBATANT'S CONTROL SYSTEM EXHIBITING MILITARY-GRADE FIREWALL SHIELDING.
NEVER MIND THAT! HAVE YOU FOUND THE SOURCE OF THE JAMMING SIGNAL?!
SCANNING...
GOLD THREE!
THEY KILLED GOLD THREE!
THOSE BASTARDS!
SCANNING...
190/90
SLOW DOWN RATE
SEQUENCE INITIATED
ZOOM 50%
CYNTHIA
ONLINE
LEFT
RANGE 100%
SATELLITE DETECTION
SUITE TEMP COOL DOWN
SIGNAL SOURCE IDENTIFIED.

THEY'VE GOT THE NUMBERS ON US, BOSS.
KEEP THEM BUSY A LITTLE LONGER. I'M GOING FOR OUR MAIN TARGET.
TARGET LOCKED AND IN RANGE.
ARE WE CLEAR?
SCANNING...
NO JAMMING SIGNAL DETECTED.
SEND THE DATA PACKAGE NOW!

S.H.I.E.L.D. PROVING CRUISE.
CURRENT LOCATION: CLASSIFIED.
COMMANDER DREW, INCOMING TRANSMISSION FROM ARNO STARK.
STARK? WE'RE NOT DUE ANOTHER CONTACT YET.
IT'S...ODD. IT'S TEXT ONLY, MA'AM. MESSAGE READS:
"YOU WERE RIGHT, I WAS WRONG. MY APOLOGIES IN ADVANCE."
IN ADVANCE? WHAT DOES HE MEAN, IN--
JUMP DRIVE IS COMING ONLINE!
WHAT?! ON WHOSE AUTHORITY?
IT'S... I THINK IT'S STARK!
HE MUST HAVE LEFT HIMSELF A BACKDOOR INTO THE DRIVE'S CONTROL SYSTEMS.
THEN THAT MEANS--
ALL HANDS PREPARE FOR EMERGENCY JUMP INTO HOSTILE COMBAT CONDITIONS!
THIS IS NOT A DRILL! REPEAT, THIS IS NOT A DRILL!

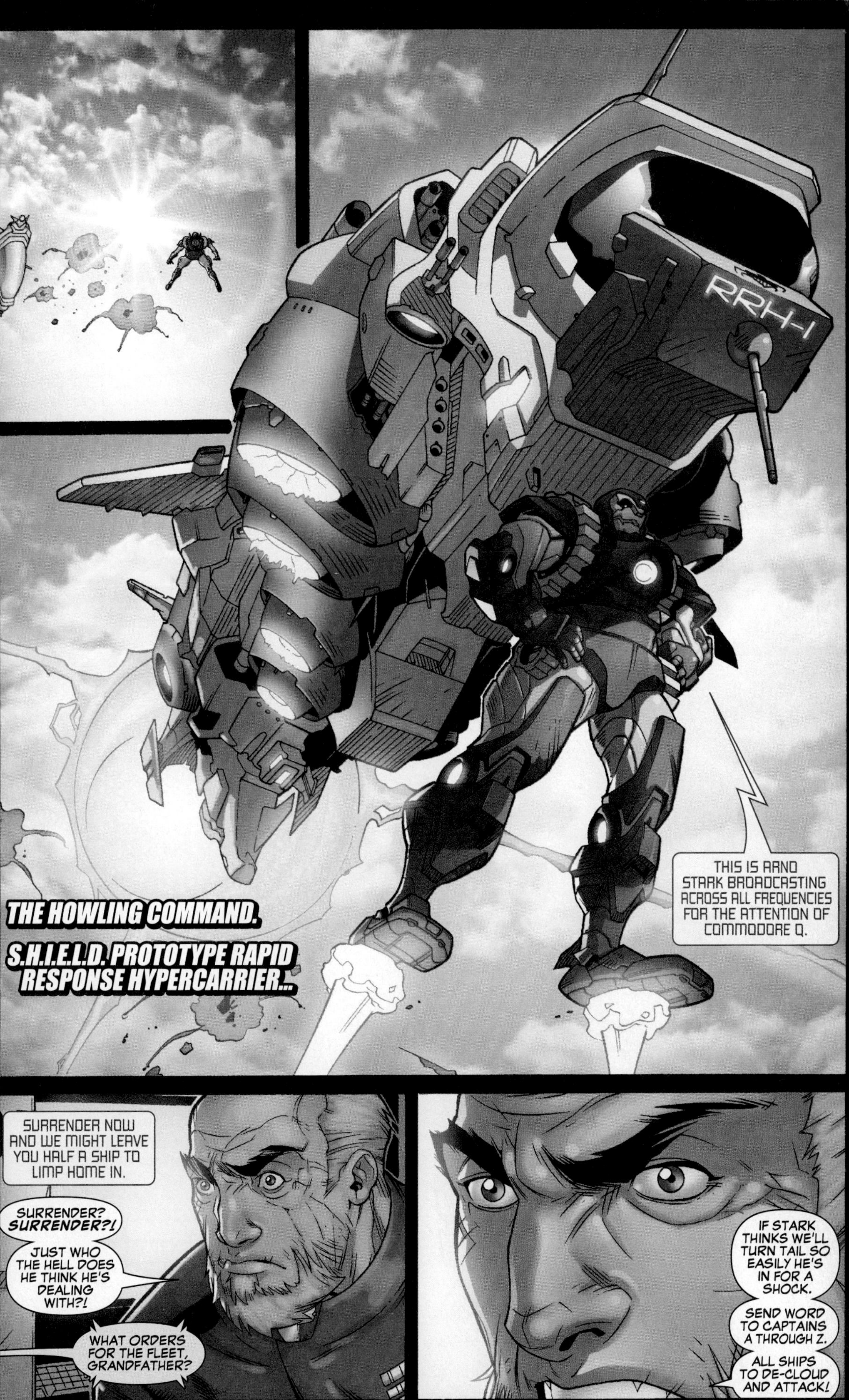
RRH-1
THE HOWLING COMMAND.
S.H.I.E.L.D. PROTOTYPE RAPID RESPONSE HYPERCARRIER...
THIS IS ARNO STARK BROADCASTING ACROSS ALL FREQUENCIES FOR THE ATTENTION OF COMMODORE Q.
SURRENDER NOW AND WE MIGHT LEAVE YOU HALF A SHIP TO LIMP HOME IN.
SURRENDER? SURRENDER?!
JUST WHO THE HELL DOES HE THINK HE'S DEALING WITH?!
WHAT ORDERS FOR THE FLEET, GRANDFATHER?
IF STARK THINKS WE'LL TURN TAIL SO EASILY HE'S IN FOR A SHOCK.
SEND WORD TO CAPTAINS A THROUGH Z.
ALL SHIPS TO DE-CLOUD AND ATTACK!

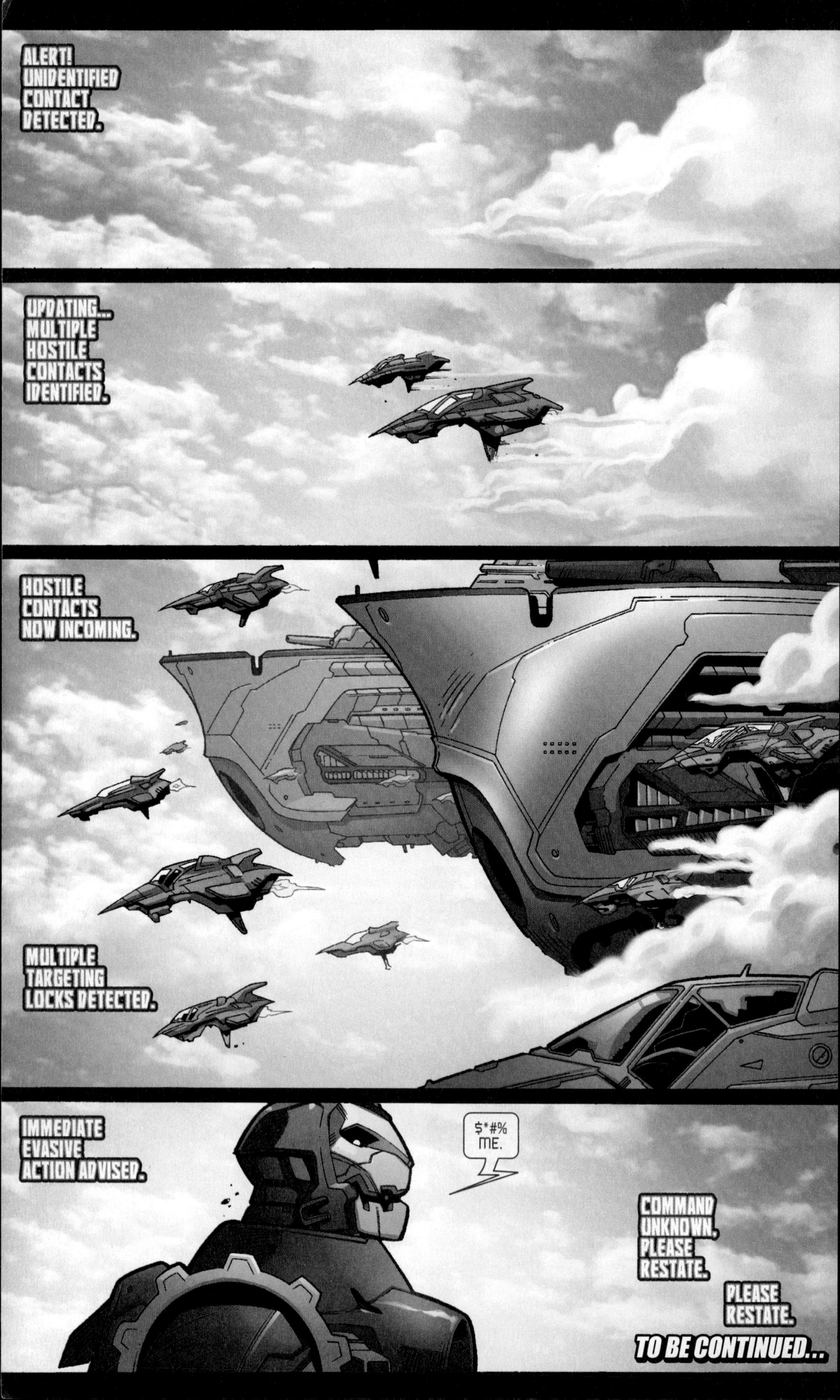
ALERT! UNIDENTIFIED CONTACT DETECTED.
UPDATING... MULTIPLE HOSTILE CONTACTS IDENTIFIED.
HOSTILE CONTACTS NOW INCOMING.
MULTIPLE TARGETING LOCKS DETECTED.
IMMEDIATE EVASIVE ACTION ADVISED.
$*#% ME.
COMMAND UNKNOWN, PLEASE RESTATE.
PLEASE RESTATE.
TO BE CONTINUED...

CORVETTE CLASS JETNAUGHT, THE CQS REDOUBTABLE. CAPTAIN Y COMMANDING.
THE CONQUEST AND THE UNREASONABLE ARE MOVING TO SUPPORT THE VENGEANCE, SIR.
FULL AHEAD TO OUR MAIN TARGET. ALL GUNNERY STATIONS PREPARE TO FIRE ON MY MARK.
FOR THE GLORY OF COMMODORE Q!
HUZZAH!
S.H.I.E.L.D. PROTOTYPE HYPERCARRIER, THE HOWLING COMMAND.
$*#%ING STARK!
MULTIPLE HEAVILY ARMED INCOMING HOSTILES, MA'AM.
COMMANDER JESSICA DREW, DIRECTOR OF S.H.I.E.L.D.
SCRAMBLE EVERYTHING WE'VE GOT!
IF IT'S GOT WINGS, ROTORS OR JETS I WANT IT IN THE AIR NOW!

ARNO STARK.
THE INVINCIBLE IRON MAN.
BASTARD BLOODY ROBOTS!
IRON MAN 2020
ENDLESS STOLEN SKY PART 5
WRITER: DANIEL MERLIN GOODBREY
PENCILER: LOU KANG
INKER: CRAIG YEUNG
COLORIST: CHRIS SOTOMAYOR
LETTERER: DAVE SHARPE
ASSISTANT EDITOR: JODY LEHEUP
EDITORS: JOHN BARBER AND NICOLE BOOSE
EDITOR IN CHIEF: JOE QUESADA
PUBLISHER: DAN BUCKLEY
EXECUTIVE PRODUCER: ALAN FINE

NCOMING TRANSMISSION FROM COMMANDER DREW.
OH JOY.
PUT HER ON.
STAAAARK!
LITTLE BUSY RIGHT NOW, COMMANDER.
WHAT THE HELL IS GOING ON HERE?
FLYING PIRATE FLEET. SOMEWHAT OBVIOUSLY, I WOULD HAVE THOUGHT.
JESUS, STARK! JUST HOW MANY PEOPLE DID YOU PISS OFF THIS TIME?
YOU KNOW, THAT'S AN EXCELLENT QUESTION.
CYNTHIA, TAKE CONTROL OF THE HYPERCARRIER'S SENSOR ARRAY.
YES, ARNO.
WHAT?! YOU CAN'T JUST--
SCAN THE ENEMY FLEET FOR LIFE SIGNS.
SCANNING...
IF YOU THINK YOU'RE GOING TO GET AWAY WITH COMMANDEERING S.H.I.E.L.D.--
END TRANSMISSION.
AND MEMO TO SELF: BUY MORE LAWYERS.

SCAN COMPLETE. ONE LIFE SIGN DETECTED.
MY GOD... THE ENTIRE FLEET'S ROBOTIC!
THAT MAKES Q THE KEY.
IF I CAPTURE HIM, HE CAN ORDER THE ENTIRE FLEET TO STAND DOWN.
GOLD ONE, WHAT'S THE SQUADRON'S STATUS?
JUST ME AND GOLD FIVE LEFT, BOSS.
DAMN ROBOTS! DAMN!
FORM ON MY POSITION.
WE'VE GOT US A TIN CAN TO OPEN.

THE CQS VENGEANCE.

THE GAME'S UP, Q!
COME ALONG QUIETLY AND--

--WHO THE HELL ARE YOU?
I'M LONG JENNY.

AND I'VE BEEN UPGRADING FOR THIS FIGHT SINCE I WAS ELEVEN YEARS OLD.

WHAT THE--
--HELL?
VIBRANIUM STRUCTURE CHARGED WITH UNKNOWN ENERGY SIGNATURE.
REPULSOR SHIELDING INEFFECTIVE.
$*#%!
REALLY? IS THAT THE BEST YOU CAN DO?
REPULSOR WEAPONRY ALSO INEFFECTIVE.
RECONFIGURE, DAMN IT!
SEARCHING ALL AVAILABLE DATABASES FOR ENERGY SIGNATURE COUNTERMEASURE.
SEARCHING...
SEARCHING...
SEARCH-- OOF!
...FASTER!

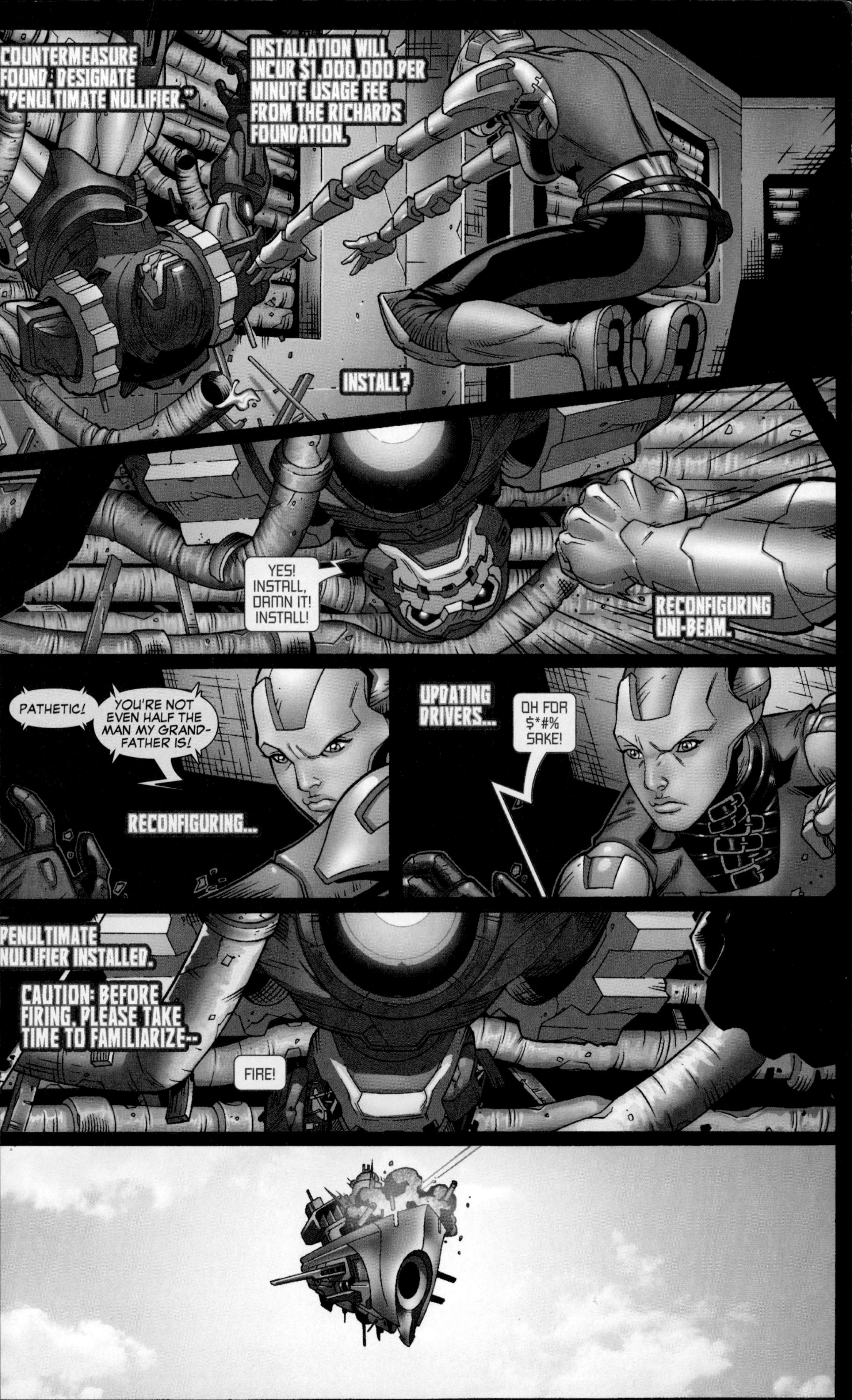
COUNTERMEASURE FOUND. DESIGNATE "PENULTIMATE NULLIFIER."
INSTALLATION WILL INCUR $1,000,000 PER MINUTE USAGE FEE FROM THE RICHARDS FOUNDATION.
INSTALL?
YES! INSTALL, DAMN IT! INSTALL!
RECONFIGURING UNI-BEAM.
PATHETIC!
YOU'RE NOT EVEN HALF THE MAN MY GRAND-FATHER IS!
RECONFIGURING...
UPDATING DRIVERS...
OH FOR $*#% SAKE!
PENULTIMATE NULLIFIER INSTALLED.
CAUTION: BEFORE FIRING, PLEASE TAKE TIME TO FAMILIARIZE--
FIRE!

STEALTH TORPEDO, THE CQS UNSTOPPABLE.
LARGE EXPLOSION REPORTED ONBOARD THE VENGEANCE, SIR.
MY GRAND-DAUGHTER'S A CLEVER GIRL. SHE'LL SEE THE VENGEANCE SAFE.
COMMODORE Q
AND I WON'T BE DISTRACTED FROM MY PRIZE WHEN WE'RE THIS CLOSE.
ENERGIZE THE PROW!
VIBRANIUM PROW FULLY ENERGIZED, SIR.
THEN CHECK YOUR WEAPONS, MEN! AND PREPARE FOR IMPACT!
AYE, AYE, CAP'N!
RAMMING SPEED!
TO BE CONCLUDED...

IRON MAN 2020
ENDLESS STOLEN SKY CONCLUSION
WRITER: DANIEL MERLIN GOODBREY
PENCILER: LOU KANG
INKER: CRAIG YEUNG
COLORIST: CHRIS SOTOMAYOR
LETTERER: DAVE SHARPE
ASSISTANT EDITOR: MICHAEL HORWITZ
EDITOR: NICOLE BOOSE
EDITOR IN CHIEF: JOE QUESADA
PUBLISHER: DAN BUCKLEY
EXECUTIVE PRODUCER: ALAN FINE
SECURE THE HOSTAGES, MEN!
AND TRY NOT TO SHOOT ANY OF THE EXCEEDINGLY RICH ONES.

WHO IS COMMODORE Q?
CANNOT... CANNOT...ORGANIC MATTER IN FAILING STATE.
YOUR BRAIN IS DYING. WHO IS COMMODORE Q?
COMMODORE Q...UNCLE QQQ...
I CAN STILL SAVE YOU. BUT ONLY IF YOU ANSWER THE QUESTION.
WHO IS COMMODORE Q?
UNCLE Q... UNCLE Q... UNCLE QQQUINN.
QUINN... QUANTRELL.
CYNTHIA, DIVERT 2% SYSTEM POWER TO JENNY'S EMERGENCY LIFE SUPPORT SYSTEM.
DOWNLOAD ANY TACTICAL DATA IN HER BACKUP DRIVES AND INITIATE A FULL DATA SEARCH FOR THE NAME QUINN QUANTRELL.
YES, TONY.

SEARCHING...
FILTERING...
QUANTRELL, QUINN, EX-EMPLOYEE OF STARK INTERNATIONAL.
HUH. DISGRUNTLED EMPLOYEE. OF COURSE.
AERONAUTIC AND ASTRONAUTIC SPECIALIST.
FIRED FROM STARK INTERNATIONAL BY TONY STARK FOLLOWING AN ATTEMPTED COVER-UP OF THE DEATHS OF THREE TEST PILOTS ATTACHED TO THE Q SERIES JETPACK TRIALS.
SO COUSIN TONY TOOK HIS JETPACK AWAY AND HE RAN OFF TO PLAY PIRATE.
BOO-HOO.
COMMODORE Q CURRENT LOCATION CONFIRMED: HELILINER *SPIRIT OF FREE ENTERPRISE* FORWARD OBSERVATION DECK.
RIGHT. LET'S FINISH THIS.

ANALYSIS OF LONG JENNY TACTICAL DATA COMPLETE.
STRUCTURAL WEAK POINT OF ROBOTIC COMBATANTS IDENTIFIED.
160 BPM
UNLOCK FIELD TURBO CONFIGURATION
ENEMY HOSTILES TARGETED AND LOCKED.
CYNTHIA ONLINE
SUGGESTION
HOMING SHURIKEN! FULL SPREAD!

YOU'RE ON YOUR OWN, Q.
ORDER THE REST OF YOUR FLEET TO STAND DOWN AND I'LL MAKE IT A QUICK DEATH.
NEVER! KILL ME NOW AND MY BOYS WILL FIGHT TO THE LAST DROP OF OIL IN THEIR ROBOTIC HEARTS!
GOOD THING I BROUGHT A BARGAINING CHIP, THEN.
F-F-FOR-GIIIIVE-
NO-- JENNY!
MY ARMOR IS ALL THAT'S KEEPING YOUR GRANDDAUGHTER'S BRAIN ALIVE, QUINN.
STAND THEM DOWN NOW OR I PULL THE PLUG.

YOU'LL FIX HER. SEE HER SAFE FROM ANY REPRISALS.
I WILL.
SWEAR IT!
I SWEAR. I'LL REBUILD HER BODY MYSELF. THE BEST STARK INDUSTRIES HAS TO OFFER.
THIS IS COMMANDER Q TO ALL SHIPS. VERIFICATION CODE REDSTONE.
ALL SHIPS AND CREW TO STAND DOWN IMMEDIATELY.
PROTOTYPE S.H.I.E.L.D. HYPERCARRIER, THE HOWLING COMMAND.
THEY'VE CEASED FIRING, COMMANDER! ALL OF THEM!
WELL LET'S NOT BE STUPID ENOUGH TO MAKE THE SAME MISTAKE.
BLOW THEM OUT OF THE SKY!

THIS IS THE END, THEN.
I'VE SAILED THE SEVEN SKIES AND SEEN ITS WONDERS. FROM THE GOLDEN SPIRES OF FAIR AIRLANTIS TO THE SKY-ISLES OF AERIE.
BUT STILL IT ISN'T ENOUGH.
IF ONLY THE WORLD HAD LET ME, I COULD HAVE SHARED IT ALL. A JETPACK IN EVERY HOME...A NEW ERA FOR AVIATION...
I COULD HAVE GIVEN US THE FUTURE WE WERE PROMISED.
BUT NO ONE WANTED IT. NO ONE WOULD LISTEN.
YOU'RE STANDING ON THE FUTURE, QUINN. HELILINER TECH IS GOING TO GIVE US BACK THE SKIES.
AND THEN EVENTUALLY PEOPLE WILL FIND OUT WHAT HYPERCARRIER JUMP ENGINES ARE REALLY CAPABLE OF.
AND I'LL HAVE GIVEN US THE STARS, TOO.

HAH! YOU STILL THINK YOU CAN SHAPE THE FUTURE, STARK? THE WORLD WON'T ALLOW ONE MAN TO CHANGE IT. THOSE DAYS ARE GONE.
BUT YOU-- YOU'LL KEEP YOUR PROMISE. YOU'LL SEE MY JENNY SAFE.
I KEEP ALL MY PROMISES. IT'S WHY I RARELY MAKE THEM. GOODBYE, COMMODORE.
ANOTHER PROMISE, QUINN; I'M GOING TO BUILD A BETTER WORLD. A BETTER FUTURE.
AND NO ONE'S GOING TO STOP ME.
NO ONE'S EVEN GOING TO SEE MY FUTURE COMING UNTIL IT'S ALREADY TOO LATE.
THE END.
ARNO STARK WILL RETURN

MARVEL COMICS
WHAT IF...
$1.95 AUS
53
DEC
02920
APPROVED BY THE COMICS CODE AUTHORITY
THREE BONE-CHILLING TALES OF ALTERNATE REALITIES!
DAVE SIMONS

HIS NAME IS ARNO STARK,
IRON MAN 2020
AND HE HAS A PROBLEM.
SEVERAL MEGATONS OF PROBLEMS!
THE PLANET BUSTER BOMB--COMMISSIONED BY THE MILITARY, BUILT BY STARK INTERNATIONAL...
...ARMED BY ROBERT SAUNDERS!
ONLY NOW SAUNDERS IS DEAD. AND HIS RETINAL PATTERNS ALONE CAN PREVENT THE BOMB'S DETONATION, NOT TO MENTION THE DEATH OF STARK'S WIFE AND SON!
DESPERATE, HE TRAVELS BACK IN TIME...
...TO COPY THE RETINAL PATTERNS OF A TWELVE YEAR OLD ROBERT SAUNDERS!
SPIDER-MAN DOES NOT SEE THE DESPERATION, THE DRIVING URGENCY. HE SEES ONLY A FRIGHTENED BOY, LEFT BLEEDING IN THE RED AND GOLD WARRIOR'S WAKE.
HE ISN'T HAPPY! NOT ONE LITTLE BIT!
HIS ARMOR DAMAGED, STARK RETREATS TO HIS OWN TIME--EMPTY-HANDED.

ONLY TO DISCOVER THE BOMB HAD ALREADY DETONATED! A FATAL FLAW IN THE TIMING SYSTEM.
IMAGINE FOR A MOMENT THAT EVENTS HAD NOT PROCEEDED IN QUITE THIS FASHION! THAT AT A CRUCIAL MOMENT SPIDER-MAN DID NOT BREAK OFF HIS ATTACK--AND STRUCK AGAIN!
DAMAGING CRITICAL MECHANISMS THAT OTHERWISE WOULD HAVE SENT STARK HOME.
STAR
IT IS IN THESE INSTANTS THAT I OBSERVE THE FORMATION OF ANOTHER, ALTERNATE REALITY, DIFFERENT FROM THE ONE YOU KNOW, BUT DISTURBINGLY SIMILAR.
AS A WATCHER, I MUST FOLLOW THIS NEW TIMELINE, SEEKING THE ANSWER TO THE QUESTION...
WHAT IF THE IRON MAN OF 2020 HAD BEEN STRANDED IN THE PAST?
SIMON FURMAN · WRITER MANNY GALAN · PENCILER
JIM AMASH · INKER JOE ANDREANI · COLORIST
JANICE CHIANG · LETTERER ROB TOKAR · EDITOR
TOM DeFALCO · EDITOR-IN-CHIEF

SIX YEARS PASS. TIME ENOUGH FOR A PRISON SENTENCE TO BE SERVED, FOR ONE DEAD END JOB TO BLUR INTO THE NEXT!

SIX YEARS CONSUMED BY HATRED AND BITTERNESS, A MAN QUITE LITERALLY OUT OF TIME! THE FIRES THAT ONCE DROVE STARK TO THE VERY PEAK OF PERSONAL AND PROFESSIONAL SUCCESS DOUSED IN BOOZE.
THE MAIN STORY AGAIN...
UNTIL NOW!

...MILLIONAIRE INDUSTRIALIST ANTHONY STARK IS DEAD!
SIX DAYS LATER. THE OFFICE OF MORGAN STARK--
DRINK?
I DON'T.
WELL, MORGAN? IS IT DONE?

OH YES, MY MYSTERIOUS FRIEND. IT'S DONE!
I GOT JIM RHODES'S EX-GIRLFRIEND--MARCY PEARSON--TO PLANT YOUR "EVIDENCE." A WORD IN THE RIGHT EAR AND IT'LL ALL BE OVER THE NEWS LIKE A RASH.
IT MAY NOT STAND UP IN COURT, BUT THE DAMAGE WILL HAVE BEEN DONE. THE WORLD WILL SUSPECT RHODES OF TONY STARK'S MURDER.
HE'LL BE FINISHED.

I LOST WHAT WAS RIGHTFULLY MINE WHEN STARK CHEATED MY FATHER OUT OF HIS SHARE OF STARK INDUSTRIES. WITH RHODES OUT OF THE WAY IT'LL BELONG TO ME...
...ALL OF IT!
MORE DAYS PASS.
UNTIL...!
GIMME ONE GOOD REASON...
...WHY I SHOULDN'T CRUSH YOUR OILY LITTLE HEAD LIKE AN EGGSHELL!
IT'S NOT ENOUGH YOU'RE TRYIN' TO BLACKMAIL ME, BUT YOU HAVE THE GALL TO DO IT HERE...
...IN MY OWN BLAMED OFFICE!
TK-TK-TK. I EXPECTED BETTER OF YOU, RHODEY--
MAY I CALL YOU RHODEY? WAR MACHINE IS SO...TACKY!
--I OFFER YOU MORGAN STARK AND HIS EVIDENCE ON A PLATE IN RETURN FOR CONTROL OF STARK ENTERPRISES AND YOU RESPOND WITH ARMOR AND THREATS.
I REALLY THOUGHT WE COULD DEAL! STILL...

...I'LL GIVE YOU YOUR ONE GOOD REASON.
FRZZAAK!
UUUUU!

I DUNNO HOW YOU DID THAT JACK... BUT YOU'VE JUST BITTEN OFF A HECK OF A LOT MORE THAN YOU CAN CHEW!
OH DEAR. IS THAT IT? BUT THEN IT ALWAYS WAS A RATHER... INFERIOR SUIT.
HERE. LET ME SHOW YOU--
BTAK!
CHAM!
KOOM!
AAAAH!
UuuUH... SHOULDN'T-- SHOULDN'T BE ABLE TO DO THAT!
SENSORS SHOWED ME YOUR ARMOR, SOON AS I WALKED IN! BUT THEY REGISTERED NO HELMET, NO CYBERNETIC, HOOK-UP TO YOUR WEAPONS SYSTEMS!

THE WAR MACHINE TECHNOLOGY IS WELL KNOWN TO ME...ALMOST REDUNDANT! I KNOW ITS SYSTEMS AS INTIMATELY AS I KNEW THE CODES THAT ALLOWED ME ACCESS TO THIS OFFICE--AND TONY'S IRON MAN WORKSHOPS!

I CERTAINLY KNOW ENOUGH ABOUT IT...

...TO DECEIVE IT?

HOW--HOW'D YOU KNOW SO MUCH ABOUT THIS PLACE? ABOUT US?
WHO THE HECK ARE YOU!
I?

I AM THE FUTURE!
KOOOM!

THERE. IT LOOKS AS THOUGH MORGAN WILL GET HIS WISH AFTER ALL. AT LEAST...
...FOR A WHILE!

AND SOON...
FACE IT, MORGAN OLD BOY, YOU'VE FINALLY MADE IT! WITH RHODES DEAD, IT WAS CHILD'S PLAY CONTESTING TONY'S WILL. THEY HANDED IT ALL TO ME... ON A PLATE!
AND NOW THAT I HAVE IT, I DON'T INTEND SHARING IT WITH ANYONE. LEAST OF ALL MY LITTLE JOHN DOE OF A PARTNER!
GLASS CO.
MORGAN STARK
AS SOON AS HE'S DONE TYING UP A FEW LOOSE ENDS... IT'LL BE HIS TURN TO MEET WITH A FATAL "ACCIDENT!"
THANKS, TONY. I OWE IT ALL TO Y--
BRAAM!
OOOW!
I'LL GIVE YOU ONE CHANCE, MORGAN, BECAUSE I LIKED YOUR FATHER, I REALLY DID.
ONE CHANCE...

...TO TELL ME WHERE HE IS!!
SPIT IT OUT, COUSIN!
KA-KU-
CU-COUSIN?
TONY?!
THAT'S RIGHT, MORGAN. AND BEING DEAD HAS NOT IMPROVED MY DISPOSITION. ESPECIALLY WHEN I FIND RHODEY DEAD AND YOUR FAT BUTT IN HIS CHAIR!
NOW, FROM THE TOP...
"...WHERE IS THIS OTHER IRON MAN?"
A TASTE. YES, I'LL LET MORGAN HAVE A TANTALIZING TASTE OF WHAT HE'S ALWAYS DESIRED... AND THEN I'LL TAKE IT ALL AWAY FROM HIM--PIECE BY PIECE!
IT'LL BE ALMOST AS SATISFYING AS KILLING RHOD--

KLAAANG!
EEEE!
YOU MADE A MISTAKE! NO, YOU MADE TWO. YOU KILLED MY FRIEND...
...AND YOU LET MY PRIVATE SURVEILLANCE SYSTEM TAPE YOU DOING IT!
BTM!
BTM!
BTM!
BTM!
YOU'RE GOING TO PAY. LEGALLY, BY THE BOOK...

I CAME BACK FROM THE DEAD FOR THIS, MISTER--IT WAS WHAT BROUGHT ME BACK FROM THE BRINK!
...AND AFTER I'VE TAKEN A PIECE OF YOUR HIDE!
CHOK!

T-TONY? OH GOD NO...NOT YOU! YOU'LL WIN...YOU ALWAYS WIN!
Muh-MONSTER! YOU-YOU'VE COME TO TAKE IT... ALL AWAY!

WON'T LET YOU! I WON'T!
UHH!
BLAST IT, MAN--LISTEN TO ME! I MUST HAVE DAMAGED A COMMAND ROUTE! YOUR BOOT JETS, THEY'VE CUT--

--OUT.
WHAAM!

DEAD.
BLAST! I NEVER MEANT FOR THIS TO HAPPEN! BUT HE WOULDN'T LISTEN!
WHO IS HE ANYWAY? NO ONE I RECOGNIZE... AND YET HE SEEMED TO KNOW STARK ENTERPRISES LIKE THE BACK OF HIS HAND.
STILL, I SUPPOSE I CAN TAKE VAGUE COMFORT FROM THE FACT...

"...THAT HE'LL NEVER TROUBLE ME AGAIN!"
CENTRAL AMERICA. FIVE YEARS LATER.
HE ALWAYS WINS! DON'T YOU UNDERSTAND...
...TONY STARK ALWAYS WINS!
I HAD IT ALL, AND HE TOOK IT AWAY FROM ME! JUST LIKE HE TOOK IT AWAY FROM MY OLD MAN!
AND YOU, YOU STUPID COW--YOU DON'T CARE, DO YOU?
MORGAN, PLEASE!

YOU'RE FRIGHTENING OUR SON!
MOM?

IT'S OKAY, SWEETIE. YOUR FATHER'S...ILL AGAIN. LET'S GET YOU TO BED!
BUT--BUT MY DRAWING...

TOMORROW ARNO. YOU CAN FINISH IT TOMORROW.
END.

## Machine Man article from *Marvel Age* #7

# MACHINE man™ RETURNS!

by **Mark Lerer**

**Machine Man** is coming back! He'll be starring in an all-new Limited Series written by **Tom DeFalco** and drawn by **Herb Trimpe** which will be coming your way this fall.

This is the world of 2020 A.D., where we find **Machine Man** caught between an old nemesis and new threats to society. Dismantled in the late nineteen-eighties, our mechanical protagonist re-emerges to avenge the injustices perpetrated upon him and upon the rest of the American civilization.

Picture a world in which every family owns a house, a car – and a robot. Imagine a society in which the robotics industry plays a powerful role in the national economy. Robots perform domestic and industrial tasks so well that they have started to take jobs away from humans – and unemployed American workers are angry. Meanwhile, a powerful few control the large robotics corporations, hand-in-hand with corrupt government officials

"**Machine Man** always appealed to me," **Tom DeFalco** told **MARVEL AGE MAGAZINE**, "because he has a firm sense of his own identity. Unlike Marvel's other famous artificial man, **the Vision, Machine Man** always knew who he was. A naive sort, **Machine Man** is less doubtful of his own place in the world than simply concerned with the plight of others." **DeFalco** isn't the only one who likes **Machine Man**'s style – Marvel has received literally hundreds of letters in the past year demanding that we bring the character back to the fold.

"By setting the series in the future,"**Tom** continued, "**Herb** and I will take **Machine Man** into situations he's never dealt with before. He'll encounter an American government which pacifies its angry citizens with a federally-funded program of high tech home entertainment. He'll meet the **Midnight Wreckers**, a band of black-marketeers who provide the public with robots cheaper than the large corporations can. Are the **Wreckers** good or evil? And of course, **Machine Man**'s old enemies, **Madame Menace** and **Senator Brickman**, will threaten him as never before. All this and **Jocasta**, too!"

So unplug that home computer – turn off that video game – and head down to your local comic book store for **MACHINE MAN #1**, on sale in September. We'll be waiting.

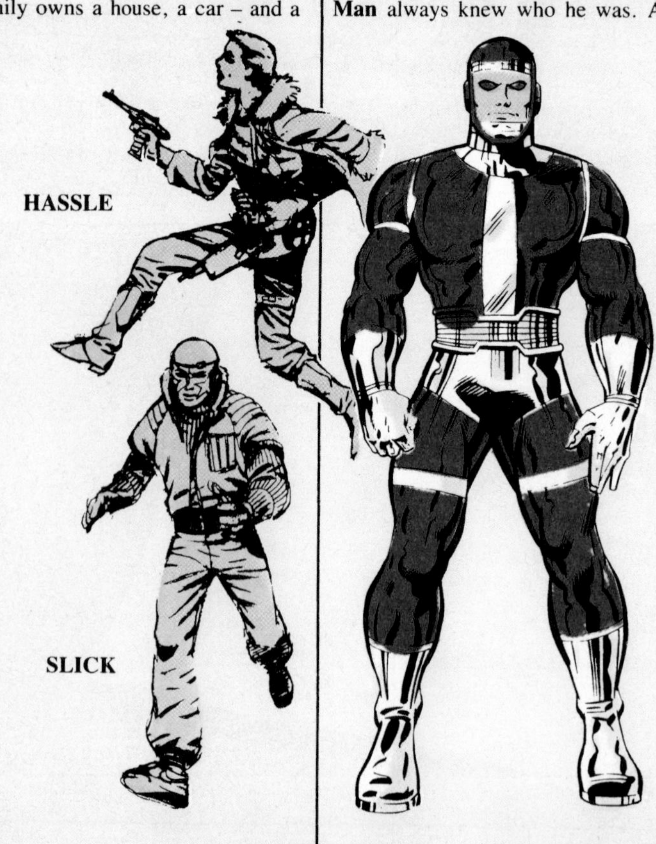

**Machine Man** and his new supporting cast.

The covers to *Machine Man* #1–4
show the robotic hero being gradually assembled.

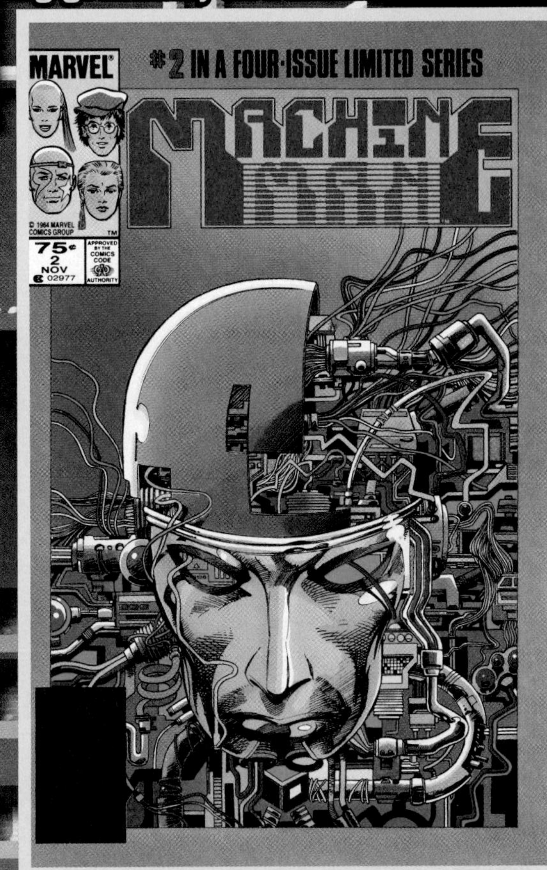

GIRLS

*Machine Man TPB* (1988)
cover by Barry Windsor-Smith

MARVEL® COMICS

MACHINE MAN™

DeFALCO • TRIMPE • WINDSOR-SMITH

*Machine Man 2020* #1 reprinted *Machine Man* #1–2.
Cover art by Barry Windsor-Smith.

$2.00 US
$2.70 CAN
1
AUG

APPROVED BY THE COMICS CODE AUTHORITY

MACHINE MAN 2020™

*Machine Man 2020* #2 reprinted *Machine Man* #3–4.
Cover art by Barry Windsor-Smith.

$2.00 US
$2.70 CAN
2
SEP

*Astonishing Tales (2009)* #1–6 reprinted the *Astonishing Tales: Iron Man 2020* digital comics along with several other digital exclusives, with new covers by Kenneth Rocafort. (Cover to issue #1 shown.)

*Incomplete Death's Head* #11 reprinted *Death's Head* #10.
Cover art by Gary Frank & Georgio Bambos.

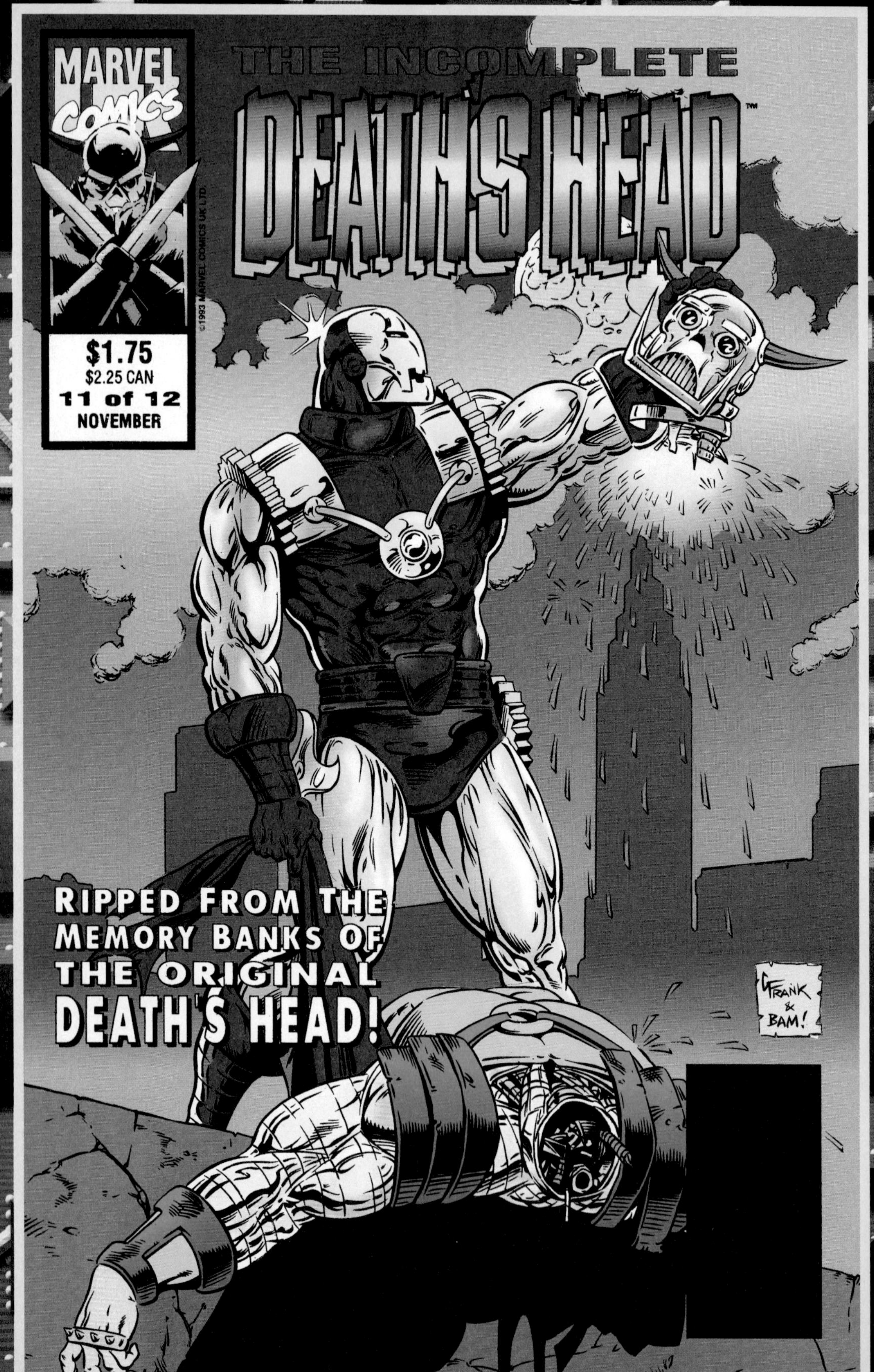

Panini's *Death's Head Vol. 2 TPB* reprinted *Death's Head* #8 – 10, along with several of Death's Head's appearances in U.S. comics. Cover art by Lee Sullivan & James Offredi.

Original art from *Machine Man* #3, page 21
Courtesy Heritage Auctions

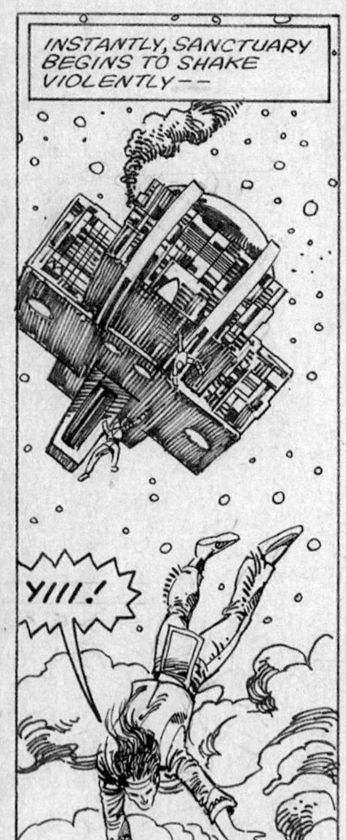

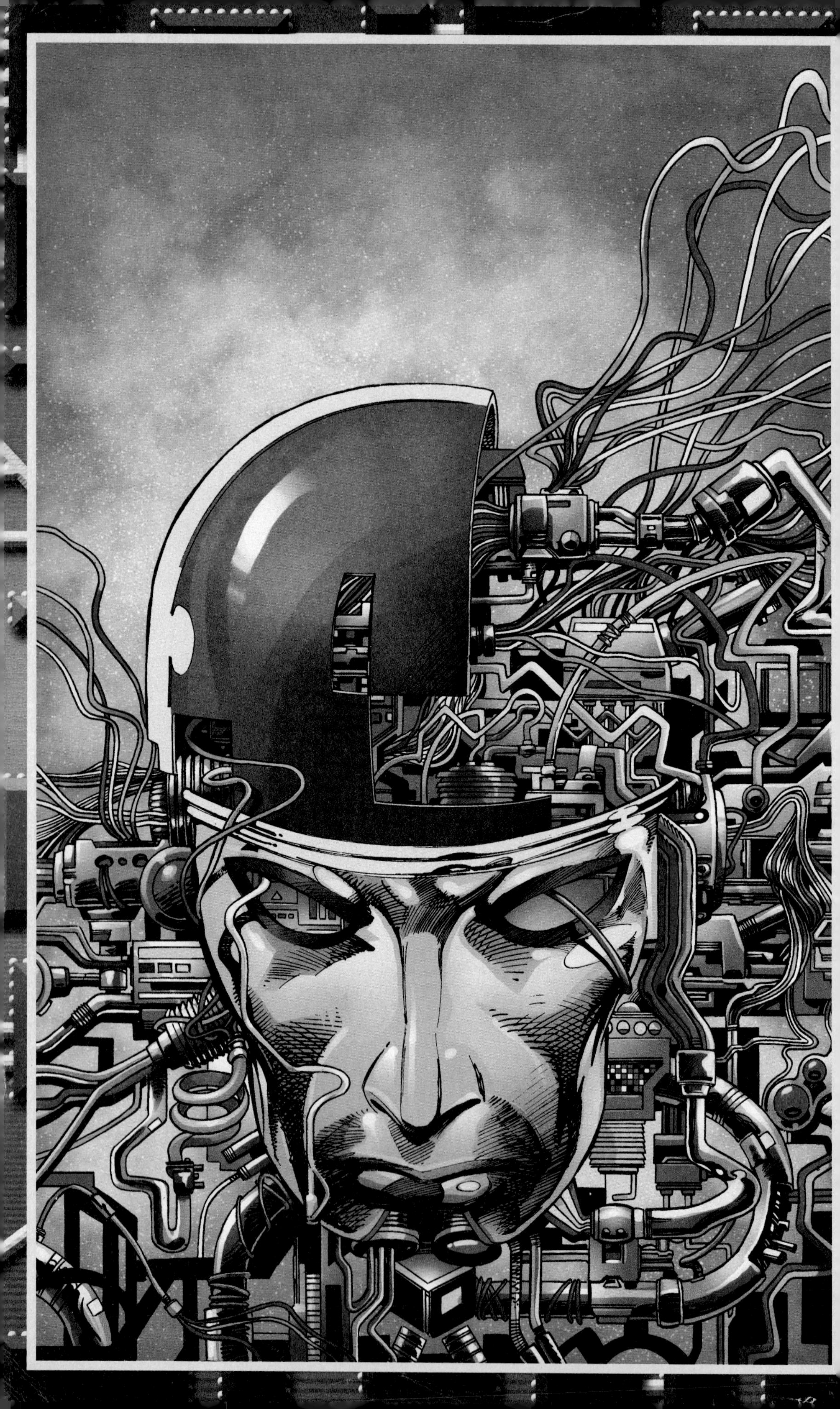